GRE • GMAT • LSAT • MCAT
Reading Comprehension
Workbook

MARK ALAN STEWART

MACMILLAN • USA

Macmillan General Reference
A Pearson Education Macmillan Company
1633 Broadway
New York, NY 10019

An ARCO book

ARCO and colophon is a registered trademark of Macmillan USA
MACMILLAN and colophon is a registered trademark of Pearson Education

Manufactured in the United States of America

10 9 8 7 6 5 4 3 2 1

International Standard Serial Number available upon request

ISBN: 0-02-863249-4

contents

About *the Author*

Mark Alan Stewart is an attorney (J.D., University of California at Los Angeles), college and law school instructor, and private test preparation consultant in Southern California. He is one of today's leading authorities in the field of standardized exam preparation, bringing to this publication more than a dozen years of experience in coaching college students as they prepare for the their graduate entrance exams. His other Macmillan (ARCO) publications for graduate-level admission include:

- *Teach Yourself the GRE in 24 Hours*
- *Teach Yourself the GMAT CAT in 24 Hours*
- *30 Days to the LSAT*
- *30 Days to the GMAT CAT*
- *GRE-LSAT Logic Workbook*
- *GRE Writing Assessment Test — Answers to the Real Questions*
- *GMAT CAT — Answers to the Real Essay Questions*
- *Perfect Personal Statements — Law, Business, Medical, Graduate School*
- *Words for Smart Test-Takers*
- *Math for Smart Test-Takers*

You'll find detailed information about all these ARCO books at the author's Website:

www.west.net/~stewart

About *Reading Comprehension Workbook*

Why a special book just for reading comprehension?

☐ **Reading Comprehension questions account for a large portion of all four exams.** On the computer-based GRE and GMAT these questions will account for about one-third of your Verbal Ability score. On the LSAT and MCAT one of your four scored sections will contain nothing but Reading Comprehension questions.

☐ **You can improve your Reading Comprehension score by practicing certain basic techniques over and over until they become instinctive.** Many test-takers neglect Reading Comprehension when getting ready for their exam, assuming that there's very little they can do to improve their performance in this area. Big mistake! The typical result: a shockingly low test score. By learning how the test-makers think, then applying this knowledge over and over to exam-style questions, you'll be surprised how much your test scores will improve.

Special features of this book

☐ *Reading Comprehension Workbook* **is fully applicable to all four exams (GRE, LSAT, GMAT and MCAT).** Although the length and number of reading passages, as well as the number of questions, vary among these four exams, the basic style and potential range in difficulty level of the questions is similar on all four exams.

☐ *Reading Comprehension Workbook* **will take you into the mind of the test-makers.** By learning how the test-makers create questions and answer choices, you'll learn how to spot "sucker bait" and to zero in on the best choice. You'll even gain a knack for predicting what the questions and answer choices will look like!

☐ *Reading Comprehension Workbook* **will help you develop a flexible and more practical approach to reading comprehension.** No single strategy or technique works for every test taker or for any one test taker in all circumstances. Accordingly, you'll learn the pros and cons of various strategies and techniques so you can determine when and to what extent to use them yourself.

☐ *Reading Comprehension Workbook* **is packed with exam-style question sets for experimenting and practicing.** Determine through experimentation which strategies and techniques work best for you, and under what circumstances each one works or doesn't work. Then apply those strategies and techniques over and over until they become comfortable, then habitual, then instinctive.

Go online for more GRE, LSAT and GMAT help from the author.
🖱 **www.west.net/~stewart**

Point your Web browser to the author's website. There you'll find free online tutorials and mini-tests for every section of the GRE, GMAT and LSAT! You'll also find FAQ's for these exams, test-taking tips, and much more.

personal acknowledgments

I wish to acknowledge and thank the following persons for their contributions to this publication: Eva Anda, Patrick Cunningham, Susan Brooks and Eric Paton. I also wish to thank Linda Bernbach and Eve Steinberg at ARCO for their cooperation and assistance.

I am particularly grateful to Annette Davis for her editorial assistance and for her support and encouragement.

Finally, a special canine and feline "thank you" to Sunny Loperfido and April-Kitty (respectively) for their patience and understanding, especially at dinner time.

MARK ALAN STEWART

Credits

"Images of Dorothea Lange," by Therese Thau Heyman, *Humanities*, Vol. 14, No. 5 (September/October 1993), pp. 6, 8–10. Published by The National Endowment for the Humanities.

"Large Format Expands *Little Buddha*," by Bob Fisher, *American Cinematographer*, Vol. 75, No. 5 (May 1994), p. 41. Reprinted by permission of *American Cinematographer*.

" 'I Am Christina Rossetti,' " by Antony H. Harrison, *Humanities*, Vol. 14, No. 4 (July/August 1993), pp. 33–37. Published by The National Endowment for the Humanities.

"Arnold's Double-Sided Culture," by John P. Farrell, *Humanities*, Vol. 12, No. 3 (May/June 1991), pp. 26–30. Published by The National Endowment for the Humanities.

"The Artful Encounter," by Richard Wendorf, *Humanities*, Vol. 14, No. 4 (July/August 1993), pp. 9–12. Published by The National Endowment for the Humanities.

"The Debate Over Mozart's Music," by Neal Zaslaw, *Humanities*, Vol. 14, No. 5 (September/October 1993), pp. 26–27. Published by The National Endowment for the Humanities.

"Has the Life Industry Forgotten Its Mission?" by John C. Scully, *Best's Review* (February 1994), pp. 46, 48. Reprinted by permission of A.M. Best Company.

"Restoration or Preservation: Reflections on a Clash of Environmental Philosophies," by G. Stanley Kane, *The Humanist* (November/December 1993), pp. 27–30. Reprinted by permission of The American Humanist Association, © 1993.

"Health Care and the Constitution: Public Health and the Role of the State in the Framing Era," by Wendy E. Parmet, *Hastings Constitutional Law Quarterly*, Vol. 20, No. 2, pp. 279–281, 285–286; reprinted by permission of University of California, Hastings College of Law and Wendy E. Parmet. © 1993 by University of California, Hastings College of Law.

"The *Encyclopédie*: banned, burned—and bought," by Robert Wernick, *Smithsonian* (May 1997), pp. 72–83. Published by the Smithsonian Institution.

questions and answers about reading comprehension

Q: How should I use this book?

A: Your first step is to read the lesson materials (Parts 1–3) straight through from beginning to end. They contain a variety of strategies, tips, and techniques for reading the passages and handling the questions. But the lessons will help you on your exam only if you practice what you learn over and over again. You'll use the Sample Passages (Part 4) and Practice Sets (Part 5) for this purpose. As you practice, experiment with the strategies you learned in the lessons. Determine which techniques work best for you and under what circumstances. Once you settle on your favorite strategies and techniques, stick with them for the remaining practice sets so they become habits.

Try to limit your time for each practice set to the recommended time limits. Then be sure to read the explanations for each question set *immediately* after you attempt the questions in that set. If it looks like you're responding incorrectly to the same type of question over and over again, go back to the lessons and review the discussion about that question type. Perhaps you fell into one of the traps that the lessons warned you about. If so, a bit of reflection will help you avoid the same mistake next time. Also reflect on whether your basic strategy is working for you. If not, modify it or try a different strategy next time.

Q: Can I really improve my reading skills in a few weeks, or even a few months?

A: One or two months is enough time to break bad reading habits and train yourself to read more actively and efficiently. A few weeks, although probably not sufficient time to drastically alter your reading habits, is enough time to learn and apply some of the techniques presented in this book— for example, how to spot "sucker bait" answer choices and make close judgment calls between best and second-best answer choices.

Q: Should I try to increase my vocabulary for Reading Comprehension questions by learning as many new words as possible?

A: No, at least not specifically for Reading Comprehension. The test-makers don't design the passages and questions to test your vocabulary. Sure, you'll find the occasional erudite word in the passages ("erudite" is a good example). But don't worry; the test-makers don't intentionally pack the passages with obscure words that only Webster would know. Also, if a passage includes a technical term rest assured that the passage will supply all you need to know about the term to respond to the questions.

Q: Should I use materials in addition to this book to get ready for the Reading Comprehension portion of my exam?

A: Yes. The practice sets in this book are not grouped together as timed sections as they will be on your exam. So you should also obtain a comprehensive test-preparation book that contains full-length exam sections, then practice under timed conditions. This is the best way to determine your optimal pace for working through Reading Comprehension sets.

Q: What abilities are Reading Comprehension questions designed to measure?

A: Reading Comprehension question sets are designed to measure your ability to read and understand materials of complexity similar to the ones you'll encounter in graduate-level study. More specifically, the questions are designed to measure your ability to:

- read *carefully* and *accurately*

- determine the *relationships* among the various parts of the passage

- draw *reasonable inferences* from the material in the passage

You'll discover that while the easiest Reading Comprehension questions test your ability to simply *recall* information from the passage, most questions go further to test your ability to *understand*, to *reason from*, and even to *apply* what you've read. So unless you actively think about a passage's ideas as you read it, expect to have trouble responding intelligently to many (if not most) of the questions.

Most test-takers are lazy—they'll "kick back" and read a passage passively from beginning to end, taking no notes along the way. As their eyes pass over the words, they'll simply hope to absorb most of the information they'll need for the questions. The result: Although passive readers will recall some details and gain a sense for what the passage was about, they're unlikely to gain enough insight about the passage's ideas to respond effectively to any but the easiest questions.

The only way to beat the test is to think actively about the passage's ideas and about what you can infer from them. In fact, you'll learn in the lessons that follow that the most effective approach for most test-takers is to actually carry on a dialogue—a "Q&A" of sorts—with the passage as you read it and as you tackle the questions.

Q: What are the sources for the Reading Comprehension passages?

A: Passages are drawn from a variety of subjects—including the humanities (literature, art, music, etc.), the social sciences (sociology, psychology, political science, economics, etc.), the physical sciences (biology, physics, chemistry, etc.), ethics, philosophy, and law. Specific sources include professional journals and periodicals, dissertations written by doctoral-degree candidates, as well as periodicals and books that deal with sophisticated subjects of intellectual interest. Some LSAT passages are excerpts from law review articles (publications of law students).

The typical reading passages is contemporary—written within the last 10 or 20 years. But there's a chance you'll encounter a passage from an older source. In fact, you might even see a passage—particularly in the area of philosophy—from a pre-1900 work in which the language and syntax used are noticeably archaic. But don't expect it; older source material shows up very rarely on the exams.

Almost all passages are excerpts from longer works and are edited so that they're packed densely with testable material. A passage might be taken from the beginning, middle, or end of the larger work. Or it might be the result of cutting and pasting from various parts of the source work.

Q: Am I at an advantage if a passage involves a topic that is familiar to me?

A: Before I answer this question, consider the following remarks:

- The test-makers are very careful to ensure that all questions are answerable based solely upon the information provided in the passage, so that outside knowledge that a test-taker might possess about the topic will not provide that test-taker with any real advantage.

- The test-makers try to select source material that is narrow and somewhat obscure in its subject matter, so that no test-taker will have enough expertise on the particular specific topic to gain an advantage.

- Different passages on a test are always drawn from different academic areas; so it's unlikely that any particular test-taker will be knowledgeable enough about two or more of the areas included on the test to hold a significant advantage over other test-takers.

Despite the test-makers' efforts to level the paying field, you might be at a slight advantage if you have some familiarity with the particular topic. You might find the passage more interesting, be more relaxed and at ease with the passage if the terminology is familiar, and be able to concentrate more easily. But even if you're already familiar with the topic, don't expect to have an advantage when it comes to responding to the questions.

How do Reading Comprehension questions fit into the format of my exam?

As you can see directly to the right, Reading Comprehension questions account for a significant portion of each of the four exams listed. The tables below and on page 4 indicate the format of each exam in greater detail. For each exam you'll see:

- The overall format of the exam
- The format of the specific exam section that contains Reading Comprehension sets
- How the exam is scored

- **GRE** *Computer-Based Test (CBT)*
  27% of your Verbal Ability score
  (8 out of 30 questions)
- **LSAT** 28% of your total score
  (28 out of 100 questions)
- **GMAT** *Computer-Adaptive Test (CAT)*
  30% of your Verbal Ability score
  (12 out of 41 questions)
- **MCAT** 30% of your total score
  (65 out of 219 questions)

Format of the Computer-Based General GRE

The computer-based General GRE consists of three scored sections—Verbal, Quantitative and Analytical—and a trial section. The trial section will look just like one of the three scored sections, but the trial section itself is not scored; the test-taker does not know which section is the trial section. These four sections may appear in any order on your exam.

Verbal Ability	30 Questions	30 Minutes
Quantitative Ability	28 Questions	45 Minutes
Analytical Ability	35 Questions	60 Minutes
Trial Section	28–35 Questions	30–60 Minutes
TOTAL allotted time (minimum)		3 Hours, 45 Minutes
TOTAL number of *scored* questions		93

A 30-Minute GRE Verbal Ability Section

A GRE Verbal Ability section includes four different types of questions, interspersed with one another in no predetermined sequence. Reading Comprehension questions account for 8 of the 30 total questions in the section. Four of the Reading Comprehension questions are based on a long passage 400–450 words in length. The other four questions are split equally between two short passages, each about 200 words in length.

Reading Comprehension (short passage)	2 Questions
Reading Comprehension (short passage)	2 Questions
Reading Comprehension (long passage)	4 Questions
Analogies	9 Questions
Sentence Completion	6 Questions
Antonyms	7 Questions
TOTAL	30 Questions

How the Computer-Based GRE is Scored

Separate scores are computed for Verbal Ability, Quantitative Ability, and Analytical Ability. Each of the three scores is reported on a scale of 200–800. The scaled scores are determined based on (1) the number of questions to which the test-taker responds correctly and (2) the difficulty level of the questions that the computerized testing system poses to each individual test-taker.

Format of the LSAT

The LSAT consists of four 35-minute scored sections, a 35-minute trial section, and a 30-minute Writing Sample. The sections may appear in any order on the actual exam, except that the Writing Sample section is always the last administered section. The trial section will resemble one of the three different types of scored sections, although the trial section itself is not scored; the test-taker does not know which section is the trial section.

Reading Comprehension	28 Questions	35 Minutes
Analytical Reasoning	24 Questions	35 Minutes
Logical Reasoning	24–26 Questions	35 Minutes
Logical Reasoning	24–26 Questions	35 Minutes
Trial Section	24–28 Questions	35 Minutes
Writing Sample	–	30 Minutes
TOTAL exam time		3 Hours, 25 Minutes
TOTAL number of *scored* questions		100–102

A 35-Minute LSAT Reading Comprehension Section

An LSAT Reading Comprehension section consists of four passages. Each passage is 450–550 words in length and is accompanied by 6–8 questions.

Passage #1	6–8 Questions
Passage #2	6–8 Questions
Passage #3	6–8 Questions
Passage #4	6–8 Questions
TOTAL	28 Questions

How the LSAT is Scored

The test-taker receives a single score on a scale of 120–180 for the multiple-choice exam sections. The scaled score is determined from the test-taker's raw score (number of correct responses). NO PENALTY IS ASSESSED FOR INCORRECT RESPONSES. No scores for individual sections are computed or reported to the test-taker or to the law schools. The trial section is not scored. The Writing Sample is not scored; however, a photocopy of the writing sample is provided to each law school receiving the test-taker's LSAT score report.

Format of the GMAT CAT (Computer Adaptive Test)

The GMAT CAT consists of two multiple-choice sections–Verbal and Quantitative–and two Analytical Writing sections (essay writing). Both essay sections will precede the two multiple-choice sections. Of the 41 Verbal questions and 37 Quantitative questions, some will be *unscored*. But you won't know which questions are unscored, so don't worry about it.

Analytical Writing Assessment (AWA)

Analysis of an Issue	1 topic	30 Minutes
Analysis of an Argument	1 topic	30 Minutes

Verbal Ability — 41 Questions — 75 Minutes

Reading Comprehension	(12 Questions)
Critical Thinking	(14 Questions)
Sentence Correction	(15 Questions)

Quantitative Ability — 37 Questions — 75 Minutes

Problem Solving	(24 Questions)
Data Sufficiency	(13 Questions)

TOTAL allotted time — 3½ Hrs.

Reading Comprehension and the GMAT Verbal Section

The GMAT Verbal Ability section contains four Reading Comprehension sets—three shorter ones (about 200 words each) and on slightly longer one (about 300 words). Each set includes three questions.

Passage #1	3 Questions
Passage #2	3 Questions
Passage #3	3 Questions
Passage #4	3 Questions
TOTAL	12 Questions

How the GMAT CAT is Scored

GMAT test-takers receive four scaled GMAT scores:

1. A Verbal Ability score, on a scale of 0–60
2. A Quantitative Ability score, on a scale of 0–60
3. A composite score, on a scale of 200–800, based on Verbal Ability and Quantitative Ability scores
4. One overall Analytical Writing Assessment (AWA) score, on a scale of 0–6 (0 is low), which averages the grades awarded by four GMAT readers

Format of the MCAT

The MCAT consists of four distinct sections, which always appear in the order indicated below:

Verbal Reasoning	65 Questions	85 Minutes
Physical Sciences	77 Questions	100 Minutes
(lunch break)	–	(1 Hour)
Essay Writing	2 Questions	60 Minutes
Biological Sciences	77 Questions	100 Minutes
TOTALS	221 Questions	5 Hrs., 45 Min.

An 85-Minute MCAT Verbal Reasoning Section

The verbal reasoning section consists of 9 Reading Comprehension passages and 65 questions. Each passage is 550–700 words in length and is accompanied by 6–8 questions.

Reading Comprehension Passage #1	6–8 Questions
Reading Comprehension Passage #2	6–8 Questions
Reading Comprehension Passage #3	6–8 Questions
Reading Comprehension Passage #4	6–8 Questions
Reading Comprehension Passage #5	6–8 Questions
Reading Comprehension Passage #6	6–8 Questions
Reading Comprehension Passage #7	6–8 Questions
Reading Comprehension Passage #8	6–8 Questions
Reading Comprehension Passage #9	6–8 Questions
TOTAL	65 Questions

How the MCAT is Scored

MCAT test-takers receive four separate scores, one for each section of the exam. Scaled scores of 1–15 are computed for verbal reasoning, for physical sciences, and for biological sciences. The scaled scores are determined from the test taker's raw score (the number of correct responses). NO PENALTY IS ASSESSED FOR AN INCORRECT RESPONSE. The Writing Ability section is scored on a scale of J–T (J is low).

Pacing and Time Allocation—Questions and Answers

Most test-takers feel the same way about Reading Comprehension: The test-*makers* force you to hurry. In other words, the test simply doesn't allow you enough time to read each passage carefully and to give full and careful attention to all the questions. Yet reading speed is not the key to success in Reading Comprehension. The test-makers are not interested in how fast you read, but rather how effectively—or how "smart"—you read.

Smart reading means thinking like the test-makers as you read. (You'll learn this skill a bit later.) But it also means managing your time well. Make it your goal to pace yourself so that you: (1) read *all* the material the test offers (passages, questions and answer choices), and (2) have enough time to consider each question so you're never forced to make a random guess. Here's a Q&A that will help you attain both these goals.

Q. Would I improve my score if I skip one entire question set so that I can spend more time on each of the others?

A: Why not slow down your pace, take your time with fewer than all of the question sets offered, and random guess quickly on the set you skip? Perhaps you might actually improve your overall score this way. In theory, this strategy seems plausible. But in practice, it usually doesn't work.

Let's assume that you're taking the LSAT. A 35-minute LSAT Reading Comprehension section includes four question sets, and 28 questions altogether. That's an average of just under 9 minutes per question set if you tackle all four sets, but an average of just under 12 minutes per question set if you tackle only three of the four sets. Let's assume that you've taken some simulated tests, and you've been responding correctly, on average, to 18 of the 28 questions. Could you improve on that by spending 12 minutes on each of three passages, while random guessing on the fourth?

Consider the two alternative scenarios to the right (**Figure 1–1**). Notice that the test-taker didn't improve her score at all by slowing down and tackling only three of the four passages. In fact, most of my students discover that this strategy actually results in *lower* scores. After experimenting with both approaches for a few weeks, the students conclude that their optimal pace is actually faster than they first thought, and by slowing down their overall performance actually suffers.

Why doesn't the strategy work? For two reasons:

1. You end up reading *too* slowly and *too* carefully; the result is that you tend to focus on details and lose sight of the larger picture—the flow of the argument and the passage's primary purpose and main idea.

2. If you have extra time to think about a question, you begin to overanalyze it, read too much into it, and ignore your intuition.

But try this strategy anyway, especially if English is your second language. Some test-takers find that slowing down and handling fewer than all question sets alleviates that time-pressure panic that can so easily destroy your concentration.

GRE and GMAT Strategy: The computerized testing system does not allow you to return to questions or passages once you've moved on. Also, incorrect responses move you down the ladder of difficulty to easier ones, and your reward for easier

questions is less than for tougher ones. So on the GRE or GMAT, use this strategy ONLY to skip the *last* reading set, and ONLY if you're sure that you need to slow way down to get anywhere with the questions.

FIGURE 1–1

Two LSAT Scenarios

**Scenario 1
(Test-taker attempts all question sets)**

Question Set 1: 5 of 7 correct responses
(didn't have time to check the passage to confirm responses to detail questions)

Question Set 2: 3 of 7 correct responses
(surprised at poor outcome, since passage was fairly easy to understand–in retrospect, chose second-best answer on three of the questions)

Question Set 3: 6 of 7 correct responses
(understood passage well, but took too much time to answer questions, so not enough time left for last passage)

Question Set 4: 4 of 7 correct responses
(only had five minutes left; read passage hurriedly; had trouble concentrating due to concern for lack of time; made some educated guesses along with some random stabs)

Total Number of correct responses: 18

**Scenario 2
(Test-taker approaches all but one question set, random guessing on the remaining set)**

Question Set 1: 6 of 7 correct responses
(had time to check passage to locate information for a scattered detail question)

Question Set 2: 4 of 7 correct responses
(additional time to reconsider scope of passage and author's purpose resulted in one additional correct answer)

Question Set 3: 6 of 7 correct responses
(finished first two passages quicker than expected; thinking clear due to lack of time pressure)

Question Set 4: 2 of 7 correct responses
(statistically average random-guess result)

Total number of correct responses: 18

Q: Should I move on to the next question set after a certain number of minutes, even if I haven't finished the question set?

A: Not necessarily. You've invested a certain amount of time in reading and assimilating the materials in each passage; having made this investment, you should by all means take the time to consider every question in the set. But if you've already made at least an educated guess at all the questions, it's probably not the best use of your precious time to go back and reexamine those questions that you are least certain about. In fact, even if you're ahead of your predetermined pace (e.g., 9 minutes per passage), move forward to the next question set. Once you begin losing momentum, you're in trouble; you'll either begin to overanalyze the questions or find yourself hunting through the passage again just to eliminate one answer choice for one question—both results are a highly unproductive use of your time. [NOTE: On the GRE and GMAT remember that you can't return to a question once you've moved on.]

Q: On the LSAT or MCAT, should I save some time at the end to go back and reexamine questions that I was uncertain about?

A: Not as a hard-and-fast rule. By all means, earmark those questions for which you think another 30 seconds of thought would help, just in case you have extra time at the end of the timed section. But don't assume that you'll have extra time, and by all means don't hurry through the test or skip questions or passages just to ensure that you have extra time left over. Also, if you do have time to go back to a previous question set, *don't go back too far*. The memory of the first passage that you read may have faded, so consider limiting your review to the last one or two question sets. [NOTE: On the GRE and GMAT remember that you can't return to a question once you've moved on.]

Q: On the LSAT or MCAT, should I read the passages in the order in which they appear?

A: Begin with a passage that looks comfortable to you. Take a few seconds to size up the first passage. Consider starting with another passage if: (1) the topic is intimidating or unfamiliar, (2) the passage appears to be especially dense in details (terminology, names, dates, and so forth), or (3) the passage is longer than average. [NOTE: On the GRE and GMAT remember that you can't return to a question once you've moved on.]

Q: On the LSAT and MCAT, do the passages appear in ascending order of difficulty? If not, is there any pattern at all?

A: The passages do not necessarily appear either in ascending or descending order of difficulty. To make this point to my students, I ask them to rank the passages of every timed section that we take in class (but before they check the answer key) according to level of difficulty. The only pattern I've noticed is that the first passage is rarely the most difficult one. If there's a lesson to be learned here, it's that you should probably not skip the first question set. [NOTE: On the computerized GRE and GMAT the pattern of difficulty level depends on each taker's own responses (see page 7).]

Q: On the LSAT or MCAT, should I skip a passage if it is not accompanied by as many questions as the other passages?

A: No. In theory this may seem like a good strategy, since the return on your investment of time (to read and assimilate the information in a passage) would seem to be greater for passages with more questions. But the number of questions from passage to passage is not likely to vary by more than one. In any case, your comfort level with the subject of the passage should be the determining factor when deciding whether to skip a passage. [NOTE: On the GRE and GMAT "skipping" a question requires a random guess (see page 7).]

Q: Are some types of questions inherently more difficult than others? If so, should I skip them?

A: Questions that require you merely to recall or locate factual information ("explicit detail" questions) do not require any insight or understanding on your part, and so these questions would seem to be inherently easier. But if the passage is extremely dense in details, it may be so difficult to recall or locate the specific information that you need to respond to one of these "easy" questions that in actuality the question is rather difficult.

Also, certain question types may seem more difficult than others to you, depending upon your own strengths and weaknesses. For example, if you have a great memory for details but often have trouble understanding broader concepts, you'll probably find that the detail-oriented questions are easier than the more general questions. Even if so, this fact would probably not justify your skipping other questions, unless you're quickly running out of time.

Q: In terms of difficulty level, what sort of "mix" should I expect among the Reading Comprehension questions on my exam?

A: Every question you'll encounter on any of the exams has appeared on a prior exam as a "trial" (unscored) question. The test-makers tabulate the percentage of test-takers responding correctly to each trial question. Then they use this data to determine the appropriate question mix for upcoming exams. On the LSAT and MCAT, you're sure to see a fairly even mix of easier, more moderate, and more difficult questions. But on the computerized GRE and GMAT, there's no preset mix; the difficulty level of later questions depends on your responses to earlier ones, as explained in the next section (below).

Does all this suggest any particular strategy? On the LSAT and MCAT, easy questions are worth the same number of points as difficult questions. So whatever you do, be sure to attempt all of the easier questions in the section (you can often spot an easier question at a glance). So by all means, shop around for easier questions; otherwise, you might defeat yourself by getting bogged down in the toughies and never getting to the "gimmies." [NOTE: The GRE and GMAT testing systems don't allow you to "shop around" for easy questions; for your strategy on these two exams, see below.]

The GRE and GMAT Computerized Testing Systems—Questions and Answers

Q: How do the GRE and GMAT computerized testing systems measure my reading comprehension ability?

A: The passages and questions on the computerized GRE and GMAT are similar to the ones on the old paper-and-pencil versions in terms of content, style, and the basic skills tested. However, these new computerized versions depart from the paper-and-pencil versions in three important ways:

- On each section of the test, you must confirm your response to at least one question for a score for that section to be tabulated and reported.

- Your responses to earlier questions dictate which questions the test subsequently presents to you. More specifically, the system is designed to adapt to your ability level by choosing questions that are appropriate in difficulty, as determined by your earlier responses. During each section, the test will initially pose questions of average difficulty. As you respond correctly, the test will move you up the ladder of difficulty; conversely, incorrect responses will prompt easier questions (but see below).

- But the test won't necessarily present an easier question after you answer a question incorrectly or a tougher one after you respond correctly. The system is designed to take three different factors into account in determining which questions to present to you and in determining your score:

1. The *difficulty level* of the questions to which you respond correctly and incorrectly (a correct response to a more difficult question is given more weight than a correct response to an easier question)

2. The *diversity of question types* to which you respond correctly (responding correctly to diverse types of Reading Comprehension questions will enhance your Verbal score)

3. *Coverage of specific content* (if the Reading Comprehension questions that you answered correctly, considered together, cover a great deal of the passage's content, this will enhance your Verbal score)

Q: On the computer-based GRE why do the time limits for the different sections vary so widely?

A: On the old paper-based GRE the time limit for each section was 30 minutes, so you'd spend the same amount of time on each of the three ability areas (Verbal, Quantitative and Analytical). But the time limits on the computer-based GRE vary widely:

Section	Number of Questions	Time	Average Time Per Question
Verbal	30	30 min.	1 min.
Quantitative	28	45 min.	1.5 min.
Analytical	35	60 min.	1.8 min.

Why such a wide difference in time limits and average time allowed per question? Three reasons:

1. Analytical questions are more time-consuming (on average) than Quantitative questions, which are more time-consuming (on average) than Verbal questions.

2. You'll need to use your scratch paper for Analytical questions more than for Quantitative questions, and more for Quantitative questions than for Verbal questions. Working back and forth between a computer screen and scratch paper eats up more time than you might think.

3. Analytical questions are tougher (on average) than Verbal and Quantitative questions.

Q: Isn't reading comprehension more difficult when reading text on a computer screen?

A: The computer-based GRE and GMAT do present some unique challenges to the test-taker, no doubt about it. This is particularly true when it comes to Reading Comprehension, in three respects:

1. You can't annotate the passage (for example, underline or circle key words) because it's on a computer screen rather than on paper. But *scratch paper is provided* to make notes and outlines.

2. You can't view an entire passage at once. And the computer interface won't allow you to enlarge or reduce the text. So you'll have to scroll vertically to read the entire passage.

3. You'll only see one question at a time, and you can't return to a question once you've moved on. So it's impossible to cross-check answers to make sure they're consistent with one another. (This is a key strategy on the LSAT and MCAT, which are still paper-based.)

Q: Are there specific Reading Comprehension strategies that apply just to the computerized tests (the GRE and GMAT)?

A: Emphatically, yes. Remember these three tips:

1. *Try to minimize vertical scrolling.* Scrolling takes time and contributes to eye strain. Read the first question presented before you begin reading the passage, so you're less likely to have to scroll up or down later just to answer that question.

2. *Take your time with the first few questions.* Remember that your response to initial questions will move you either up or down the ladder of difficulty. You want to move up, of course, because correct responses to tougher questions earn you more points. So spend a bit more time than average on the first few questions; otherwise, you'll waste the next several questions trying to reverse direction by convincing the test that you're smarter than it thinks you are!

3. *Use your scratch paper to outline the passage.* You can't annotate a reading passage (mark it up and make margin notes) on a computer screen. So on your scratch paper take *brief* notes, or even make a brief outline, to keep the passage's main points and details straight in your mind. With a good outline you'll be able to recall the flow of the passage. Then as you tackle the questions, your outline will tell you where to go in the passage to find the information you need for each question. So a good outline will save you time and help minimize vertical scrolling.

Also, remember that your score is determined in part by the *diversity* of question types and content among the questions to which you respond correctly. A good outline will help you keep in focus all different areas of the passage, which will help you respond to diverse questions. The end result: a high test score!

Q: I heard that the computer-based GRE might also include a writing task and a Mathematical Reasoning section. Is this true?

A: On the computer-based GRE you *might* encounter a separate *research* section called "Mathematical Reasoning." If so, it'll be the last section of your exam, it will be clearly identified as a research section, and your responses to the questions on this section won't affect your test scores. So don't worry about it.

Effective October, 1999, ETS is offering a GRE Writing Assessment Test. It isn't administered as part of the multiple-choice GRE. You register, pay for, and take the Writing Assessment Test separately. It's administered by computer, just like the multiple-choice GRE; you'll use a word processor to compose two essays in response to two specific writing topics, which the testing system selects randomly from a bank of topics. Your essays are read and scored by ETS "readers." Check with the graduate programs to which you are applying for admission to see if they require GRE Writing Assessment Test scores.

approaching the passages

The Operating Principle

Almost everyone who struggles with Reading Comprehension on one of the graduate-level entrance exams suffers from one or more of the problems indicated in **Figure 2–1**. The first and third problems are particularly common. All of these problems are results of the same bad habit: PASSIVE READING. The materials here in Part 2 are designed to help you break this old habit (at least long enough to take your exam) and to develop a highly active (even *interactive*) approach toward the passages. But the only way to break old reading habits and to develop new and better ones is through practice. So in addition to reading Part 2, you should also use the practice sets in Part 5 of this book to experiment with the techniques discussed here.

Every Reading Comprehension question is designed to measure one of two basic abilities:

1. your ability to *remember* what you read, or

2. your ability to understand—or *comprehend*—what you read.

The second skill is a higher one in that it requires independent thinking on your part. More important, you'll find that *the majority of the questions are comprehension questions, not memory questions*; and it's this fact that should drive your approach in reading the passages. In order to understand (comprehend) a passage, you must be able to:

- identify the thesis (or main idea) and the author's primary purpose

- follow the author's line of reasoning from paragraph to paragraph.

Beginning right now, embrace the following operating principle:

UNDERSTAND THE PASSAGE WELL ENOUGH TO BE ABLE TO BRIEFLY EXPLAIN THE AUTHOR'S MAIN POINT AND LINE OF REASONING TO SOMEONE WHO HAS NOT READ THE PASSAGE.

FIGURE 2–1

COMMON READING COMPREHENSION PROBLEMS	SOLUTIONS
1. Poor concentration due to • high density (too many details) • obscure or unfamiliar terminology/jargon • apparent lack of structure (passage seems to ramble) • lack of interest in subject matter	1. • Engage passage's author in a dialogue • Strive to understand line of reasoning rather than remembering facts and figures • Annotate, take notes, or make an outline
2. Slow reader, so cannot finish in time	2. • Shop for information • Focus on main ideas and overall structure instead of details
3. When answering questions, too much time searching the passage for information needed to respond to question	3. Annotate, take notes, or make an outline
4. Cannot narrow answer choices down to one clear best answer	4. Learn to think like test maker (see Part 3)

The Four Modes of Reading

If there's one key to succeeding in Reading Comprehension, it's developing a highly active approach toward the question sets. In this portion of the lesson I'll explain what this approach involves and how to develop it.

Let's refer to your frame of mind as you tackle a question set as your reading "mode." Consider the four basic modes and corresponding approaches listed in **Figure 2–2**. They differ in the reader's level of activity and basic strategy. You'll learn in the pages that follow that only the *Interactive* and the *Question-Driven* modes are likely to help you improve your performance in Reading Comprehension.

FIGURE 2–2

MODE	APPROACH	LEVEL OF ACTIVITY
Passive	straight read-through	low
Preview	preview, then read-through	moderate
Interactive	work back and forth between passage and questions	high
Question-Driven (LSAT/MCAT)	respond to selected questions without reading entire passage	very high

The Passive Mode

Most test-takers take a rather passive approach toward Reading Comprehension, adopting the following three steps:

1. Read the passage carefully from beginning to end. As you read, underline what strikes you as being particularly important points.

2. Respond to the questions in the order presented. Go back to the passage as required if you have trouble answering a question or remembering the relevant portion of the passage.

3. On the LSAT or MCAT, place a question mark next to any questions you're uncertain about, hoping you'll have time at the end of the test section to reconsider the question. (By the way, you won't have time!)

The typical test-taker gives equal time and attention to every sentence in the passage, reading the passage from beginning to end without interruption and with very little thought as to what particular information is most important in order to respond to the specific questions. This strategy is actually better characterized as a NON-strategy.

What is the likely result of this approach? Although the reader might remember some scattered factual information as well as some of the points the author makes along the way, the reader isn't likely to respond effectively to questions that require any degree of insight or understanding about the author's ideas.

The Preview Mode

Many test-preparation books and courses advocate this mode, in which you follow these steps:

1. Preview the question stems (or on the GRE and GMAT, the first question stem), but *not* the answer choices, for hints about the passage's subject and possible thesis. This step is intended to help you anticipate what you're about to read—in other words, to help put you in an active reading mode.

2. Preview the passage by reading the first (and perhaps last) sentence of each paragraph. This preview is intended to give you an idea as to the structure of the passage and flow of the discussion.

3. Read the passage carefully from beginning to end, paying particular attention to excerpts that look familiar to you from your reading of the question stems (or on the GRE and GMAT, that first question stem). Underline these excerpts as well as any other information that strikes you as particularly important. (On the GRE and GMAT you jot this information down on your scratch paper.)

In theory, this sounds like good advice. So should you use this approach? The bottom line is: Previewing works better for the paper-based exams (LSAT and MCAT), and it's more useful of you're short on time. Otherwise, the preview mode does not make the most effective use of your time. Beginning on Page 12 we'll try applying this mode to some question stems and passages, and you can see for yourself if you agree.

The Interactive Mode

This is the approach I advocate for *most* test-takers under *most* circumstances. My students find that this is the only approach that actually helps them improve their overall performance to any significant extent. In the interactive mode, although you should by all means read the passage in its entirety, you should NOT read the entire passage without interrupting your reading to answer questions. Here are the basic steps:

1. Do NOT preview the question stems (or on the GRE or GMAT, the first question stem) or passage. Begin immediately with the passage itself.

2. After reading the first paragraph, scan the question stems for ones you might respond to at this point, at least tentatively. The first paragraph will most certainly provide enough information for you to respond, at least tentatively, to any question that asks about the overall thesis, topic, or author's purpose. (GRE-GMAT NOTE: The first paragraph usually contains information useful in responding to the first question presented.)

3. Return to the passage and read the next paragraph. On the LSAT or MCAT, scan the question stems for any additional questions that you can respond to at this time.

4. Take a few seconds to reconsider any questions that you responded to after reading the first paragraph. Have you changed your mind about your tentative response after reading the second paragraph? Or has the second paragraph confirmed that your initial response was correct?

5. Perform step 3 for the remaining paragraphs; work back and forth between passage and questions.

6. After reading the entire passage, apply the operating principle indicated on Page 9. Take a few seconds to recap the passage in your mind. What was the author's main point and what were the major supporting points? Just remind yourself right now about the flow of the discussion; don't be concerned with remembering all of the detailed factual information.

Practice this approach in Part 5, and you'll discover:

- *Your concentration will improve.* From the first second, you're interacting with the passage, engaged in a Q&A session with the test-maker.

- *Your accuracy will improve.* You don't need to remember everything in the passage. Because you're focusing only on a single question and on shopping for the answer to that specific question,

you're less likely to forget or be confused by the relevant information in the passage.

- *You'll finish the exam section in the allotted time.* By using every second of your time as productively as possible, you won't get bogged down by a particularly tedious or difficult passage.

- *Your skill in identifying wrong answers will improve.* Making tentative or educated guesses forces you to interact with the test-maker and to try to determine what the test-maker was thinking in drafting the questions and answer choices. You'll develop an intuition for spotting wrong answers.

REMEMBER: You'll have to practice this interactive approach in order to become comfortable with it. Old habits die hard. Apply this approach to the question sets in Part 5 of this book until the interactive mode becomes second nature to you.

The Question-Driven Mode

Suppose you had only one or two minutes to handle an entire Reading Comprehension set. How would you spend that brief time? On the LSAT or MCAT I'd "shop around" for two question types:

1. Questions that ask about the author's primary concern or about the passage's main idea

2. Questions that includes specific line references (e.g., "in lines 20–22...")

Then I'd preview the first few and last few sentences of the passage to try to get a sense for the scope of the topic at hand, the author's perspective (or attitude), and possible thesis. Then I'd tackle any questions of the first type listed above. Next, I'd consider the second type (if any): I'd quickly read the enumerated lines, as well as the ones immediately preceding and following them, and attempt the question.

The GRE and GMAT hurry-up drill is a bit different. Think twice before taking random stabs at questions just to move ahead to ones you think you can answer quickly. (Remember: Incorrect responses move you down that difficulty ladder, which is not what you want!) Instead, preview the passage (just as in the LSAT and MCAT drill discussed above). Then use your intuition on each question in turn; eliminate answer choices that run contrary to your sense of the passage. Your goal during a GRE or GMAT hurry-up drill is simple: *Make at least a reasoned guess on every Reading Comprehension question the test is willing to offer you during your Verbal Ability section.*

Pre-Reading Techniques

As I mentioned on page 10 (see *The Preview Mode*), many test-preparation books and courses recommend that before you read a passage straight through you (1) preview the question stems, and (2) preview the first and perhaps the last sentence of each paragraph. On the LSAT and MCAT previewing can be very useful if you're running out of time and need to make some quick educated guesses on that last question set. Otherwise, while some LSAT and MCAT test-takers find previewing helpful, others find that it eats up more time than it's worth. The best way to decide for yourself is to try it using the practice sets in Part 5.

GRE/GMAT NOTE: On these computer-based tests, you can only preview the first question anyway, and previewing the passage requires a lot of vertical scrolling—more trouble than it's worth. So the next four pages applies only to the LSAT and MCAT.

Previewing LSAT and MCAT Question Stems

Reading the question stems (but not necessarily the answer choices) prior to reading the passage might help you focus on the topic (thereby improving your concentration) and anticipate what you're about to read. Question stems often provide hints about the subject of the passage and possible thesis, as well as providing information or clues about some of the details in the passage.

Reading the question stems first can also give you an idea as to what particular information in the passage you should pay particular attention to. As you read the passage, you might come across a subtopic (perhaps a particular name, event, theory, or title) that you recall was mentioned in one of the questions. Obviously, you should pay close attention to this particular discussion because you know that there is a question about it. Perhaps you might consider interrupting your reading at this point to respond to that particular question while the information is fresh in your mind.

Examine the question stems in **Figure 2–3** , along with the following commentary about the clues and ideas that you might obtain solely by reading these question stems.

AUTHOR'S POINT OF VIEW: None of the questions suggest that the author has a point of view on an issue. While Question 3 might suggest otherwise, I really doubt that the passage discusses various opinions or

FIGURE 2–3

> **QUESTION STEMS**
>
> 1. Which of the following statements about the Italian madrigal is best supported by the passage?
>
> 2. In the passage above, the author's primary purpose is to:
>
> 3. Based upon the information provided in the passage, which of the following persons would the author agree made the most significant contribution to the development of the madrigal?
>
> 4. Which of the following statements about the *frottola* is best supported by the passage?
>
> 5. According to the passage, all of the following are characteristics of early sixteenth-century madrigals EXCEPT:
>
> 6. Which of the following is the most readily inferable reason for the use of the term "madrigal proper" in line 29 to identify a particular poetic form?

theories as to who "made the most significant contribution to the development of the madrigal." The other question stems do not point in that direction.

QUESTION 1: The passage describes the Italian madrigal, perhaps comparing it with something else. I probably won't find a *list* of characteristics in the passage; if a list of characteristics were included, the question would ask "all of the following statements about the Italian madrigal are supported by the passage EXCEPT...."

QUESTION 2: This stem does not provide any clues. However, I bet I could make an educated guess at the correct response without even looking at the passage, just by considering all of the question stems. As a whole, the passage concerns the "madrigal." The author is presenting the material objectively, and in an historically chronological fashion. Thus, the author's primary concern might be to trace the historical development of the madrigal or to compare the madrigal to other poetic forms that emerged during certain centuries. I'm not quite sure, but I bet I can narrow the answer choices from five down to perhaps two.

QUESTION 3: The passage will probably mention at least five specific names (one for each answer choice). They will be easy to locate in the passage because they are capitalized. I could probably answer this question now (before reading the passage straight through) by scanning the passage and reading the material immediately preceding and following the names.

QUESTION 4: Okay, while Questions 1, 3, 5, and 6 all mention the term "madrigal," this question mentions a different term: *frottola*. It looks as if the passage as a whole is about madrigals, while the *frottola* (whatever that is) will be discussed only in one portion of the passage. Maybe it's a specific type of madrigal, or maybe it is compared to or contrasted with the madrigal. In any event, I could probably find the relevant portion of the passage very quickly, especially since the word *frottola* is italicized, read the material immediately preceding and following the

term, and respond to the question without reading any other part of the passage.

QUESTION 5: This question provides a clue about the structure of the passage. The author probably discusses historical periods chronologically. Perhaps each paragraph is devoted to a different century. I could probably locate key terms such as "fifteenth century" and "sixteenth century" quickly by scanning the passage. All four wrong answer choices to Question 5 are probably listed in the same paragraph. Since there are four characteristics that are discussed, I will probably have to read an entire paragraph to see them all. As with Questions 3 and 4, I probably won't have to read any other part of the passage to respond to this question.

QUESTION 6: I bet I can answer this one merely by reading the material immediately preceding and following line 29. I wonder if "madrigal proper" is one type of madrigal while *frottola* (Question 4) is another? Does each term refer to a specific poetic form? Question 6 seems to suggest so.

Now try this previewing technique yourself. Read the question stems in the left-hand column below (**Figure 2–4**), then try to anticipate the content of the passage by asking yourself the questions in the right-hand column. After you're done, ask yourself whether you'd be likely to get more out of the passage by thinking about these questions beforehand.

FIGURE 2–4

QUESTION STEMS

1. The author of the passage is primarily concerned with

2. Based upon the author's interpretation of Arnoldian culture, with which of the following statements would Arnold most likely disagree?

3. It can be inferred from the passage that the two-cultures debate

4. All of the following statements about multiculturalists are supported by the passage EXCEPT:

5. In criticizing Arnold's dissenters, the author employs all of the following methods EXCEPT:

6. It can be inferred from the information in the passage that Arnoldian culture is perpetuated today by

Based upon these 6 questions, ask yourself:

- What is the topic of the passage? (NOTE: it must be broad enough to embrace all of the questions.)

- Can you identify one or more subtopics (areas of discussion)?

- Does the author present the topic objectively, or does the author have a point of view about the topic?

- If the passage is subjective, does the author side with one school of thought in opposition to another, or does the author offer a new theory or explanation about the topic?

- Which question(s) could you answer tentatively without reading any part of the passage?

- For which question(s) do you think you could find the information by quickly scanning the passage for the relevant information (rather than reading every word from the beginning)?

Previewing an LSAT or MCAT Reading Passage

FIGURE 2–5

Would it help to read key excerpts of an LSAT or MCAT passage—perhaps the first and last sentence of each paragraph—before you read the entire passage? This technique might provide clues about:

- the scope of the topic

- the structure of the passage (how the author has organized the information among the paragraphs)

- the author's thesis or major conclusions.

- whether the author resolves the issue, problem, or question posed in the passage.

Figure 2–5 and **Figure 2–6** each present a passage and a set of question stems. Notice that I've included only the first and last sentences of each paragraph. Examine each figure; pretend you're taking an actual LSAT or MCAT under the pressure of time. Ask yourself:

- How much time did it take to preview the passage and question stems?

- What clues did I obtain about the items listed above?

- What clues did I obtain about where to go in the passage to find the information I need to answer each question?

- Are these clues helpful enough to justify the time spent using this strategy?

FIGURE 2–5

QUESTION STEMS

1. The author of the passage is primarily concerned with

2. Based upon the author's interpretation of Arnoldian culture, with which of the following statements would Arnold most likely disagree?

3. It can be inferred from the passage that the two-cultures debate

4. All of the following statements about multi-culturalists are supported by the passage EXCEPT:

5. In criticizing Arnold's dissenters, the author employs all of the following methods EXCEPT:

6. It can be inferred from the information in the passage that Arnoldian culture is perpetuated today by

(PARAGRAPH 1)

Late Victorian and modern ideas of culture are always, in some sense, indebted to Matthew Arnold, who, largely through his *Culture and Anarchy* (1869), placed the word at the center of debates about the goals of intellectual life and humanistic society. · · · · · · · · · · · · · · · ·

· Although Arnold's thinking about culture helped to define the purposes of the liberal arts curriculum in the century following the publication of *Culture*, three concrete forms of dissent from Arnold's views have had considerable impact of their own.

(PARAGRAPH 2)

The first can be seen as protesting Arnold's fearful designation of "anarchy" as culture's enemy. · · · · · · ·

· The writer who regarded the contemporary condition with such apprehension in *Culture* is the poet who wrote "Dover Beach," not an ideologue rounding up all the usual modern suspects.

(PARAGRAPH 3)

Another form of opposition saw Arnold's culture as a perverse perpetuation of classical and literary learning, outlook, and privileges in a world where science had become the new *arch* and from which any substantively new order of thinking must develop. · · · · · · · · · · ·

· However, Arnold himself had viewed culture as enacting its life in a much more broadly conceived set of institutions.

(PARAGRAPH 4)

Today, however, Arnoldian culture is sustained, if indirectly, by multiculturalism, a movement aimed largely at gaining recognition for voices and visions that Arnoldian culture has implicitly suppressed. · · · · · · · · · · · ·

· · · · · · · · · · · · · · · The multiculturalists' conflict with Arnoldian culture has clear affinities with the radical critique; yet multiculturalism affirms Arnold by returning us more specifically to a tension inherent in the idea of culture rather than to the culture-anarchy dichotomy.

(PARAGRAPH 5)

The social critics, defenders of science, and multiculturalists insist that Arnold's culture is simply a device for ordering us about. ·

· · This capacity which all humans possess, Arnold made the foundation and authority of culture.

FIGURE 2-6

(PARAGRAPH 1)

A "radiative forcing" is any change imposed on the Earth that affects the planetary energy balance. · · · · · · · ·
· ·
· ·
· ·
· ·
· ·
· ·
· · · Radiative feedbacks include changes in such phenomena as clouds, atmospheric water vapor, sea-ice cover, and snow cover..

(PARAGRAPH 2)

The interplay between forcings and feedbacks can be quite complex. ·
· ·
· ·
· ·
· ·
· ·
· · · However, scientists do not know how the balance might shift in the future as cloud formation and dissipation are affected by ozone depletion.

(PARAGRAPH 3)

Contributing to this uncertainty is the complexity of the mechanisms at work in the process of ozone depletion. · ·
· ·
· ·
· ·
· ·
· ·
· · · · · · · · · · These findings have called into question conventional explanations for ozone depletion, which fail to adequately account for the new evidence.

QUESTION STEMS

1. It can be inferred from the information in the passage that "the burning of fossil fuels" (lines 9-10)

2. According to the passage, radiative forcings and radiative feedbacks can be distinguished from each other in which of the following ways?

3. Based upon the information in the passage, decreased evaporation is most likely to result in which of the following?

4. The author discusses the effect of clouds on atmospheric temperature most likely in order to show that

5. Based upon the information in the passage, the author would probably agree that scientists could more accurately predict the extent and direction of the greenhouse effect if they were to

6. The information in the last paragraph does NOT:

7. Which of the following best expresses the author's primary concern in the passage?

I think you'll find that, although previewing the passages makes sense in theory, in practice it isn't very helpful, for three reasons:

1. Once you begin to read the passage in its entirety, you'll probably forget most, if not all, of what you learned from previewing.

2. Previewing calls for you to read the same material twice. Does that sound efficient to you?

3. Previewing takes time—perhaps 30 seconds to a minute—time that you probably can't afford during the real test.

4. While previewing might be useful for some passages, for others this technique will be of little or no help. Previewing the passage in **Figure 2–5** was more helpful than it was for the passage in **Figure 2–6**, wasn't it?

There is one exceptional situation in which you should preview the passage and the question stems. If you're running out of time and only have a few minutes to handle that last set of questions, you might be able to take reasoned guesses to certain questions without reading the entire passage. (This is the question-driven approach I described on page 11.)

But remember: Previewing the passage won't work equally well for all passages. A passage that is more technical in subject, or one in which the questions require you to pull together bits and pieces from different parts of the passage, is certainly not the ideal candidate. (It's difficult to know beforehand how well previewing will work, but the question stems might offer clues.) Be sure to try previewing as part of a hurry-up drill for at least a few of the practice sets in Part 5, just to get the hang of it.

Dialogue, Anticipation and Recap

To help develop an interactive approach, think about Reading Comprehension as a three-way conversation between you, the author and the test-maker. The moment you start reading, begin a conversation, or dialogue. As silly as it might seem to you as you read this, a rather informal three-way conversation is the best way to shift into your interactive mode, and stay there.

During my workshops I'll take a question set and literally converse aloud with the author and test-maker through the entire passage and question set, for all of my students to hear, so they can get a better idea of what I'm thinking as I approach a Reading Comprehension question set. The following suggestions should help you to develop a conversational approach.

Continually form and reform a mental outline.

Learn to ask questions that bear directly on tested information. Although what sort of questions are most useful depends in part on the passage, here are some questions that you can ask while reading any passage:

- What is your purpose, author, in making this particular statement at this particular point in the passage?

- What part does this point play in your overall argument, author?

- Does this idea continue a line of thought or begin a new one?

- What does this evidence prove or exemplify?

- Do you have an opinion about the statement you just made, author? If so, is it positive or negative? Can you justify your opinion?

- What are you going to talk about next, author?

After you read each paragraph, pause for a moment to evaluate the paragraph as a whole. Try to recap the paragraph as one, two, or perhaps three basic ideas. It's important to express these ideas in your own words; otherwise, you'll revert to a passive mode. Recap all of the points the author has made up to this point in the passage. After each paragraph, answer the following questions for yourself:

- How would I sum up the passage to this point?

- At what point is the discussion now?

- What basic points is the author trying to get across in this paragraph? Do these ideas continue a line of thought, or do they begin a new one?

- Where is the discussion likely to go from here?

Get to know the author.

Do not allow the author to intimidate you. Discard your mental image of the world's foremost authority on the subject at hand, whose insight into a highly complex subject far exceeds that of any other human. Instead, picture a struggling graduate student, perhaps 24 to 28 years old, probably no more intelligent or experienced in the world than you, sitting at a library carrel trying desperately to produce a research paper of publishable quality so that he or she can earn a degree and land a decent teaching job. I've got news for you: the second image is probably closer than the first one to reality. The following dialogue will render the author more approachable to you:

Before reading the passage:

- About what particular subject are you supposed to be such an expert, author?

- Is there some important insight that you have into this subject that you're telling the world about here?

As you read the passage:

- Prove to me, author, that what you're saying here is true. I demand that you show me one or two pieces of evidence to support this brilliant and important idea of yours.

- There must be some other legitimate opinion about this subject other than your own, author. Will you at least acknowledge one other point of view?

Think out loud as you practice.

This will help you to concentrate and chase away distracting and unproductive thoughts. As you become more proficient at interactive reading, you can begin conversing silently instead.

Example

Figure 2–7 below includes the entire first paragraph from the passage on page 14, followed by some comments that indicate what you should be thinking after reading this paragraph. Notice that these thoughts include anticipation as well as recap. After examining **Figure 2–7**, look again at the six question stems in **Figure 2–5** (page 14). Would you consider interrupting your reading to respond tentatively to one or more of the questions? Perhaps to answer questions 1 and 2?

FIGURE 2–7

Late Victorian and modern ideas of culture are always, in some sense, indebted to Matthew Arnold, who, largely through his *Culture and Anarchy* (1869), placed the word at the center of debates about the goals of intellectual life and humanistic society. Arnold defined culture as "the pursuit of total perfection by means of getting to know, on all matters which most concern us, the best which has been thought and said in the world." It was Arnold's hope that, through this knowledge, we can turn "a fresh and free thought upon our stock notions and habits." Although Arnold's thinking about culture helped to define the purposes of the liberal arts curriculum in the century following the publication of *Culture*, three concrete forms of dissent from Arnold's views have had considerable impact of their own.

Thoughts about scope of topic:
• Limited to historical period from 1869–1969 (century following publication of *Culture*)
• Does not appear to be limited geographically (e.g., to Europe or America)

Thoughts about possible thesis:
• Must acknowledge Arnold's contribution and forms of dissent, and will probably include some evaluative statement about the forms of dissent

Thoughts about author's attitude toward subject:
• Admiring attitude toward Arnold
• Will author agree with any of the "three forms of dissent?" Probably not—author will probably criticize all three forms

Thoughts about possible structure/organization of passage:
• Look for separate paragraph describing each form of dissent
• Look for author's opinion and possible thesis statement in final paragraph/sentences of passage

Don't let the test-maker intimidate you.

Maybe you haven't thought consciously about the individuals who write the questions; but your subconscious impression is probably that the questions are the product of a disembodied intellect, infallible in its reasoning and almost divine in its judgment as to the true meaning of the passage and the best responses to the questions. Well, discard that image right now; it only serves to intimidate you and discourage you from interacting and dialoguing with the test.

Instead, picture the test-maker as three or four individuals about your age and intellect, all sitting around a table with their shirt sleeves rolled up, each with three items: (1) a copy of the passage; (2) a list of question types to choose from; and (3) a list of wrong-answer types (in case they run out of ideas for wrong answers). This image isn't quite accurate, but if you picture yourself as an active participant in the brainstorming session, the test will become far more approachable—it will become easier for you to interact with the test, to get inside the mind of the test-maker, and to score some points.

Look for structural triggers

"Triggers" are key words and phrases that provide clues about the structure and organization of the passage and the direction the discussion is flowing. If you're interacting with the passage, these words should trigger a mental response. *See page 20 for more about structural triggers.*

Annotate and make margin notes

On the LSAT and MCAT circle or underline key words and phrases in the passage to help you maintain an active mind set, to provide an outline of sorts, and to help you to locate the information you need to answer the questions. For some passages annotating won't be enough (and on the GRE and GMAT you can't annotate anyway). You might need to jot down some notes—in the margin, at the bottom of the page, or on your scratch paper—to help keep the details straight in your mind. *See pages 20 and 21 for more about annotating, margin notes and outlining.*

Apply the operating principle to each paragraph.

REMEMBER: Understand each paragraph well enough to be able to briefly explain the main point and line of reasoning to someone who has not read the passage.

Common Organizational Patterns

An important part of interactive reading is to *anticipate* how the material in the passage is organized. By anticipating how the materials are organized, you can predict the direction the discussion is heading, thereby improving:

- your ability to focus
- your ability to understand with insight
- your ability to discern between main points and details
- your reading speed

Because the organization of the passage reveals the flow of the author's argument, focusing on structure will also help you to:

- understand the author's main idea and primary purpose
- identify supporting evidence
- understand the author's purpose in mentioning various details

In sum, identifying the overall structure helps you to answer the questions correctly. In fact, you will discover that you can probably respond correctly to all of the more "general" questions (e.g., "main idea," "primary purpose," and "author's attitude" questions) just by determining the basic structure of the passage and organization of the materials.

No two passages will reflect identical patterns of organization; however, if you read enough passages, you will begin to see certain organizational patterns. Three general organizational patterns appear most often among the passages:

1. theory and critique
2. chronological tracing
3. classification

The materials that follow describe in greater detail how a passage of each type is likely to flow—from the introductory sentences, through the main body of the discussion, to the concluding remarks. Familiarizing yourself with these patterns will help you to anticipate the flow of the discussion in a passage. As you examine these patterns, bear in mind that not all passages fall neatly into one of these common patterns. A particular passage might, for example, (1) reflect two patterns (2) present a variation of one of the three common patterns, or (3) reflect a less common pattern not discussed below.

PATTERN #1
Theory and Critique

Introductory Sentences/First Paragraph:

The author identifies the conventional (older, established, traditional) view, theory, or explanation of a phenomenon. The introduction also either implies or states that the conventional view is flawed. (If the conventional view could not be criticized, the author probably would not be interested in writing about the topic in the first place.)

Body:

Look for one of the following patterns:

- The author focuses on one (or perhaps two) newer, more enlightened views. The author may attribute the new view either to a particular individual (scientist, author, sociologist, etc.) or to a school of thought in general (e.g., the leaders of the feminist movement of the 1970s).

- The author points to specific examples, observations, data, or other evidence that support a different theory. The author may also point out that the evidence is conflicting (and so no firm conclusions can be reached).

Final Sentences:

Look for one of the following typical patterns:

- The author admits that both views have their merits and shortcomings.
- The author suggests that all views are incomplete in their understanding and insight and that we need to study the subject further.
- The author introduces (but does not describe in detail) a new piece of evidence that suggests either yet another view, an explanation for conflicting views, or a synthesis of numerous views.

In any case, the author will almost always have an opinion on the subject.

PATTERN #2
Chronological (Historical) Tracing

Introductory Sentences/First Paragraph:

The author describes the state of affairs either currently or at a relatively recent time in history; the author asserts that this state of affairs can be attributed to (i.e.—has directly or indirectly resulted from) certain previous historical phenomena.

Body:

Look for one of the following typical patterns:

- The author discusses alternative theories regarding historical cause and effect (e.g., some historians believe X was the primary contributing cause of Y, while other historians disagree and believe instead that Z…). However, if this discussion turns out to be the author's primary concern, you are really dealing with a "theory and explanation" pattern rather than a "historical influence" pattern.

- The author traces in chronological order the events leading up to and contributing to a phenomenon.

Final Sentences:

Look for one of the following typical patterns:

- The author recaps by concluding that the current phenomenon is rooted in one or more particular ideology, movement, school of thought, event, etc.

- The author concludes that no single influence adequately explains the course of events; instead, we should recognize all contributing factors.

PATTERN #3
Classification

Introductory Sentences/First Paragraph:

The author identifies two or three basic types, categories, or classes of a phenomenon.

Body:

Look for the author to accomplish all of the following:

- describe each class in some detail

- compare and contrast characteristics of members of the different classes

- further divide one or more classes into subclasses.

Final Sentences:

Look for one of the following patterns (the first pattern is by far the most common):

- The discussion concludes simply by finishing the description of the classes and subclasses (in other words, no conclusions or arguments are made).

- The author points out new evidence that suggests an additional class or subclass.

- The author explains briefly how the classification system is used by practitioners to observe and test theories.

- The author points out a problem with the current classification system and suggests that some modification may be appropriate.

Structural Clues

While the passage as a whole will present a thesis (main idea), the author constructs his or her thesis by asserting various secondary points and presenting factual information. The supporting points and details are the building blocks with which the thesis is constructed. To follow the flow of the author's discussion, you should attempt to break up the passage into these building blocks and examine each block to determine what purpose it serves in the author's overall thesis.

The author has already broken the passage down into large building blocks called *paragraphs*. While paragraph breaks do indeed provide important clues about the organization of the passage, you need to break these paragraphs down further into more basic building blocks. A typical paragraph contains at least two or three smaller building blocks. As you identify each building block, mark the passage (either by annotations or margin notes, discussed later) so that you can see after you have read the passage where each building block begins and ends.

In constructing a house, building blocks are connected with mortar. Instead of mortar, specific words are used to connect the logical building blocks in a passage. **Figure 2–8** on page 20 lists many common connectors—*key words and phrases that provide clues as to the structure and organization of the passage and the direction in which the argument is flowing.* Underline or circle trigger words as you read the passage. By reviewing your annotations, you can effectively recap the structure and organization of the passage. (The subject of annotating is examined next.)

Annotating, Taking Notes and Outlining

On the LSAT and MCAT you can use a pencil to scribble directly in your test booklet, and on the computer-based GRE and GMAT pencils and scratch paper are provided. Here we'll go into more detail about how to use your pencil to get the most out of a Reading Comprehension passage.

Annotating an LSAT or MCAT Passage

Why annotate ("mark up") an LSAT or MCAT reading passage? Well, selective annotating can:

- help you maintain a question-oriented frame of mind

- provide a pre-written outline of sorts

- help you to locate passage information quickly

How much information should you annotate? If you *under*-annotate, you won't be able to effectively recap the passage by reviewing your annotations. On the other hand, if you *over*-annotate, your annotations lose their meaning, and you might as well not have annotated at all. So annotating is a balancing act, and a bit of an art form.

What sort of information should you annotate? Here are some suggestions for annotating a passage:

1. Mark information that strikes you as testable. In other words, earmark the ideas and information that you think you'll need to know to answer the questions.

2. Try to annotate so that your annotations provide a pre-written outline. This way you can recap the passage simply by reviewing your annotations.

3. Avoid underlining complete sentences. Instead, select key words (or phrases) that "trigger" for you the idea or point of a sentence or part of a paragraph. (Remember: avoid over-annotating.)

4. Mark structural connectors—key words that connect the logical building blocks of the passage. (See *Structural Triggers*, below.)

5. In chronological passages, annotate historical benchmarks—centuries, years, decades, or historical periods—that form a bridge from one part of the passage to another:
   - "prior to 1860…"
   - "During the years just after World War I…"
   - "During the latter half of the 17th century,…"
   - "Before the Renaissance period Italian art…"

6. Annotate to match specific individuals, works, events, dates and time periods to one another.

FIGURE 2–8

STRUCTURAL TRIGGERS	
Signals an item in a list (of examples, classes, reasons, or characteristics):	Signals that the author is comparing (identifying similarities) two things:
first, secondly (etc.) in addition also moreover	similarly in the same way analogous parallel likewise just as to also as
Signals that the author is contrasting two things:	
alternatively by contrast however on the other hand rather than while yet	Signals evidence (factual information) used to support the author's argument:
Signals a logical conclusion based upon preceding material:	because since in light of
consequently in conclusion then thus therefore as a result accordingly	Signals an example of something: for instance e.g. such as — is an illustration of

The Annotation "Toolbox" (LSAT and MCAT)

There are many ways to annotate an LSAT or MCAT passage. Your annotations will be more helpful if you use a variety of tools, such as these:

- underlined words and phrases
- circled words and phrases
- numbered items
- arrows
- stars, asterisks, and other icons

Here are some ideas for how to use these tools:

1. Put boxes around words and phrases that suggest the author's attitude, opinion, or perspective. Quickly review the boxed words to answer "primary purpose" and "author attitude" questions.

2. Use circled numbers to identify items in a list of examples, characteristics, reasons, etc.

3. Use arrows to physically connect particular words that represent logical, chronological or conceptual links; for example:

   - to clarify cause and effect in the natural sciences or in the context of historical events

   - to indicate who was influenced by whom in literature, music, psychology, etc.

   - to connect names (philosophers, scientists, authors, etc.) with dates, events, other names, theories or schools of thought, works, etc.

   - to indicate the chronological order in which historical events occurred

4. Create your own visual cues to earmark

   - possible thesis statements
   - major supporting points
   - points of author disagreement

IMPORTANT: Whatever tools you use, be sure to use the same ones *consistently for the same purpose*. Take advantage of the practice sets in Part 5 of this book to develop your own arsenal of annotating tools.

Margin Notes (LSAT and MCAT)

Don't overdo it when annotating directly on the text. You should also take shorthand notes in the left-hand margin to summarize paragraphs, earmark areas of discussion, and otherwise provide signals to help you locate details and recap each paragraph of the passage. Keep your margin notes brief (a few key words usually suffice to get across an idea), and abbreviate wherever possible. (On the GRE or GMAT you'll need to take notes on your scratch paper instead.)

Outlining a Passage

I don't recommend that you create an outline *per se* of the passage, for two reasons. First, it's time consuming. Secondly, many passages are not all that well organized because they're products of cutting and pasting from longer works (although some do hold up better on their own than others). So trying to construct an outline with headings and subheadings might be futile, or at least frustrating and time consuming.

On the LSAT or MCAT your annotations and margin notes might suffice as an outline. For the GRE and GMAT I suggest taking some brief notes on your scratch paper. Be sure to mark clearly which notes go with which paragraphs. Even on the LSAT and MCAT, for high-density passages arrows and other annotating tools might not be adequate to keep the details straight; use the bottom of the page to organize those details. The following scenarios typically call for note-taking:

- The passage categorizes or classifies various things (a few good notes will clarify which things belong in which categories)

- The passage mentions numerous individual names (authors, artists, political figures) who are interconnected according to influence, agreement or disagreement, and so forth.

Two Sample Passages with Annotations and Notes

On pages 22 and 23 you'll find two passages with question stems. (You'll recognize them from earlier in Part 2). Examine the handwritten annotations and notes. Do you get a sense of the overall structure of the passages and the flow of the discussion from these annotations and notes? Perhaps you would have used different symbols, or perhaps you would have circled or underlined other words and phrases. That's fine. Use whatever tools work best for you.

[NOTE: Beginning on page 39 you'll find these two question sets again, this time with answer choices and an analysis of each question.]

SAMPLE PASSAGE #1

Late Victorian and modern ideas of culture are always, in some sense, indebted to Matthew Arnold, who, largely through his *Culture and Anarchy (1869)*, placed the word at the center of debates about the
(5) goals of intellectual life and humanistic society. Arnold defined culture as "the pursuit of total perfection by means of getting to know, on all matters which most concern us, the best which has been thought and said in the world." It was Arnold's hope
(10) that, through this knowledge, we can turn "a fresh and free thought upon our stock notions and habits." Although Arnold's thinking about culture helped to define the purposes of the liberal arts curriculum in the century following the publication of *Culture,* three
(15) concrete forms of dissent from Arnold's views have had considerable impact of their own.

The first can be seen as protesting Arnold's fearful designation of "anarchy" as culture's enemy. This dichotomy seems to set up simply one more version
(20) of the old struggle between a privileged power structure and radical challenges to its authority. Arnold certainly tried to define the *arch*—the legitimizing order of value—against what he saw as the *an-arch* of existentialist democracy, yet he himself was plagued
(25) in his soul by the blind arrogances of the reactionary powers in his world. The writer who regarded the contemporary condition with such apprehension in *Culture* is the poet who wrote "Dover Beach," not an ideologue rounding up all the usual modern suspects.
(30) Another form of opposition saw Arnold's culture as a perverse perpetuation of classical and literary learning, outlook, and privileges in a world where science had become the new *arch* and from which any substantively new order of thinking must develop. At
(35) the center of the "two cultures" debate were the goals of the formal curriculum in the educational system, which is always taken to be the principal vehicle through which Arnoldian culture operates. However, Arnold himself had viewed culture as enacting its life
(40) in a much more broadly conceived set of institutions.

Today, however, Arnoldian culture is sustained, if indirectly, by multiculturalism, a movement aimed largely at gaining recognition for voices and visions that Arnoldian culture has implicitly suppressed. At
(45) the level of educational practice, the multiculturalists are interested in deflating the imperious authority that "high culture" exercises over the curriculum while bringing into play the principle that we must learn what is representative, for we have overempha-
(50) sized what is exceptional. The muliculturalists' conflict with Arnoldian culture has clear affinities with the radical critique; yet multiculturalism affirms Arnold by returning us more specifically to a tension inherent in the idea of culture rather than to the
(55) culture-anarchy dichotomy.

The social critics, defenders of science, and multiculturalists insist that Arnold's culture is simply a device for ordering us about. Instead, it is designed to register the gathering of ideological clouds on the
(60) horizon. There is no utopian motive in Arnold's celebration of perfection. The idea of perfection mattered to Arnold as the only background against which we could form a just image of our actual circumstances, just as we can conceive finer sunsets
(65) and unheard melodies. This capacity which all humans possess, Arnold made the foundation and authority of culture.

1. The author of the passage is primarily concerned with

2. Based upon the author's interpretation of Arnoldian culture, with which of the following statements would Arnold most likely disagree?

3. It can be inferred from the passage that the two-cultures debate

4. All of the following statements about multiculturalists are supported by the passage EXCEPT:

5. In criticizing Arnold's dissenters, the author employs all of the following methods EXCEPT:

6. It can be inferred from the information in the passage that Arnoldian culture is perpetuated today by

SAMPLE PASSAGE #2

A "radiative forcing" is any change imposed on the Earth that affects the planetary energy balance. Radiative forcings include changes in greenhouse gases (such as carbon dioxide and ozone), aerosols
(5) in the atmosphere, solar irradiance, and surface reflectivity. A forcing may result from either a natural or an anthropogenic cause, or from both, as in the case of atmospheric aerosol concentrations, which can be altered either by volcanic action or the
(10) burning of fossil fuels. Radiative forcings are typically specified for the purpose of theoretical global climate simulations. In contrast, radiative "feedbacks" are environmental changes resulting from climate changes and are calculated from scien-
(15) tific observation. Radiative feedbacks include changes in such phenomena as clouds, atmospheric water vapor, sea-ice cover, and snow cover.

The interplay between forcings and feedbacks can be quite complex. For example, an increase in the
(20) concentration of atmospheric water vapor increases solar irradiance, thereby warming the atmosphere and, in turn, increasing evaporation and the concentration of atmospheric water vapor. A related example of this complex interplay also shows the
(25) uncertainty of future climatic changes associated with forcings and feedbacks. Scientists are unsure how the depletion of ozone will ultimately affect clouds and, in turn, the Earth's temperature. Clouds trap outgoing, cooling radiation, thereby providing a
(30) warming influence. However, they also reflect incoming solar radiation and thus provide a cooling influence. Current measurements indicate that the net effect of clouds is to cool the Earth. However, scientists do not know how the balance might shift
(35) in the future as cloud formation and dissipation are affected by ozone depletion.

Contributing to this uncertainty is the complexity of the mechanisms at work in the process of ozone depletion. The amount of radiation reaching the
(40) earth's surface and the amount of reradiated radiation that is trapped by the greenhouse effect influence the Earth's temperature in opposite directions. Both mechanisms are affected by the vertical distribution of ozone. Also, the relative importance
(45) of these two competing mechanisms depends on the altitude at which ozone changes occur. In a recent NASA-sponsored aircraft study of the Antarctic ozone hole, chlorine monoxide was measured at varying altitudes. The measurements suggest that
(50) chlorine plays a greater role, and oxides of nitrogen a lesser role, than previously thought in the destruction of ozone in the lower atmosphere. The study concluded that simultaneous high-resolution measurements at many different altitudes (on the
(55) scale of 0.1 kilometer in vertical extent) are necessary

to diagnose the operative mechanisms. These findings have called into question conventional explanations for ozone depletion, which fail to adequately account for the new evidence.

1. It can be inferred from the information in the passage that "the burning of fossil fuels" (lines 9-10)

2. According to the passage, radiative forcings and radiative feedbacks can be distinguished from each other in which of the following ways?

3. Based upon the information in the passage, decreased evaporation is most likely to result in which of the following?

4. The author discusses the effect of clouds on atmospheric temperature most likely in order to show that

5. Based upon the information in the passage, the author would probably agree that scientists could more accurately predict the extent and direction of the greenhouse effect if they were to

6. The information in the last paragraph does NOT:

7. Which of the following best expresses the author's primary concern in the passage?

approaching the questions

PART 3

The "best" response? Isn't this awfully subjective?

The official directions for responding to reading-comprehension questions admonish you to choose the "best" answer among the five choices. Frequently, you will be required to weigh two or more answer choices of which each is a plausible answer, at least considered separately. Thus, there is an element of subjective judgment involved. Right? If your job is to choose the best response, isn't it just a matter of opinion as to which answer is correct?

Well, yes and no. In my workshops, students practice reading comprehension by taking actual previously-administered exams. After considering a particular passage and question set, students always react as follows:

- "Oh, I don't agree with their answer, because I interpret the passage differently; it's a matter of interpretation, and it's all subjective."

- "I think (C) is just as good an answer choice as (A); you can make an argument for either one; I don't understand how they can get away with saying that (A) is better than (C)."

- "It all depends on what they mean by this or that particular word; it's so subjective, that I might as well just guess randomly."

Are these students right or wrong? Well, they are always WRONG. In nearly every instance, after discussing the particular question in class, an alert, reasonably intelligent student with a fair command of the English language comes to understand that there is a single qualitatively-best response among the five choices. In sum, despite the apparent subjectivity of the questions (except for the explicit detail questions), the test maker is nearly always quite justified in the decision as to which is "best" among the five choices.

The test makers do a very fine job at avoiding ambiguities and problems of interpretation. You might see the occasional awkwardly-phrased or wordy question or response; if so, it is probably necessary to avoid ambiguity. Remember that these questions are reviewed, tested, and revised several times before they appear as scored questions on an actual exam. DO NOT SECOND GUESS THE TEST MAKER'S JUDGMENT OR COMMAND OF THE ENGLISH LANGUAGE. If you think there are two or more viable "best" responses, you (not the test maker) have either misread or misinterpreted the passage, the question, or the answer choices.

Introduction to question types

Think about the test-taking process as a dialogue between you and the test maker. In order to assess your ability both to remember and to understand what you have read, here is what the test maker really wants to find out:

- Did you catch the overall message--in other words, did you get the main point?

- Do you remember the little details mentioned along the way?

- Did you understand the author's purpose in mentioning the little details?

- Did you follow the author's line of reasoning, even where it wasn't spelled out for you?

- Did you see the overall structure of the passage?

- If the author had an opinion about the subject, did you get a feel for the author's perspective, beliefs, and attitude?

- Can you predict how the author would react to different or new ideas, information, or events?

- Can you predict how the passage would continue?

Instead of posing these queries directly to you in this form, the test maker has created a series of very specific multiple-choice questions designed to approximate the foregoing queries. According to the Educational Testing Service, there are six basic types of reading comprehension questions, distinguished from one another by their areas of focus:

- questions that focus on the main idea or primary purpose of the passage;

- questions that focus on information explicitly stated in the passage;

- questions that focus on information or ideas implied or suggested by the author;

- questions that focus on possible applications of the author's ideas to other situations;

- questions that focus on the author's logic, reasoning, or persuasive techniques; and

- questions that focus on the author's attitude as it is revealed in the language used.

I suppose this is good to know; and the test makers are absolutely correct—every reading-comprehension question does indeed exemplify one of these six question types. But so what? How can you use your newfound knowledge of question types to improve your test score? Read on, and you will learn how.

Why is it important to identify distinct question types?

If you know in advance what kind of information and ideas you are expected to glean from the passage, you are one step ahead of the game. You are no longer resigned to merely sit back and read the words that have been thrust in front of you; instead, you can "survey" the passage's ideas for test-worthy material. In short, you will be able to shift from your passive mode to your active mode.

What's next?

Next, we are going to look more closely at each of the various question types. I will be using nine different categories instead of six because a few of the six types listed above can be divided further into sub-types for us to examine. For each question type, you will learn:

- typical question stems (how the question is posed)

- ability tested with this question type

- frequency of appearance

- how to think about this question type

- some recommended approaches and techniques for handling each question type

- some typical wrong-answer ploys and hints for discerning best responses from among the others.

We will also examine a typical example of each question type. You will learn that you can develop a sense for what wrong answer choices look like without having read the passage! It is very important for you to develop this sense, because it will help you to eliminate wrong answers more quickly and confidently as well as to make educated guesses if you are short on time.

❶ "Main Idea" Questions

Typical Question Stems

- Which of the following best expresses the main idea of the passage?

- Which of the following would be the most appropriate title for the passage?

- Which of the following best expresses the author's main point?

Ability Being Tested

The test maker wants to know if you caught the main point or overall message that the author is trying to convey in the passage. This question type requires you to *discern between the forest and the trees*—that is, to distinguish broader and larger ideas from supporting evidence and details.

Frequency of Appearance

The odds are about 50/50 that any particular passage will include a "main idea" question (although nearly every passage includes either a "main idea" question or a "primary purpose" question, or both).

Comments and Suggestions

1. Every passage has a "main idea" (thesis). Sometimes, the main idea is expressed somewhere in the passage, usually in one sentence. If it is there, you will probably find it either somewhere in the *first paragraph or at the very end of the passage*. Do not expect, however, that the author will be so explicit as to state: "My thesis is..." or "The purpose of this article is..." or to otherwise provide some obvious indicator.

2. If no specific sentence fairly expresses the author's thesis or main point, that does not mean that there is no main idea. What it means is that the thesis can be determined and expressed only by considering the passage as a whole.

3. Try to tentatively answer the "main idea" question before you read through the passage from beginning to end, following these two steps:

- *Scan the first paragraph and the final few sentences of the passage* for possible thesis statements. If you see a sentence that looks as if it might be a viable thesis statement, check the answer choices quickly for a similar statement.

- If you do not see any viable thesis statement in either of these two places, *read the first and last sentence of each paragraph* to get a general sense of the passage as a whole. Then, read the answer choices and choose a tentative response or earmark the more viable responses.

4. After a complete reading of the passage, follow these steps:

   - *Formulate your own thesis statement* before considering the answer choices. Then, scan through the answer choices for a similar statement. By knowing what sort of response to look for, you will be far less tempted by the other (wrong) responses.

   - If your earlier, tentative, response is different from your updated response, consider the answer choices in light of wrong-answer ploys discussed below.

Look for These Wrong Answer Ploys

1. The response that is *too narrow in scope*. The response focuses on one element of the passage, ignoring other important elements. Be particularly suspicious of a response that refers to a *single specific person, event, idea, or work* (book, composition, etc.). For example:

   - If the passage is concerned with comparing two phenomena, a response that ignores this concern and focuses on only one of the two phenomena is too narrow to be a viable best response.

   - If the author uses specific examples to support an argument, a response that ignores the author's larger point and focuses on one of the examples is too narrow to be a viable best response.

2. The response that is *too broad in scope*. The response encompasses the author's main concern or idea but extends that concern or idea *beyond the author's intended scope*. Look for these common scenarios:

   - *Geographic region*. The passage concerns events in one country or region of the world, but the response extends beyond the region.

   - *Time frame*. The passage concerns events occurring during a particular historical period, but the response extends outside that period.

   - *Population*. The passage concerns a narrowly and clearly-defined population (usually a group of people)—e.g., botanists, black feminists, German neo-Nazis—but the response extends beyond that population.

An Illustrative Example

You can often spot answer choices that are likely to be too broad or too narrow without reading the passage. In the following example, do you agree that (C) and (D) appear to be appropriate in scope for a thesis statement? Do you also agree that (A) looks too broad while (B) and (E) are probably too narrow?

Q. Which of the following best expresses the author's main point in the passage above?

   (A) Nature transforms itself in a variety of ways, as illustrated by plant metamorphosis.

   (B) The process of plant metamorphosis occurs as one of three types.

   (C) Plant metamorphosis is a gradual process whereby each new form shares common characteristics with the neighboring or prior forms.

   (D) One can best understand the process of plant metamorphosis through careful observation of abnormal metamorphosis.

   (E) The study of contingent metamorphosis reveals little about the process of plant development.

❷ "Primary Purpose" Questions

Typical Question Stems

- The primary purpose of the passage is to

- The author of the passage is primarily concerned with

- The passage can be best described as a

Ability Being Tested

As with "main idea" questions, the test maker wants to know if you can see the forest from the trees—that is, if you can discern between main points and supporting points and details.

Frequency of Appearance

As with "main idea" questions, the odds are about 50/50 that any particular passage will include a "primary-purpose" question (although nearly every passage includes a "main idea" question, a "primary purpose" question, or both).

Comments and Suggestions

1. Ask yourself: "Toward what point is the author's effort primarily directed?" In other words, what is the main idea of the passage? There should be a consistency between the main idea of the passage and the author's primary purpose. Thus, if both question types appear in the question set, be sure your answers to these two questions are consistent with each other.

2. *Focus on the operative verb* (probably the first word) in each answer choice. That word will be an action verb or an action verb with an "ing" or "tion" on the end (these verbs in noun form are called "gerunds" in English grammar). Based on the action verb, you can probably eliminate all but one or two answer choices.

3. As you read the passage, *pay particular attention to all words and phrases that indicate or suggest the author's attitude* (tone, opinion, perspective). In fact, circle all such words and phrases. The *operative verb* in the best response must reflect or at least show consistency with the words and phrases that you have circled.

4. After a complete reading of the passage, follow these steps:

- *Formulate your own statement of the author's purpose.* Then, scan through the answer choices for a similar statement. If you know what sort of response to look for, a quick scan through the answer choices will usually reveal the best response; also, you will be far less tempted by the other (wrong) responses. However, you will never see a sentence that explicitly states: "My primary concern here is..." or some other obvious statement of purpose, so don't waste your time looking for help from the author to formulate your ideal response.

- If your earlier tentative response is different from your updated response, consider the answer choices in light of wrong-answer ploys below.

Look for These Wrong Answer Ploys

1. The response that *misses the author's attitude* toward the subject. For example, if the author's ultimate concern is to argue for a particular position or to propose a new and better explanation for some phenomenon, any response that ignores the author's opinion and instead implies objectivity on the author's part is not a viable best response.

2. The response that is *too narrow* in scope. Sometimes it helps to look at what the author spends most of his or her time discussing. This may sound simplistic, but it helps to keep your thinking straight for this type of question. If a particular topic is discussed in only one of five paragraphs, you can pretty safely conclude that the author's "primary" concern is not with that specific topic.

3. The response that is *off focus*. This type of response emphasizes a secondary function or purpose of the passage. For example, if the author describes two existing theories and goes on to propose and describe a new and better theory, the author's primary purpose is not to examine, describe or criticize current theories; the best response would go further and include the author's concern with proposing a new theory.

An Illustrative Example

Notice the operative words in the answer choices below. What sort of structural clues (trigger words) would you look for in the passage that would suggest that the author is "arguing" for a particular position or "weighing" advantages against disadvantages? Do you agree that it might be possible to find these structural clues quickly enough to allow for an educated guess or tentative response without a complete reading of the passage? Also, do any of the answer choices below appear inappropriate as a primary purpose—either because they appear too broad or too narrow in scope? Do you agree, for example, that (A) is probably too broad? Finally, compare (D) and (E). Their focus is quite different. If one of these choices is actually the best response, the other choice is quite off focus, and it will probably be rather easy to see this even by previewing or skimming the passage.

Q. The passage is primarily concerned with

(A) analyzing the effects upon society of various features of modern capitalism

(B) demonstrating the impact of Western culture's economic structure upon literature and upon social relationships

(C) arguing that the unique characteristics of contemporary capitalism adversely affect modern man's social character

(D) tracing the development of capitalism as it relates to the social character of man

(E) weighing the economic advantages of modern capitalism against the resulting social disadvantages

❸ "Explicit Detail" Questions

Typical Question Stems

* According to the passage, all of the following are

* The author mentions all of the following as examples of … EXCEPT:

* The author makes which of the following statements about …

* The passage provides information for answering which of the following questions?

Ability Being Tested

Although it would seem that the test maker is testing your short-term memory by asking you about the little details mentioned in the passage that you just read, that is not really what is going on here. Most readers cannot remember all of the details, and the test maker does not expect you to remember them either. What the test maker really wants to see is how quickly you can find the clues in the passage; if you are alert, you will have the passage well-enough outlined to know right away where to look.

Frequency of Appearance

All question sets include at least one or two "explicit detail" questions. If the passage itself contains a lot of detailed information, 50% (or possibly more) of the total number of questions might be this type.

Comments and Suggestions

1. There are really two types of explicit detail questions, and the location of the clues depends upon the type:

   Type 1: All answer choices are mentioned (as a characteristic, example, etc., of…) EXCEPT the correct answer choice. The wrong answers are probably clustered together in the same paragraph; the correct answer is either mentioned somewhere else in the passage or is not mentioned at all.

   Type 2: Only the correct answer choice is mentioned (as a characteristic, example, etc.). The correct answer is located within one sentence (either preceding or following) the relevant line(s) in the passage; each wrong answer is either mentioned somewhere else in the passage or is not mentioned at all.

2. Wherever some sort of list occurs in the passage—whether it be a list of characteristics, a list of examples, or some other list—you can be sure that there will be an explicit detail question that focuses on that list.

3. Most explicit detail questions focus on information contained in only one paragraph. Less commonly, the details will be scattered throughout the passage.

4. Try to answer the "explicit detail" question before you read the passage from beginning to end. The question will probably refer to a particular line (or lines) or to a particular paragraph in the passage. In any event, you will discover that on the basis of the information in the question stem, you can locate the relevant portion of the passage very quickly (5 to 10 seconds).

5. Do not insist on finding a best response that repeats word for word what is stated in the passage. The best answer is usually not expressed exactly as it is in the passage but rather paraphrases the language used in the passage.

6. Do not rely on your short-term memory for details to answer these questions. Always go to the relevant portion of the passage at the time you are considering the question and read around (from the preceding sentence to the following sentence) the particular text referred to in the question stem.

Look for These Wrong-Answer Ploys

1. The response that *refers to unrelated details*. In a "Type 1" question (see Comments), the correct answer is usually mentioned somewhere in the passage. If you recall reading it, you may be reticent to select it as the correct response. In a "Type 2" question (see Comments), some (and perhaps all) of the wrong answers are mentioned somewhere in the passage, and you might be reticent here as well to eliminate those responses.

2. *Not mentioned in the passage.* In a "Type 2" question (see Comments), one or more of the wrong answers might provide information completely unsupported by or not mentioned anywhere in the passage. These wrong answers can be quite tempting—your natural reaction is that the information appeared somewhere in the passage, but you missed it. Well, probably not! Don't fall for this ploy.

An Illustrative Example

The following example is a "Type 1" question. Accordingly, the correct response either will relate to a time period other than the early sixteenth century or will involve something other than madrigals. You can probably locate the relevant portion of the passage (the paragraph where the wrong answers are listed) quickly by scanning the passage for the term "sixteenth century." Also, a discussion of historical periods will probably flow in chronological order, which should make it even easier for you to locate the relevant discussion.

Q. According to the passage, all of the following are characteristics of early sixteenth-century madrigals EXCEPT:

(A) The poetry was of greater literary value than the poetry of earlier madrigals.

(B) Varying styles reflected the influence of composers from other countries.

(C) Emotionally-charged lyrics were given special musical treatment.

(D) They became increasingly polyphonic in nature, with the structure of the poem dictating their form.

(E) They initially resembled secular songs of the fifteenth century.

❹ "Inference" Questions

Typical Question Stems

- It can be inferred from the passage that the most probable reason…disagreed with…about…is that

- The author suggests that a major contributing cause of…is

- It can be inferred from the discussion of --- in the second paragraph that the author believes which of the following about --- ?

- Which of the following statements concerning --- is most directly suggested by the passage?"

Ability Being Tested

Are you able to interpret what the author infers or implies but does not state explicitly?

Frequency of Appearance

On average, this type of question will account for about one third of the questions—perhaps 2 or 3 out of 7–8—in a single question set.

Comments and Suggestions

1. In most cases, the question stem will begin with: "It can be inferred…" A question that asks what is *suggested* by the author or by the passage might be either an inference question or an explicit-detail question. Which it is is usually made clear after reading the entire question stem. For example, look at the last question stems accompanying *Sample Passage #1* (page 22). Without reading the passage or the answer choices, it should be clear enough that the question is asking for an inference rather than referring to an explicit statement.

2. This question type calls for you to make only very "tight" inferences—in other words, *the inference will be so strongly suggested in the passage that there really is no other reasonable interpretation*. Remember: do not fight the test maker by groping for a colorful or creative argument for more than one possible interpretation of the passage. The test maker does not select material that is ambiguous.

3. You probably won't have to read the entire passage or understand the passage as a whole to respond to an inference question. In fact, after reading the entire passage from beginning to end, your mind will be swimming with so many ideas that you probably won't remember the particular inference—that is, if you caught it in the first place.

4. The question stem might refer to specific lines or a specific paragraph in the passage. In any event, you will discover that, based upon the information in the question stem, you can locate the relevant portion of the passage very quickly (5 to 10 seconds).

5. An author inference usually requires that you fit together (logically speaking) no more than two consecutive sentences. Accordingly, do not waste your time reading more than you need to in order to respond to the question. To analyze the question, *locate the relevant line or lines in the passage, read around those lines*—the sentence preceding and the sentence following—and the inference should be clear enough to you.

Look for These Wrong-Answer Ploys

1. *The unwarranted inference*. This response will leap to a conclusion that is not supported by the area of the passage where the inference occurs. It might refer to a point made elsewhere in the passage, bring in material that is outside of the passage altogether, or, less commonly, exaggerate or distort the author's relatively narrow inference.

2. *The response that is contrary to the passage*. You might be surprised how easy it is to turn around the author's meaning or opinion, to confuse who or what the author agrees with and what the author disagrees with, or to confuse the author's opinion with the opinion of someone else mentioned in the passage. The test maker knows this and may include an answer choice that is contradicted by or that runs contrary to the passage.

3. *The response that is partly right, but partly wrong*. The test maker is hoping that, in your haste to complete the test within the allotted time, you will evaluate answer choices without reading the entire answer. If the first part of the answer contains accurate information and seems to respond to the question, it is tempting to select the answer as the best response without reading on. Don't fall for this one. *Remember*: always read every answer choice in its entirety.

An Illustrative Example

The question stem in the following example does not refer to a particular line or paragraph in the passage. Accordingly, it may be inappropriate to examine the question before reading the passage. However, you may want to scan the passage quickly for the term "Italian madrigal." If this term appears only in one particular paragraph, then consider reading around the term (from the preceding through the following sentence), and respond tentatively to the question.

Q. Which of the following statements about the Italian madrigal is best supported by the passage?

(A) The evolution of the madrigal may be viewed as a process toward the attainment of an ideal form.

(B) The overall quality of the madrigal improved over time through the use of simpler forms of musical expression.

(C) The latter part of the sixteenth century marked a return to the purer madrigal form of the fourteenth century.

(D) The Italian madrigalists both influenced and were influenced by their contemporaries in the Netherlands and in France.

(E) A madrigal of high literary quality generally required a collaborative effort between poet and musician.

❺ "Purpose of Detail" Questions

Typical Question Stems

- The author mentions --- (lines X–X) most probably in order to:

- The example discussed in lines X–X is intended by the author to illustrate ---

- The author quotes --- in the first paragraph most probably in order to

Ability Being Tested

The test maker hopes that you will become lost in the details themselves, thereby losing sight of the author's reason for including the details. To avoid falling into this trap, keep your mind on the flow of the argument.

Frequency of Appearance

The odds are about 50/50 that any particular passage will include a "purpose of detail" question, and rarely will you see more than one of these in a question set.

Comments and Suggestions

1. Compare this question type with the "explicit detail" question. The latter type requires that you find the "list" of examples, characteristics, etc., and take note of each item in the "list." *The "purpose of detail" question isn't concerned with whether you remember or understand the detail itself.* Instead, you should ask yourself why the author would take the time to mention the detail.

2. *You will not find an explicit answer to this question in the passage.* In other words, the author is not going to come right out and state, "The reason I am mentioning this particular detail is to support my assertion that..." Instead, you must infer that this is the author's purpose.

3. As with "inference" questions, "purpose of detail" questions call for you to *make only very "tight" inferences*—in other words, the author's purpose will be so strongly suggested in the passage that there really is no other reasonable interpretation.

4. *Consider answering the question before you read the passage in its entirety.* After reading the entire passage continuously from beginning to end, your mind will no doubt selectively store in memory certain details and minute bits of information from the passage. However, if someone were to ask you immediately after reading the passage, "Why do you suppose the author mentioned this little detail or that little detail?," you might be hard pressed to respond intelligently. The question stem will typically refer to specific lines or a specific paragraph in the passage. To analyze the question, locate the relevant line or lines in the passage, read around those lines—the sentence preceding and the sentence following—and the author's purpose will probably be clear enough. If not, read the answer choices for suggestions and choose a tentative response (or earmark the more viable responses).

5. During your complete reading of the passage, *examine the "purpose of detail" question immediately after reading the relevant area of the passage, while it is fresh in your mind.* Confirm your earlier (tentative) response (if any) or reevaluate.

Look for These Wrong-Answer Ploys

1. The response that is *true but unresponsive to the question.* The response will restate a point made elsewhere in the passage. This response will be tempting if you recall reading the statement and are confident that the statement is true or accurately states the author's position. Don't be fooled. By focusing your attention on only the relevant portion of the passage, you can be confident that this response, while it may be an accurate statement, is a wrong answer.

2. The response that is *too broad.* The response will accurately reflect the author's purpose, but the point will be too broad. In other words, the purpose of a detail is likely to be a narrow and limited one. Be suspicious of the answer choice that looks more like a primary purpose than a secondary one.

An Illustrative Example

Considering the following example, you would probably be able to locate and read the relevant portion of the passage and respond to the question

before reading the passage in its entirety. Also, do you agree that (B) appears to be too broad, even without looking at the passage?

Q. The author mentions the "process by which a single flower becomes double" (lines X-X) in order to:

(A) illustrate that plant metamorphosis may occur in more than one direction

(B) prove a theory about a particular law of nature

(C) support the author's assertion that external parts of plants assume the form of the nearest series

(D) convey, by way of example, the concept of plant metamorphosis

(E) show the resemblance of flowers in form and color to other leaves of the corolla

⑥ "Logical Continuation" Questions

Typical Question Stem

- Which of the following would be the most logical continuation of the passage?

- The author would probably continue the discussion by

Ability Being Tested

The test maker is testing your ability to see the overall structure and flow of the discussion. As with "main idea" and "primary purpose" questions, you will be able to handle this question type more effectively if you are able to see the forest from the trees—i.e., to set aside the details in the passage and form a picture of the passage as a whole.

Frequency of Appearance

This is not a common question type. Perhaps one out of three question sets will include a question of this type.

Comments and Suggestions

1. Before you read the passage, scan the questions to see if a "logical continuation" question appears. If so, you have been forewarned to pay particular attention to the last paragraph. However, this is usually not a question that can be answered by reading only a small portion of the passage (but see [2] below). You will also need to *develop a good general outline of the passage* to get a sense for how the argument flows. Then consider the final paragraph in light of that flow to determine how far downstream the passage has ended.

2. *You can probably make an educated guess by reading the final paragraph in isolation* from the rest of the passage. The final sentences will almost certainly provide enough information for you to eliminate some of the wrong answer choices.

3. Note in particular the *operative word* in each answer choice; as in "primary purpose" questions, the operative word will in all likelihood be a verb in noun form (i.e., a gerund). Focusing on the operative word alone may be sufficient to narrow the choices considerably. Remember, however, always read each answer choice completely before settling on a final choice.

Look for These Wrong-Answer Ploys

1. The response that *covers old ground*. The author's discussion is unlikely to reverse its "flow" and rehash material already treated in the earlier parts of the passage. However, don't rule out this possibility. For example, the author might continue by examining in more detail one of two or three points made in the passage. If this is the case, the last paragraph will in all likelihood provide a clue that this is the next area of discussion.

2. The response that *expounds on a secondary point*. Keep your attention on the primary concern of the passage. A response that involves a secondary point—i.e., supporting evidence or details—is probably not a viable best response.

An Illustrative Example

In the following example, notice the operative word in each answer choice ("classifying," "proposing," etc.). Do you agree that by considering just these key words in light of the overall structure of the passage, you may very well be able to respond correctly to the question?

Q. Of the following, it is most likely that the author would continue the passage by

(A) further classifying various types of retrograde metamorphosis among flowering plants

(B) proposing an alternative classification scheme for plant metamorphosis to the one already presented

(C) explaining why the study of contingent metamorphosis is not as valuable as the study of other types of plant metamorphosis

(D) proposing certain theories of plant transmutation, citing specific examples of progressive metamorphosis in support of those theories.

(E) further examining the process of sexual reproduction among flowering plants

❼ "Method of Argumentation" Questions

Typical Question Stems

- Which of the following techniques does the author use to discredit ---?

- The author's argument is developed primarily by the use of

- Which of the following best describes the relationship of the first paragraph of the passage to the passage as a whole?

- The author's argument proceeds by

Ability Being Tested

The test maker want to know if you can follow the author's logic and line of reasoning.

Frequency of Appearance

This is not a common question type. Perhaps one out of three question sets will include a question of this type.

Comments and Suggestions

1. In examining a "Method of Argumentation" question, consider the question in light of the overall structure of the passage. *Review your annotations and margin notes, particularly the key structural clues* (trigger words) that you circled or underlined as you read the passage.

2. The question stem often reveals that the author has a point of view about the subject—that is, that the passage is subjective rather than objective. For example, the first Illustrative Example on this page strongly suggests a point of view, while the second question is really rather neutral. Thus, *a question of this type may help you to respond to other questions in the set*—e.g., "primary purpose," "main idea," or "author's attitude" questions.

Illustrative Examples

Q. In criticizing Arnold's dissenters, the author employs all of the following methods EXCEPT:

(A) pointing out the paradoxical nature of an argument against Arnoldian culture

(B) presenting evidence that conflicts with a claim made by Arnold's dissenters

(C) asserting that a claim made by the dissenters is an oversimplification

(D) drawing an analogy between one of the dissenters' claims and another insupportable theory

(E) suggesting that the focus of one of the dissenters' arguments is too narrow

Q: The author uses all of the following in presenting the subject EXCEPT:

(A) illustrative example

(B) logical deduction

(C) analogy

(D) analysis of experimental data

(E) distinction between two ways of viewing a phenomenon

❽ "Author's Attitude" Questions

Typical Question Stems

- The author's attitude toward --- is best described as

- The theories espoused by --- are regarded by the author as

Ability Being Tested

The test maker wants to know if you have a sense for the author's opinion, perspective, or position on the subject of the passage.

Frequency of Appearance

This is not a common question type. Perhaps one out of three question sets will include a question of this type.

Comments and Suggestions

1. As you read every passage, you should *circle, underline, or otherwise take note* of all words and phrases that indicate the author's opinion, perspective, or position on the subject. For example:

   - "--- rightly concludes that..."

   - "The narrow view held by most..."

   - "A more enlightened view of..."

   - "--- fails to take into account..."

2. There are essentially *two types* of "author's attitude" questions. One type asks about the author's attitude toward the subject in general, while the other type focuses on the author's attitude toward a specific and narrower subject— e.g., toward one particular author (not the main subject of the passage) whose style differed from that of most of her contemporaries. Your approach to these two types should differ:

   Type (1): Focus your attention on the author's primary purpose to ensure that your choice is consistent with the author's primary purpose. For example, if the author's primary purpose is to critique, the author has a critical attitude. The best response should be consistent with the author's primary purpose.

Type (2): You can probably respond to this question without considering the passage as a whole. Instead, scan the passage for the relevant discussion, then read only that portion of the passage for key words and phrases that suggest the author's attitude.

Look for These Wrong-Answer Ploys

1. The extreme response that *exaggerates* the author's attitude. Answer choices that might fit into this category would include the following terms:

   (overly positive) enthusiastic approval, unqualified endorsement, deeply respectful, openly favorable

   (overly negative) condemnatory, outraged, unfairly biased, naively credulous, disdainful, resentful

2. The *neutral* response. While some passages are strictly objective in presenting factual information along with the ideas of others, most are subjective in that the author will have a point of view. Be suspicious of the answer choice that fails to suggest that the author is even the least bit critical—for example, "ambivalent," "strictly objective," or "indifferent."

An Illustrative Example

In the following example, note that (A), (C) and (E) seem too extreme. Also, do you agree that (B) seems an unlikely tone for a scholarly discussion?

Q. Based upon the passage, the author's attitude toward contemporary capitalism can best be described as

(A) resentful

(B) appreciative

(C) disdainful

(D) objective but critical

(E) laudatory

⑨ "Extrapolation" Questions

Typical Question Stems

- The passage suggests that the author would be most likely to agree with which of the following statements?

- Which of the following new discoveries, if actually occurring, would most strongly support the author's hypothesis about ---?

- Which of the following, if true, would most seriously weaken the author's assertion in line X?

Ability Being Tested

The test maker is interested in measuring your ability to apply the ideas presented in the passage to new situations or changed circumstances.

Frequency of Appearance

This is not a common question type. Perhaps one out of three question sets will include a question of this type.

Comments and Suggestions

1. Approach this question in much the same way as you would approach an "author's attitude" question. A question of this type will appear only if the author has a clear point of view about the subject. Accordingly, *pay particular attention to words and phrases in the passage that indicate or suggest the author's opinion, perspective, or position.*

2. It is unlikely that you will be able to respond confidently to this type of question without a complete reading of the passage.

Look for These Wrong-Answer Ploys

1. The response that *confuses the author's opinion with those of others.* When reading the passage, be careful not to confuse the author's opinion with those of others mentioned in the passage. Also pay careful attention to who or what the author is agreeing with. This typical wrong answer will prey on your confusion. Don't fall into this trap!

2. The response that is *unsupported* by the passage. This response will appear consistent with the author's attitude toward the subject, and thus will be quite tempting. However, the passage will fail to provide adequate support for the statement. Avoid extrapolating from the author's attitude toward the specific subject of the passage to conclude what the author might think about unrelated topics. However, just because an answer choice appears to be off the topic, it may still be the best of the five choices.

3. The response that is an *accurate statement but is off the topic.* If the question asks which statement the author would agree (or disagree) with, respond by disregarding whether the statements are in reality accurate statements. In other words, answer the question, without regard to the truth or accuracy of the five statements.

An Illustrative Example

Notice that the answer choices below seem to invite you to inject your own opinions or outside knowledge. As noted above, do not evaluate the answer choice based upon your understanding of the truth or accuracy of the statement. Look only at the author's words.

Q. Which of the following, if true, would most seriously weaken the author's argument?

(A) The process of centralization and concentration of capital has reversed in recent decades.

(B) Most social relationships are not dictated by economic relations.

(C) Most individual workers do not feel alienated from themselves, their jobs, or their fellow workers.

(D) In general, the physical needs of modern man are not met to the extent they were in Huxley's *Brave New World.*

(E) The disparity in the standard of living within most contemporary capitalistic cultures is generally far greater than the author assumes.

sample question sets

Reprinted on the following pages are the two sample passages that we examined in Part 2. Here, however, the passages appear as they do on the actual exam—accompanied by questions *and* answer choices. Also, following each question set is an answer key as well as a detailed analysis of each question.

Work through both sample passages as if this were your first exposure to them. ALLOW YOURSELF 8–9 MINUTES PER PASSAGE. As you read each passage, annotate and make margin notes as you deem appropriate and helpful. Interrupt your reading to respond tentatively to particular questions as you deem appropriate.

When you finish working through a question set, READ THE ACCOMPANYING ANALYSIS IN ITS ENTIRETY, EVEN FOR THOSE QUESTIONS THAT YOU ANSWERED CORRECTLY. The analysis exposes the various wrong-answer ploys used by the test maker, thereby illustrating and reinforcing the materials in Part 3 of this book.

Sample Passage #1 begins on page 40.

Sample Passage #2 begins on page 46.

SAMPLE PASSAGE #1

Late Victorian and modern ideas of culture are always, in some sense, indebted to Matthew Arnold, who, largely through his *Culture and Anarchy* (1869), placed the word at the center of debates about the
(5) goals of intellectual life and humanistic society. Arnold defined culture as "the pursuit of total perfection by means of getting to know, on all matters which most concern us, the best which has been thought and said in the world." It was Arnold's hope
(10) that, through this knowledge, we can turn "a fresh and free thought upon our stock notions and habits." Although Arnold's thinking about culture helped to define the purposes of the liberal arts curriculum in the century following the publication of *Culture*, three
(15) concrete forms of dissent from Arnold's views have had considerable impact of their own.

The first can be seen as protesting Arnold's fearful designation of "anarchy" as culture's enemy. This dichotomy seems to set up simply one more version of
(20) the old struggle between a privileged power structure and radical challenges to its authority. Arnold certainly tried to define the *arch*—the legitimizing order of value—against what he saw as the *an-arch* of existentialist democracy, yet he himself was plagued
(25) in his soul by the blind arrogances of the reactionary powers in his world. The writer who regarded the contemporary condition with such apprehension in *Culture* is the poet who wrote "Dover Beach," not an ideologue rounding up all the usual modern suspects.
(30) Another form of opposition saw Arnold's culture as a perverse perpetuation of classical and literary learning, outlook, and privileges in a world where science had become the new *arch* and from which any substantively new order of thinking must develop. At
(35) the center of the "two cultures" debate were the goals of the formal curriculum in the educational system, which is always taken to be the principal vehicle through which Arnoldian culture operates. However, Arnold himself had viewed culture as enacting its life
(40) in a much more broadly conceived set of institutions.

Today, however, Arnoldian culture is sustained, if indirectly, by multiculturalism, a movement aimed largely at gaining recognition for voices and visions that Arnoldian culture has implicitly suppressed. At
(45) the level of educational practice, the multiculturalists are interested in deflating the imperious authority that "high culture" exercises over the curriculum while bringing into play the principle that we must learn what is representative, for we have overempha-
(50) sized what is exceptional. The muliculturalists' conflict with Arnoldian culture has clear affinities with the radical critique; yet multiculturalism affirms Arnold by returning us more specifically to a tension inherent in the idea of culture rather than to the
(55) culture-anarchy dichotomy.

The social critics, defenders of science, and multiculturalists insist that Arnold's culture is simply a device for ordering us about. Instead, it is designed to register the gathering of ideological clouds on the
(60) horizon. There is no utopian motive in Arnold's celebration of perfection. The idea of perfection mattered to Arnold as the only background against which we could form a just image of our actual circumstances, just as we can conceive finer sunsets
(65) and unheard melodies. This capacity which all humans possess, Arnold made the foundation and authority of culture.

1. The author of the passage is primarily concerned with

   (A) arguing against those who have opposed Arnold's ideas
   (B) describing Arnold's conception of culture
   (C) explaining why Arnold considered the pursuit of perfection to be the essence of culture
   (D) tracing Arnold's influence on the liberal arts educational curriculum
   (E) examining the different views of culture that have emerged since the mid-eighteenth century

2. Based upon the author's interpretation of Arnoldian culture, with which of the following statements would Arnold most likely disagree?

   (A) The capacity to conceive perfection is the foundation of culture.
   (B) Culture operates in a wide array of social institutions.
   (C) Existential democracy is culture's enemy.
   (D) The educational curriculum should de-emphasize what is representative.
   (E) The anarchy-culture dichotomy embraces the struggle against the privileged power structure.

3. It can be inferred from the passage that the two-cultures debate

   (A) emerged as a reaction to the multiculturalist movement
   (B) developed after 1869
   (C) influenced Arnold's thinking about culture
   (D) was carried on by American as well as European scientists
   (E) led to a schizophrenic educational system

4. All of the following statements about multiculturalists are supported by the passage EXCEPT:

   (A) They affirm Arnold's thesis through their opposition to his culture.
   (B) They protest Arnold's designation of anarchy as culture's enemy.
   (C) They seek to suppress the voices and visions of Arnold's allies.
   (D) They oppose the pursuit of perfection in schools of higher education.
   (E) They consider Arnold's culture to be imperious and arrogant.

5. In criticizing Arnold's dissenters, the author employs all of the following methods EXCEPT:

   (A) pointing out the paradoxical nature of an argument against Arnoldian culture
   (B) presenting evidence that conflicts with a claim made by Arnold's dissenters
   (C) asserting that a claim made by the dissenters is an oversimplification
   (D) drawing an analogy between one of the dissenters' claims and another insupportable theory
   (E) suggesting that the focus of one of the dissenters' arguments is too narrow

6. It can be inferred from the information in the passage that Arnoldian culture is perpetuated today by

   (A) the two-cultures debate
   (B) postmodernists
   (C) imperious elitists
   (D) existentialists
   (E) social critics

Analysis of Sample Passage #1

Answer Key

1. A
2. E
3. B
4. B
5. D
6. C

QUESTION 1

The author of the passage is primarily concerned with

(A) arguing against those who have opposed Arnold's ideas
(B) describing Arnold's conception of culture
(C) explaining why Arnold considered the pursuit of perfection to be the essence of culture
(D) tracing Arnold's influence on the liberal arts educational curriculum
(E) examining the different views of culture that have emerged since the mid-eighteenth century

Question Type: Primary Purpose
Difficulty Level: Moderate

(A) is the best response. The author's threshold purpose, articulated in the final sentence of the first paragraph, is to identify the significant forms of dissent to Arnoldian culture. But the author proceeds to do more than merely identify and describe these forms of dissent; the author is also critical of the dissenters—for example, because they have misunderstood Arnold. Response (A) embraces both the author's threshold and ultimate concerns.

Incorrect Responses

(B) is off focus. Although the author does define and describe throughout the passage Arnold's conception of culture, the author is more concerned with how others have reacted to and been influenced by his ideas.

(C) is off the topic. Although the author does claim that Arnold considered the pursuit of perfection to be the essence of culture, the author offers little explanation as to why Arnold believed as he did.

(D) is off focus. The passage includes no detail about specific ways that Arnold's ideas molded or otherwise influenced the liberal arts curriculum.

(E) is too broad. The passage concerns only Arnold's views and the views of those who opposed Arnoldian culture.

QUESTION 2

Based upon the author's interpretation of Arnoldian culture, with which of the following statements would Arnold most likely disagree?

(A) The capacity to conceive perfection is the foundation of culture.
(B) Culture operates in a wide array of social institutions.
(C) Existential democracy is culture's enemy.
(D) The educational curriculum should de-emphasize what is representative.
(E) The anarchy-culture dichotomy embraces the struggle against the privileged power structure.

Question Type: Explicit Detail
Difficulty Level: Challenging

(E) is the best response. Admittedly, the author does state that "[t]his dichotomy seems to set up simply one more version of the old struggle between a privileged power structure and radical challenges to its authority" (lines 18-21). However, the author continues by suggesting strongly that the resemblance between Arnold's anarchy-culture dichotomy and the struggle against established authority is only an apparent one: in light of Arnold's "Dover Beach" and in light of the fact that Arnold was himself plagued by the "blind arrogances of the reactionary powers in the world" (lines 25-26), the interpretation of Arnold's dichotomy as "simply one more version of the old struggle..." misunderstands Arnold.

Incorrect Responses

(A) is consistent with Arnold's views as described in the final sentence of the passage. The "capacity" to which the author refers in the final sentence is the ability of humans to conceive the ideal (perfection is the ideal) for the purpose of "forming a just image of our actual circumstances" (lines 63-64).

(B) is consistent with Arnold's views as described in the third paragraph. The author states that "Arnold himself had viewed culture as enacting its life in a much more broadly conceived set of institutions" than just the educational system (lines 39-40).

(C) is consistent with Arnold's views as described in the second paragraph: the author states that Arnold designated "anarchy" as culture's enemy (line 18) and that he sought to define *arch* "against what he saw as the *an-arch* of existential democracy" (lines 23-24). Considering these two statements together, it can be inferred that Arnold viewed existential democracy as an enemy of culture.

(D) is consistent with Arnold's views. The author emphasizes throughout the passage Arnold's argument for the pursuit of perfection (i.e., culture); thus, Arnold would probably agree that we should study the "exceptional" (see line 50) rather than the "representative." Also, Response (D) is inconsistent with the multiculturists' viewpoint as described in the third paragraph: "we must learn what is representative, for we have overemphasized what is exceptional" (lines 48-50). By implication, Arnold would probably agree with Statement (D).

QUESTION 3

It can be inferred from the passage that the two-cultures debate

(A) emerged as a reaction to the multiculturalist movement
(B) developed after 1869
(C) influenced Arnold's thinking about culture
(D) was carried on by American as well as European scientists
(E) led to a schizophrenic educational system

Question Type: Inference
Difficulty Level: Easier

(B) is the best response. Arnold's *Culture and Anarchy* was published in 1896. The three forms

of opposition to Arnold's ideas as presented in this work, therefore, must have emerged later than 1869.

Incorrect Responses

(A) distorts the information in the passage. The author identifies the two-cultures debate and the multiculturalist movement as two distinct forms of dissent (opposition to Arnoldian culture). However, the author neither states nor implies that either form resulted in the emergence of or had any influence upon the other.

(C) confuses the information in the passage. It was Arnold's earlier ideas that sparked the two-cultures debate, not the other way around.

(D) brings in information not mentioned in the passage. Nowhere in the passage does the author identify or refer specifically to American or European scientists.

(E) calls for an unwarranted inference. While opposing forces in the debate did have their own opposing ideas about what an educational curriculum should include, the author neither states nor implies that the debate resulted in a schizophrenic system.

QUESTION 4

All of the following statements about multiculturalists are supported by the passage EXCEPT:

(A) They affirm Arnold's thesis through their opposition to his culture.
(B) They protest Arnold's designation of anarchy as culture's enemy.
(C) They seek to suppress the voices and visions of Arnold's allies.
(D) They oppose the pursuit of perfection in schools of higher education.
(E) They consider Arnold's culture to be imperious and arrogant.

Question Type: Interpretation
Difficulty Level: Moderate

(B) is the best response. Response (B) confuses the information in the passage. It is the radical critique discussed in the second paragraph, not the multiculturists, that "can be seen as protesting

Arnold's fearful designation of "anarchy" as culture's enemy" (lines 17-18).

Incorrect Responses

(A) is consistent with the author's view of multiculturalism as expressed in the fourth paragraph: the multiculturalists' conflict with Arnold is inherent in ("returns us to") the (Arnold's) idea of culture. Thus, this conflict actually supports (affirms) Arnold's notion of culture.

(C) is consistent with the author's description of the multiculturist agenda. According to the author, the multiculturists "are interested in deflating the imperious authority that "high culture" exercises over the curriculum" (lines 46-47). Response (C) restates this idea.

(D) is consistent with the author's description of the multiculturist agenda. According to the author, the multiculturists are interested in "bringing into play the principle that we must learn what is representative, for we have overemphasized what is exceptional" (lines 48-50). Response (D) restates this idea.

(E) is consistent with the author's description of the multiculturist agenda. According to the author, the multiculturists "are interested in deflating the imperious authority that "high culture" exercises over the curriculum" (lines 46-47). Considered in the context of the author's broader discussion, the multiculturists are clearly referring here to Arnold and his allies.

QUESTION 5

In criticizing Arnold's dissenters, the author employs all of the following methods EXCEPT:

(A) pointing out the paradoxical nature of an argument against Arnoldian culture
(B) presenting evidence that conflicts with a claim made by Arnold's dissenters
(C) asserting that a claim made by the dissenters is an oversimplification
(D) drawing an analogy between one of the dissenters' claims and another insupportable theory
(E) suggesting that the focus of one of the dissenters' arguments is too narrow

Question Type: Method of Argumentation
Difficulty Level: Challenging

(D) **is the best response.** The only analogy in the passage is found in the final paragraph, in which the author compares striving for perfection (i.e., culture) to conceiving "finer sunsets and unheard melodies" (lines 64–65). Although the author uses this analogy to help the reader understand the author's final argument against Arnold's dissenters, this analogy is not in the nature of "an insupportable theory" which the author compares to a claim made by Arnold's dissenters, as Response (D) suggests.

Incorrect Responses

(A) The method suggested in (A) is used by the author in the fourth paragraph to criticize multiculturalists, whose conflict with Arnold, according to the author, only serves to affirm Arnold's notion of culture.

(B) The method suggested in (B) is used by the author in the second paragraph to criticize those who protested Arnold's culture-anarchy dichotomy. The author counters such protests by asserting that the protesters misinterpret Arnold. The author bases this assertion on two pieces of evidence: (1) Arnold's "Dover Beach," and (2) the fact that Arnold was "plagued in his soul by the blind arrogances" of reactionary powers.

(C) The method suggested in (C) is used by the author in the final paragraph to criticize all three schools of dissent. According to the author, the social critics, defenders of science, and multiculturists "insist that Arnold's culture is simply a device for ordering us about" (lines 57-58). The author then suggests that this criticism is too simple in that Arnold's culture is about much more than merely suggesting what humans should do.

(E) The method suggested in (E) is used by the author in the third paragraph to criticize the "defenders of science." The author suggests that the defenders of science, by placing the formal curriculum (in the educational system) at the center of the two-cultures debate, miss Arnold's much-broader view as to the social institutions in which culture enacts its life (lines 39-40).

QUESTION 6

It can be inferred from the information In the passage that Arnoldian culture is perpetuated today by

(A) the two-cultures debate
(B) postmodernists
(C) imperious elitists
(D) existentialists
(E) social critics

Question Type: Explicit Detail
Difficulty Level: Moderate

(C) **is the best response.** In the first paragraph, the author states that Arnold helped to define the purposes of the liberal arts curriculum in the century following the publication of his *Culture and Anarchy*. In the fourth paragraph, the author claims that today's multiculturists movement, which opposes Arnoldian culture, is interested in deflating the "imperious authority that 'high culture' exercises over the curriculum" (lines 46-47). It is reasonably inferable, then, that these imperious elitists are modern-day allies of Arnold who have perpetuated his ideas about culture through their authority over today's educational curriculum.

Incorrect Responses

(A) runs contrary to the information in the passage. The first sentence of the fourth paragraph ("Today, however, Arnoldian culture is sustained, if indirectly, by multiculturalism") implies that the two forms of dissent discussed earlier—the protest against Arnold's culture-anarchy dichotomy and the two-cultures debate—cannot be credited with sustaining Arnoldian culture today. Moreover, the author neither states nor implies affirmatively that the two-cultures debate continues to this day.

(B) brings in information not mentioned in the passage. Nowhere in the passage does the author mention or allude to "the postmodernists."

(D) confuses the information in the passage. The only mention of existentialism is in the first paragraph, where the author describes Arnold's view of existential democracy. The author ncithcr states nor implies that existentialists are in any way responsible for sustaining Arnoldian culture today.

(E) runs contrary to the information in the passage. The first sentence of the fourth paragraph ("Today, however, Arnoldian culture is sustained, if indirectly, by multiculturalism") implies that the two groups of dissenters discussed earlier— the social critics who protested Arnold's culture-anarchy dichotomy and the defenders of science—cannot be credited with sustaining Arnoldian culture today.

SAMPLE PASSAGE #2

A "radiative forcing" is any change imposed on the Earth that affects the planetary energy balance. Radiative forcings include changes in greenhouse gases (such as carbon dioxide and ozone), aerosols in the
(5) atmosphere, solar irradiance, and surface reflectivity. A forcing may result from either a natural or an anthropogenic cause, or from both, as in the case of atmospheric aerosol concentrations, which can be altered either by volcanic action or the burning of
(10) fossil fuels. Radiative forcings are typically specified for the purpose of theoretical global climate simulations. In contrast, radiative "feedbacks" are environmental changes resulting from climate changes and are calculated from scientific observation. Radiative
(15) feedbacks include changes in such phenomena as clouds, atmospheric water vapor, sea-ice cover, and snow cover.

The interplay between forcings and feedbacks can be quite complex. For example, an increase in the
(20) concentration of atmospheric water vapor increases solar irradiance, thereby warming the atmosphere and, in turn, increasing evaporation and the concentration of atmospheric water vapor. A related example of this complex interplay also shows the uncertainty of
(25) future climatic changes associated with forcings and feedbacks. Scientists are unsure how the depletion of ozone will ultimately affect clouds and, in turn, the Earth's temperature. Clouds trap outgoing, cooling radiation, thereby providing a warming influence.
(30) However, they also reflect incoming solar radiation and thus provide a cooling influence. Current measurements indicate that the net effect of clouds is to cool the Earth. However, scientists do not know how the balance might shift in the future as cloud
(35) formation and dissipation are affected by ozone depletion.

Contributing to this uncertainty is the complexity of the mechanisms at work in the process of ozone depletion. The amount of radiation reaching the
(40) earth's surface and the amount of reradiated radiation that is trapped by the greenhouse effect influence the Earth's temperature in opposite directions. Both mechanisms are affected by the vertical distribution of ozone. Also, the relative importance of these two
(45) competing mechanisms depends on the altitude at which ozone changes occur. In a recent NASA-sponsored aircraft study of the Antarctic ozone hole, chlorine monoxide was measured at varying altitudes. The measurements suggest that chlorine plays a
(50) greater role, and oxides of nitrogen a lesser role, than previously thought in the destruction of ozone in the lower atmosphere. The study concluded that simultaneous high-resolution measurements at many different altitudes (on the scale of 0.1 kilometer in vertical
(55) extent) are necessary to diagnose the operative

mechanisms. These findings have called into question conventional explanations for ozone depletion, which fail to adequately account for the new evidence.

1. It can be inferred from the information in the passage that "the burning of fossil fuels" (lines 9-10)

   (A) is an anthropogenic cause of radiative forcings
   (B) results in both radiative forcings and radiative feedbacks
   (C) does not affect atmospheric forcings or feedbacks
   (D) is a significant type of radiative forcing
   (E) is an anthropogenic cause of radiative feedback

2. According to the passage, radiative forcings and radiative feedbacks can be distinguished from each other in which of the following ways?

   (A) whether the radiative change is global or more localized
   (B) the precision with which the amounts of radiative change can be determined
   (C) that altitude at which the radiative change occurs
   (D) whether the amount of radiative change is specified or calculated
   (E) whether the radiative change is directed toward or away from the earth

3. Based upon the information in the passage, decreased evaporation is most likely to result in which of the following?

   (A) an increase in water vapor concentration
   (B) a decrease in atmospheric absorption of longwave radiation
   (C) a decrease in other radiative forcings
   (D) an increase in atmospheric temperatures
   (E) a decrease in surface reflectivity

4. The author discusses the effect of clouds on atmospheric temperature most likely in order to show that

   (A) radiative feedbacks can be more difficult to isolate and predict than radiative forcings
   (B) the distinction between radiative feedbacks and radiative forcings is somewhat arbitrary
   (C) some radiative feedbacks cannot be determined solely by global climate model simulations
   (D) the climatic impact of some radiative feedbacks is uncertain
   (E) the NASA-sponsored study is inconclusive as to the effect of ozone on cloud formation and dissipation.

5. Based upon the information in the passage, the author would probably agree that scientists could more accurately predict the extent and direction of the greenhouse effect if they were to

   (A) monitor radiative feedbacks and forcings over a longer time period
   (B) change the direction of research away from determining amounts of radiative changes
   (C) account for the altitude at which cloud formations appear
   (D) isolate those ozone changes caused specifically by anthropogenic factors
   (E) isolate the cooling influence of ozone changes from their warming influence

6. The information in the last paragraph does NOT:

   (A) provide evidence of the variability of ozone amounts at different altitudes
   (B) underscore the complexity in measuring radiative changes
   (C) call into question current methods of determining radiative changes
   (D) support the author's position that predicting future ozone changes is problematic
   (E) explain a discrepancy between an earlier theory and more recent scientific evidence

7. Which of the following best expresses the author's primary concern in the passage?

   (A) to examine the environmental effects of radiative forcings and feedbacks
   (B) to challenge conventional theories about the impact of radiative changes on ozone depletion and the greenhouse effect
   (C) to illustrate the complexity and uncertainty of some radiative changes
   (D) to evaluate current methods of determining radiative changes
   (E) to identify the factors that contribute to ozone changes and to the greenhouse effect

Analysis of Sample Passage #2

Answer Key

1. A
2. D
3. B
4. D
5. E
6. C
7. C

QUESTION 1

It can be inferred from the information in the passage that "the burning of fossil fuels" (lines 9-10)

(A) is an anthropogenic cause of radiative forcings
(B) results in both radiative forcings and radiative feedbacks
(C) does not affect atmospheric forcings or feed-backs
(D) is a significant type of radiative forcing
(E) is an anthropogenic cause of radiative feedback

Question Type: Inference
Difficulty Level: Easier

(A) is the best response. The author states in the first paragraph that "[f]orcings can arise from either natural or anthropogenic causes." In the following sentence the author describes two specific causes of forcings, presumably to illustrate the point of the previous sentence. It can be reasonably inferred by considering both sentences together that the first example (volcanic activity) is a natural cause, while the second (the burning of fossil fuels) is an anthropogenic cause.

Incorrect Responses

(B) is only partly supported by the passage. Although it can be inferred that the burning of fossil fuels causes radiative forcings, the author neither states nor suggests that this activity also causes radiative feedback.

(C) contradicts the information presented in this part of the passage, which states explicitly that the concentration of sulfate aerosols is affected ("can

be altered") by burning of fossil fuels. Thus, although burning of fossil fuels may not affect radiative feedback, it can be inferred that such activity does affect radiative forcings.

(D) gets the passage information backwards. The burning of fossil fuels is a cause, not a type, of radiative forcing.

(E) confuses forcings with feedbacks.

QUESTION 2

According to the passage, radiative forcings and radiative feedbacks can generally be distinguished in which of the following ways?

(A) whether the radiative change is global or more localized
(B) the precision with which the amounts of radiative change can be determined
(C) that altitude at which the radiative change occurs
(D) whether the amount of radiative change is specified or calculated
(E) whether the radiative change is directed toward or away from the earth

Question Type: Explicit Detail
Difficulty Level: Easier

(D) is the best response. According to the passage, radiative forcings are normally specified in global climate model situations, whereas feedbacks are calculated changes based on observations (lines 10-14).

Incorrect Responses

(A) is wholly unsupported by the passage. The author never discusses the geographic extent of radiative changes in any context.

(B) is not supported by the passage. The fact that feedbacks are "calculated" while forcings are "specified" does not in itself suggest that one can be more precisely determined than the other.

(C) and (E) similarly confuse the information in the

passage. In the third paragraph the author discusses altitude as a factor influencing the relative effects on ozone changes (a radiative forcing) of radiation directed toward the earth and radiation directed away from the earth. But this discussion does not serve to distinguish forcings and feedbacks from each other.

QUESTION 3

Based upon the information in the passage, decreased evaporation is most likely to result in which of the following?

(A) an increase in water vapor concentration
(B) a decrease in atmospheric absorption of longwave radiation
(C) a decrease in other radiative forcings
(D) an increase in atmospheric temperatures
(E) a decrease in surface reflectivity

Question Type: Inference
Difficulty Level: Moderate

(B) is the best response. According to the passage, increased evaporation leads to increased water vapor concentration (lines 22-23), which leads to an increase in solar irradiance (lines 20-21). Accordingly, it is likely that a decrease in evaporation will lead to a decrease in the other two amounts.

Incorrect Responses

(A) runs contrary (although not explicitly) to the information in the passage, which states that increased (not decreased) evaporation leads to increased water vapor concentration (see lines 22-23).

(C) confuses the information in the passage. The pertinent part of the passage (lines 12-17) deals solely with feedbacks and not forcings.

(D) runs contrary (although not explicitly) to the information in the passage, which states that increased (not decreased) evaporation leads to a warming of the atmosphere.

(E) confuses the information in the passage. The pertinent part of the passage (lines 12-17) deals solely with feedbacks. However, surface reflectivity is a type of forcing (line 5).

QUESTION 4

The author discusses the effect of clouds on atmospheric temperature most likely in order to show that

(A) radiative feedbacks can be more difficult to isolate and predict than radiative forcings
(B) the distinction between radiative feedbacks and radiative forcings is somewhat arbitrary
(C) some radiative feedbacks cannot be determined solely by global climate model simulations
(D) the climatic impact of some radiative feedbacks is uncertain
(E) the NASA-sponsored study is inconclusive as to the effect of ozone on cloud formation and dissipation.

Question Type: Purpose of Detail
Difficulty Level: Moderate

(D) is the best response. Response (D) fairly expresses the author's point in the first sentence of the second paragraph. Immediately thereafter, the author discusses clouds as an example of this point—it is difficult to predict the impact of greenhouse gases on clouds and thus on temperature.

Incorrect Responses

(A) is unsupported by the passage. In the second paragraph, the author discusses two particular examples of radiative changes—one involving radiative forcings (lines 35-44) and the other involving radiative feedbacks (lines 25-34). The author's purpose in discussing these two phenomena is to illustrate the author's previous point that "[t]he effects of some forcings and feedbacks on climate are both complex and uncertain" (lines 24-25). However, the author makes no attempt to compare the relative complexity or uncertainty of these two effects.

(B) is unsupported by the passage. In the first paragraph, the author attempts to distinguish between forcings and feedbacks but neither asserts nor infers that the distinction is somewhat arbitrary.

(C) confuses the information in the passage and is somewhat nonsensical. It is forcings (not feedbacks) that are specified in (not determined by) global climate model simulations (lines 10-

12). Moreover, (C) is wholly unsupported by the information in the second paragraph; the author neither discusses nor mentions global climate simulations in relation to the effects of clouds on atmospheric temperatures.

(E) confuses the information in the second paragraph with the discussion in the third paragraph about the NASA-sponsored study. (E) is also unsupported insofar as the author does not indicate whether the study is conclusive or inconclusive.

QUESTION 5

Based upon the information in the passage, the author would probably agree that scientists could more accurately predict the extent and direction of the greenhouse effect if they were to

(A) monitor radiative feedbacks and forcings over a longer time period
(B) change the direction of research away from determining amounts of radiative changes
(C) account for the altitude at which cloud formations appear
(D) isolate those ozone changes caused specifically by anthropogenic factors
(E) isolate the cooling influence of ozone changes from their warming influence

Question Type: Interpretation
Difficulty Level: Challenging

(E) **is the best response.** According to the passage, a given vertical distribution of ozone affects atmospheric temperature in both directions at once (lines 39-42). Accordingly, by isolating the cooling influence of a given distribution of ozone from its warming influence, scientists might better predict whether changes in the vertical distribution of ozone will have a net cooling or a net warming effect.

(A) **is the second-best response.** Admittedly, it seems reasonable from a common-sense viewpoint that our ability to forecast the precise extent of the greenhouse effect improves as more data is acquired over time. But this is neither stated nor implied in the passage itself; thus (A) is not adequately supported.

Other Incorrect Responses

(B) runs contrary to the information in the passage. Radiative changes include changes in ozone, which are the very cause of the greenhouse effect. Thus, scientists should continue attempts to determine the amounts of such changes.

(C) confuses the information in the passage. The discussion of altitude relates to forcings, while the discussion of clouds relates to feedbacks.

(D) is off the topic. Although the author does indicate in the first paragraph that forcings arise from both anthropogenic and natural causes (lines 6-7), nowhere in the passage does the author attempt to isolate their effects from each other, nor does the author suggest that doing so would enable scientists to better predict the extent of the greenhouse effect.

QUESTION 6

The information in the last paragraph does NOT:

(A) provide evidence of the variability of ozone amounts at different altitudes
(B) underscore the complexity in measuring radiative changes
(C) call into question current methods of determining radiative changes
(D) support the author's position that predicting future ozone changes is problematic
(E) explain a discrepancy between an earlier theory and more recent scientific evidence

Question Type: Interpretation
Difficulty Level: Moderate

(C) **is the best response.** Response (C) actually runs contrary (although not explicitly) to the information in the final paragraph. The author seems to accept the findings of the recent aircraft studies, and certainly does not call into question the methods used in those studies.

Incorrect Responses

(A) is incorrect based upon the last sentence of the passage. Since high (vertical) resolution observations are required to detect concentrations of greenhouse gases, it can be inferred that changes in such concentrations vary quickly with altitude. Moreover, the author suggests in the previous paragraph that this is the case [referring to the "vertical distribution of ozone" (lines 42-43) and to the dependence of climate forcings upon the altitude of ozone changes (lines 43-45)].

(B) is incorrect because the studies discussed in the last paragraph suggest that determining the amounts of forcings is more complex than previously thought—specifically, that relative amounts vary quickly and significantly with altitude.

(D) is incorrect for essentially the same reason as (B). The new-found variability of chemical concentration among different altitudes adds to the difficulty in assessing the relative importance of competing forcings discussed in the previous paragraph (lines 43-45).

(E) is inferable. In the passage's last sentence the author refers to "conventional explanations," which can be characterized as "earlier theories." Since the new evidence calls into question those earlier theories, it is reasonable to infer that a discrepancy existed between earlier explanations and recent scientific evidence. In fact, the third paragraph as a whole explains this discrepancy.

QUESTION 7

Which of the following best expresses the author's primary concern in the passage?

(A) to examine the environmental effects of radiative forcings and feedbacks
(B) to challenge conventional theories about the impact of radiative changes on ozone depletion and the greenhouse effect
(C) to illustrate the complexity and uncertainty of some radiative changes
(D) to evaluate current methods of determining radiative changes
(E) to identify the factors that contribute to ozone changes and to the greenhouse effect

Question Type: Primary Purpose
Difficulty Level: Challenging

(C) **is the best response.** While the first paragraph introduces the topic and defines terms, the author stresses in the second paragraph that the effects of radiative changes can be complex and uncertain; in fact, the author devotes the second and third paragraphs (the bulk of the passage) to demonstrating this point. So (B) is neither too narrow nor too broad in scope. It is just broad enough to encompasses the author's concern with prediction problems.

(D) **is a second-best response.** Admittedly, the author does point out the insufficiency of certain types of data in predicting climate changes (second paragraph), as well as pointing out that previous explanations for Antarctic ozone depletion were somewhat inaccurate (final paragraph). These points are secondary, however, to the broader and primary point that predicting radiative changes is difficult due to their complexity and uncertainty. Thus, (D) is *too narrow* in its scope.

(E) **is a second-best response.** But (E) is too narrow in one sense, yet too broad in another sense. Although the author does indeed identify various factors contributing to ozone depletion, the author's concern is not merely with identifying these factors but also with pointing out problems in isolating and measuring these factors and the resulting problem of making accurate predictions about the greenhouse effect. In this sense, then, (E) is *too narrow*. In addition, there may be other factors that contribute to ozone depletion not discussed in the passage; the author does not necessarily intend to identify all such factors; in this sense, then, (E) is *too broad*.

Other Incorrect Responses

(A) is too broad a statement of the author's primary purpose. The author is primarily concerned with how radiative changes relate specifically to ozone depletion and to the resulting greenhouse effect, not to the environment in general.

(B) is entirely *off focus* and far *too narrow* to serve as a viable "best" response. The author makes no attempt in the passage to discuss the "conventional explanations" to which the last sentence of the passage refers. Moreover, the recent scientific study discussed in the final paragraph (which calls into question those "conventional explanations" about ozone depletion) serve only to illustrate the author's *broader* and *primary* point that predicting radiative changes is difficult due to their complex and uncertain interaction.

practice sets

Part 5 consists of 20 practice sets. Each practice set includes a passage, a series of questions, an answer key, and a detailed analysis of each question. Use the practice sets to experiment with the techniques discussed in Parts 1 and 2 and to improve your ability to detect the use of the various wrong-answer ploys as discussed in Part 3. Here's how the practice sets are organized:

- **Practice Sets 1–12** include passages that are similar in length (450–550 words) to the ones on the LSAT and to the longer ones on the GRE. Each set includes 6–8 questions, just like the LSAT. (*NOTE:* On the GRE your long question set might include as few as 4 questions.) ALLOW YOURSELF 8–9 MINUTES PER SET.

- **Practice Sets 13–15** reflect the format of MCAT passages. Each passage is 600–700 words in length and is accompanied by 7–8 questions. (*NOTE:* an *actual* MCAT question set may include as few as 6 questions.) ALLOW YOURSELF 9–10 MINUTES PER SET.

- **Practice Sets 16–20** include passages that are similar in length (200–300 words) to the ones on the GMAT CAT and to the shorter ones on the GRE. Each set includes 3–4 questions. (*NOTE:* On the GRE a short question set might include as few as two questions.) ALLOW YOURSELF 4–5 MINUTES PER SET.

When you finish working through a question set, READ THE ANALYSIS THAT FOLLOWS, EVEN FOR THE QUESTIONS YOU ANSWERED CORRECTLY. The analysis illustrates and reinforces the materials in Part 3 about the test-makers' various wrong-answer ploys.

PASSAGE #1

The half-decade of 1850–1855 saw the appearance of an unusually rich cluster of literary works in America. This period, known as the American Renaissance, represented the first
5   flowering of a national literature with character-istically American settings and themes. Not a rebirth in the sense of a recovery of the lost arts of the past, it was rather a confluence of two streams of thought that emerged in early
10 nineteenth-century America: a determination to cut loose from European literary forms and a desire to explore the millennial belief that an ideal world was forming in America.

When Ralph Waldo Emerson pronounced
15 America's declaration of cultural independence from Europe in his "American Scholar" address of 1837, he was actually articulating the transcen-dental assumptions of Jefferson's declaration of political independence. In the ideal new world
20 envisioned by Emerson and his transcendental associates, America was to become a perfect democracy of free and self-reliant individuals. Because the transcendentalists considered the potentialities of the individual to be infinite, the
25 possibility of achieving the democratic ideal seemed, for them, within reach. Bringing Emerson's metaphysics down to earth, Thoreau, in his *Walden* (1854), asserted that in America one can live entirely without encumbrances and thus
30 can realize the transcendental doctrine of self-reliance. Emerson wanted to visualize Thoreau as the ideal scholar in action that he had called for in the "American Scholar," but in the end Emerson regretted Thoreau's too-private
35 individualism which failed to signal the vibrant revolution in national consciousness that Emerson had prophesied.

For Emerson, what Thoreau lacked, Whitman embodied in full. On reading *Leaves of Grass*
40 (1855), Emerson saw in Whitman the "prophet of democracy" whom he had sought—the poet-seer with the charisma to propel transcendentalist ideas into the national consciousness and to awaken Americans to a sense of the sublime
45 social perfection that lay within their grasp. The other writers of the American Renaissance were less sanguine about the fulfillment of the demo-cratic ideal. In *The Scarlet Letter* (1850), while portraying Hester Prynne's assertion of transcen-
50 dental freedom as heroic, Hawthorne concluded that such antinomianism leads to moral anarchy. And Melville, who saw in his story of *Pierre* (1852) a metaphor for the misguided assumptions of democratic idealism, declared the transcen-
55 dentalist dream unrealizable. Ironically, the

literary vigor with which both Hawthorne and Melville explored the ideal showed their deep sympathy with it even as they dramatized its delusions.

60 Thus the writers of the American Renaissance waged a kind of imaginary debate over the American democratic ideal, with Emerson, Thoreau, and Whitman affirming it as vibrantly emergent and Hawthorne and Melville warning
65 that it was sadly specious. Although the Civil War seemed to corroborate the ideals of freedom and democracy, the rise of realism in literature and of pragmatism in philosophy during the latter half of the century revealed that the debate was not over.

1. The author of the passage seeks to

    (A) explore the impact of the American Renaissance writers on the literature of the late eighteenth century
    (B) illustrate how American literature of the mid-eighteenth century differed in form from European literature of the same time period
    (C) identify two schools of thought among American Renaissance writers regarding the democratic ideal
    (D) point out how Emerson's democratic idealism was mirrored by the works of the American Renaissance writers
    (E) explain why the writers of the American Renaissance believed that an ideal world was forming in America

GO ON TO THE NEXT PAGE.

2. Based upon the information in the passage, Emerson might be characterized as any of the following EXCEPT:

   (A) a literary critic
   (B) an American Renaissance writer
   (C) a public speaker
   (D) a literary prophet
   (E) a political pragmatist

3. The passage mentions works of the American Renaissance period by all of the following EXCEPT:

   (A) Emerson
   (B) Hawthorne
   (C) Thoreau
   (D) Whitman
   (E) Melville

4. With which of the following statements about Melville and Hawthorne would the author most likely agree?

   (A) Both men were disillusioned transcendentalists.
   (B) Hawthorne sympathized with the transcendental dream more so than Melville.
   (C) They agreed as to what the transcendentalist dream would ultimately lead to.
   (D) Both men believed the idealists to be misguided.
   (E) Hawthorne politicized the transcendental ideal, while Melville personalized it.

5. Which of the following statements about *Leaves of Grass* is best supported by the information in the passage?

   (A) It dramatized the delusions of the democratic ideal.
   (B) It marked the beginning of a rise of realism in literature.
   (C) Emerson read it after he read Thoreau's *Walden*.
   (D) Its form was a departure from established European literary forms.
   (E) Its main character mirrored its author's charisma.

6. The author would most likely agree that the Civil War

   (A) led to the rise of realism in American literature
   (B) affirmed that the democratic ideal was unrealistic
   (C) demonstrated that the transcendental dream in America was alive
   (D) effectively terminated the American Renaissance
   (E) provided inspiration to the writers of the American Renaissance

STOP.

PASSAGE #1—ANSWER KEY

1. C
2. E
3. A
4. D
5. D
6. C

PASSAGE #1—ANALYSIS

QUESTION 1

1. The author of the passage seeks to

(A) explore the impact of the American Renaissance writers on the literature of the late eighteenth century

(B) illustrate how American literature of the mid-eighteenth century differed in form from European literature of the same time period

(C) identify two schools of thought among American Renaissance writers regarding the democratic ideal

(D) point out how Emerson's democratic idealism was mirrored by the works of the American Renaissance writers

(E) explain why the writers of the American Renaissance believed that an ideal world was forming in America

Question Type: Interpretation
Difficulty Level: Moderate

(C) is the best response. The passage describes an imaginary debate over the American democratic ideal among the writers of the American Renaissance, in which Emerson, Thoreau, and Whitman are grouped together in one school of thought while Hawthorne and Melville are paired in another.

(D) is the second-best response. Admittedly, Emerson's idealism was reflected in the works of Thoreau and Whitman insofar as they too shared the transcendentalists' dream. However, Response (D) distorts the information in the passage. The author actually points out that Thoreau's "too-private individualism" was not in accord with what Emerson hoped for. In this sense, the author is pointing out how Thoreau's *Walden* failed to accurately mirror Emerson's idealism. In addition, although the passage does strongly suggest that, through his works, Whitman fully reflected Emerson's ideal American scholar, the passage does not discuss how Whitman's works serve this end. Thus, Response (D) is not as well supported by the passage as Response (C).

Other Incorrect Responses

(A) focuses on the wrong information. The last sentence of the passage does mention that the imaginary debate among the American Renaissance writers continued during the latter half of the century, suggesting that they influenced later writers. Indeed, the passage might have continued as indicated by Response (A). However, the passage itself does not "explore" the impact of the American Renaissance writers to any extent.

(B) focuses on the wrong information. Although the author mentions in the first paragraph that American Renaissance literature reflected a determination to cut loose from European literary forms, the author makes no further attempt to distinguish American forms from European forms.

(E) distorts the information in the passage. The only event mentioned in the passage that may have contributed to the idealist mind-set of the times was Jefferson's declaration of political independence. However, the author does not actually claim that it was because of Jefferson (in whole or in part) that the writers of the American Renaissance believed that an ideal world was forming in America. Moreover, there is no discussion in the passage of any other reasons why the American Renaissance writers might have believed as they did.

QUESTION 2

2. **Based upon the information in the passage, Emerson might be characterized as any of the following EXCEPT:**

   (A) a literary critic
   (B) an American Renaissance writer
   (C) a public speaker
   (D) a literary prophet
   (E) a political pragmatist

Question Type: Interpretation
Difficulty Level: Moderate

(E) **is the best response.** Response (E) runs contrary to the passage. The author makes clear throughout the passage that Emerson is an idealist, which is just the opposite of a pragmatist.

(D) **is a second-best response.** The author asserts that Thoreau "failed to signal the vibrant revolution in national consciousness that Emerson had prophesied" (lines 35–37). Also, the passage supports the idea that Emerson anticipated and predicted that America would become "a perfect democracy of free and self-reliant individuals" (lines 21–22). However, Emerson was not foreseeing a literary phenomenon so much as a political one; also, the passage does not support the notion that Emerson's predictions were ever realized. Thus, Response (D) is not as viable as Response (E).

(A) **is a second-best response.** Response (A) is not supported as explicitly by the passage as are (B) and (C). Nevertheless, in regretting Thoreau's "too-private individualism" (line 34), Emerson is criticizing Thoreau for the ideas presented in *Walden*, thereby playing the role of literary critic.

Other Incorrect Responses

(B) and (E) are both implied by the first sentence of the final paragraph: "Thus the writers of the American Renaissance waged a kind of imaginary debate over the American democratic ideal, with Emerson, Thoreau and Whitman affirming it as vibrantly emergent ..." It can be reasonably inferred from this statement both that Emerson was one of the American Renaissance writers and that the author considered him to be a political idealist.

QUESTION 3

3. The passage mentions works of the American Renaissance period by all of the following EXCEPT:

    (A) Emerson
    (B) Hawthorne
    (C) Thoreau
    (D) Whitman
    (E) Melville

Question Type: Explicit Detail
Difficulty Level: Easier

(A) is the best response. The only "work" by Emerson mentioned in the passage is his "American Scholar" address. Even if a public address can be considered a "work," since Emerson gave the address in 1837 and not during the American Renaissance period (1850-1855), the address would not be considered an American Renaissance work.

Incorrect Responses

The passage mentions specific works by Hawthorne (*The Scarlet Letter*), Thoreau (*Walden*), Whitman (*Leaves of Grass*), and Melville (*Pierre*), all created during the period from 1850-1855.

QUESTION 4

4. With which of the following statements about Melville and Hawthorne would the author most likely agree?

    (A) Both men were disillusioned transcendentalists.
    (B) Hawthorne sympathized with the transcendental dream more so than Melville.
    (C) They agreed as to what the transcendentalist dream would ultimately lead to.
    (D) Both men believed the idealists to be misguided.
    (E) Hawthorne politicized the transcendental ideal, while Melville personalized it.

Question Type: Interpretation
Difficulty Level: Challenging

(D) is the best response. According to the passage, Melville, through his story of *Pierre*, conveyed the notion that democratic idealism was based upon "misguided assumptions." Although the author is not so explicit that Hawthorne also believed idealists to be misguided, Hawthorne's conclusion that transcendental freedom leads to moral anarchy can reasonably be interpreted as such.

(A) is the second-best response. According to the passage, both men sympathized with the democratic ideal (line 58), which was part of the transcendental dream. In this respect, it could be argued that both men were transcendentalists at heart. Also, Hawthorne concluded that transcendental freedom would lead to moral anarchy, while Melville declared the dream unrealizable. In this sense, then, both men were disillusioned with the transcendental dream. However, in lines 23–26, the author states that for the transcendentalists, the democratic ideal seemed "within reach," while for Hawthorne and Melville, the ideal was clearly not within reach. Accordingly, to categorize them as transcendentalists would contradict the author's description of the transcendental viewpoint.

Other Incorrect Responses

(B) is unsupported by the passage. The passage states that both men sympathized with the transcendental dream (line 58). However, the author neither states nor implies that one of these two men sympathized with the transcendental dream more than the other.

(C) is unsupported by the passage. According to the passage, Hawthorne believed that antinomianism leads to moral anarchy (lines 48–51), while Melville believed that the transcendental dream was unrealizable (lines 52–55). This information suggests neither agreement nor disagreement between the two men as to what the transcendental dream would ultimately lead to.

(E) confuses the information in the passage. The passage suggests just the opposite. It can be argued that Melville politicized transcendentalism in that, through his metaphorical story of *Pierre*, he revealed the problems of democratic idealism. At the same time, Hawthorne personalized transcendentalism through the "heroic" actions of an individual character (Hester Prynne) in *The Scarlet Letter*.

QUESTION 5

5. Which of the following statements about *Leaves of Grass* is best supported by the information in the passage?

   (A) It dramatized the delusions of the democratic ideal.
   (B) It marked the beginning of a rise of realism in literature.
   (C) Emerson read it after he read Thoreau's *Walden*.
   (D) Its form was a departure from established European literary forms.
   (E) Its main character mirrored its author's charisma.

Question Type: Inference
Difficulty Level: Moderate

(D) is the best response. In lines 10–11, the author states that the literature of the American Renaissance period reflected "a determination to cut loose from the European literary forms." It is reasonable to infer, then, that *Leaves of Grass* (an example of American Renaissance literature) differed in form from European literature.

(B) is the second-best response. In the final sentence of the passage, the author suggests that the "rise of realism in literature" throughout the latter half of the eighteenth century is a continuation of the imaginary debate over the American democratic ideal waged among the writers of the Renaissance period. Admittedly, the author does include Whitman (through his *Leaves of Grass*) in this debate. However, it was the American Renaissance period in general, and not Whitman's *Leaves of Grass* specifically, that marked the beginning of the rise of realism. In this sense, then, (B) distorts the information in the passage. Moreover, Whitman sided in the "debate" with the idealists rather than with the realists; in this respect, then, (B) actually runs contrary to the information in the passage.

Other Incorrect Responses

(A) confuses the information in the passage. It was the works of Hawthorne and Melville, not *Leaves of Grass* (written by Whitman), that dramatized the delusions of the democratic ideal.

(C) calls for speculation. The passage does not indicate when Emerson read either work or which of the two works Emerson read first.

(E) is wholly unsupported by the passage. The passage indicates that, upon reading Whitman's *Leaves of Grass*, Emerson recognized Whitman's charisma. However, the passage makes no mention of any character in *Leaves*, nor does the passage suggest that any of the characters in *Leaves* resemble Whitman.

QUESTION 6

6. The author would most likely agree that the Civil War

    (A) led to the rise of realism in American literature
    (B) affirmed that the democratic ideal was unrealistic
    (C) demonstrated that the transcendental dream in America
         was alive
    (D) effectively terminated the American Renaissance
    (E) provided inspiration to the writers of the American
         Renaissance

Question Type: Interpretation
Difficulty Level: Easier

(C) is the best response. According to the passage, the Civil War "seemed to corroborate the ideals of freedom and democracy." Response (C) restates this idea.

Incorrect Responses

(A) calls for an unwarranted inference and actually runs contrary to the passage. The author makes no causal connection between the Civil War and the subsequent rise of realism in literature. In fact, insofar as the Civil War corroborated the ideals of freedom and democracy, the rise of realism in literature may have occurred in spite of, rather than as a reaction to, the Civil War.

(B) distorts the information in the passage. The author does not comment on whether the Civil War tended to show that the democratic ideal was realistic or unrealistic. The author only goes so far as to assert that the Civil War affirmed the democratic ideal.

(D) is unsupported by the passage. Whether or not the Civil War coincided with the end of the American Renaissance period, Response (D) suggests that the Civil War in some way caused the American Renaissance to end. This implication is not supported by the passage.

(E) distorts the information in the passage. Although the Civil War may have affirmed the ideals that inspired some of the American Renaissance writers, the author neither states nor suggests that the Civil War itself was a source of inspiration for the writers of the American Renaissance period.

PASSAGE #2

Tuberculosis has two general stages relevant to its transmission and infectivity: tuberculosis infection (sometimes also called latent tuberculosis) and active tuberculosis. Active tuberculosis
5 manifests itself in a variety of ways, depending in part on the primary site of infection in the body. Pulmonary tuberculosis is the most common form of the disease, leading to cavity formation and progressive destruction of lung tissue. Pathologic
10 and inflammatory processes associated with pulmonary tuberculosis produce weakness, fever, chest pain, cough, and when a small blood vessel is eroded, bloody sputum. Although only pulmonary and laryngeal tuberculosis are
15 contagious through the airborne route, another active form—extrapulmonary tuberculosis—can affect other sites in the body. Dissemination begins in the lung, which is the initial site of the infection, and travels through the body or
20 through lymphatics to regional lymph nodes, resulting in the formation of small miliary (seed-like) lesions or life-threatening meningitis.

The cellular immune system is believed to play a central role in the development of
25 tuberculosis. While some of the relevant immunologic processes have been identified, fundamental questions remain concerning the interplay and regulation of immunologic forces that both inhibit and actually contribute to the
30 disease process itself. Airborne particles containing tubercle bacilli that are inhaled and that reach the lower parts of the lung are initially engulfed by macrophages—a type of scavenger cell—in the alveoli (terminal air sacs in the lung).
35 If the bacilli are not destroyed by the alveolar macrophages, the bacilli multiply, killing the cell and attracting nonactivated macrophages from the bloodstream. In these new macrophages, the bacilli multiply logarithmically. Antigenic
40 substances present within or secreted by tubercle bacilli stimulate T-lymphocytes (CD4 cells) to produce chemical substances (lymphokynes) which activate these new macrophages, enabling them to destroy or inhibit the bacilli. This process
45 of cell-mediated immunity (CMI) forms one part of the body's immune response to tuberculosis.

A related immune process—delayed-type hypersensitivity (DTH)—is an inflammatory response that destroys bacilli-laden unactivated
50 macrophages. An overabundance of DTH is blamed for most of tissue damage characteristic of pulmonary tuberculosis. Death of tissues leads to caseating granulomas and liquefaction of solid caseous waste, producing cavities in the tissue.
55 Within the liquified caseum, tubercle bacilli

multiply outside of the cells, reaching tremendous numbers. Host resistance may be overwhelmed, and the bacilli may develop resistance to antimicrobial drugs. Liquefaction
60 and cavity formation allow the disease to become contagious because the bacilli spread via airways to other parts of the body and to the outside air.

1. In the passage, the author's primary concern is to

   (A) examine the different stages in the development of tuberculosis in the body
   (B) describe the role of the body's immune system in the development of tuberculosis
   (C) distinguish between contagious and non-contagious forms of tuberculosis
   (D) describe the physiological effects of various forms of tuberculosis
   (E) discuss the interplay between two types of immune responses to tuberculosis

2. Among the following, it is most reasonably inferable from the information in the passage that extrapulmonary tuberculosis

   (A) is contagious through the airborne route
   (B) usually begins in the lymph nodes
   (C) is less common than pulmonary tuberculosis
   (D) is more likely than pulmonary tuberculosis to result in death
   (E) is disseminated by way of activated macrophages

GO ON TO THE NEXT PAGE.

3. Among the following, which would the author probably agree contributes LEAST to the development or spread of tuberculosis?

   (A) liquefaction of caseous waste
   (B) tubercle bacilli
   (C) T-lymphocytes
   (D) caseating granulomas
   (E) unactivated macrophages

4. According to the passage, lymphokynes

   (A) are produced by tubercle bacilli
   (B) produce T-lymphocytes
   (C) attract new macrophages from the bloodstream
   (D) aid in the destruction of bacilli
   (E) destroy unactivated macrophages

5. The passage provides information for answering all of the following questions EXCEPT:

   (A) How do tubercle bacilli escape from the body to the outside air?
   (B) In what ways does the body's immune system actually contribute to the development of tuberculosis?
   (C) How do various forms of tuberculosis manifest themselves in the body?
   (D) What is the mechanism by which the body produces macrophages?
   (E) How does the body's immune system respond to the presence of tubercle bacilli?

6. Which of the following best expresses the main idea of the passage?

   (A) The body's immune system both inhibits and contributes to the development of tuberculosis.
   (B) Research suggests that airborne tubercle bacilli are primarily responsible for the development of contagious tuberculosis.
   (C) The interplay and regulation of various immunological forces affecting tuberculosis remain largely uncertain.
   (D) The immune system plays a more significant role in the development of contagious tuberculosis than in that of non-contagious tuberculosis.
   (E) Immune-system responses play a more integral part in disease processes than previously believed.

7. Among the following, the passage would most likely continue by

   (A) identifying treatments which may help to reverse the harmful effects of immune-system responses on the development of tuberculosis
   (B) defining latent tuberculosis and describing its manifestations
   (C) describing the process by which extrapulmonary tuberculosis spreads through the body
   (D) raising questions about the interplay of immunological processes pertaining to the development of tuberculosis
   (E) examining the physiological factors that determine susceptibility to contagious tuberculosis

STOP.

PASSAGE #2—ANSWER KEY

1. B   5. D
2. C   6. A
3. C   7. D
4. D

PASSAGE #2—ANALYSIS

QUESTION 1

1. In the passage, the author's primary concern is to

   (A) examine the different stages in the development of tuberculosis in the body
   (B) describe the role of the body's immune system in the development of tuberculosis
   (C) distinguish between contagious and non-contagious forms of tuberculosis
   (D) describe the physiological effects of various forms of tuberculosis
   (E) discuss the interplay between two types of immune responses to tuberculosis

Question Type: Primary Purpose
Difficulty Level: Moderate

(B) **is the best response.** While the first paragraph is introductory in nature (terms are defined and classified), the author's main concern in the remainder of the passage is to describe how different immune responses (two are described: CMI and DTH) both inhibit and contribute to the development of tuberculosis.

(E) **is the second-best response.** Admittedly, the author does indicate, in the first sentence of the final paragraph, that DTH and CMI are "related," suggesting that there is indeed some interplay between these two types of immune responses. However, the author's broader concern is to describe how each of these two responses both inhibits and contributes to the development of tuberculosis. The precise manner in which the two types of responses are related to each other is not discussed in any detail; thus, (E) is off focus.

Other Incorrect Responses

(A) is off focus. In the first sentence of the passage, the author identifies the two stages of tuberculosis—tuberculosis infection (latent tuberculosis) and active tuberculosis. However, there is no further discussion or mention of latent tuberculosis. The remainder of the passage deals with the various forms of active tuberculosis and with its development.

(C) is off focus. Although in the first paragraph the author does distinguish between contagious and non-contagious tuberculosis, the passage includes no further discussion of the differences between these two types.

(D) is off focus. Although some of the physiological effects of pulmonary and extrapulmonary tuberculosis are listed in the first paragraph, there is no further discussion of symptoms or manifestations.

QUESTION 2

2. **Among the following, it is most reasonably inferable from the information in the passage that extrapulmonary tuberculosis**

   (A) **is contagious through the airborne route**
   (B) **usually begins in the lymph nodes**
   (C) **is less common than pulmonary tuberculosis**
   (D) **is more likely than pulmonary tuberculosis to result in death**
   (E) **is disseminated by way of activated macrophages**

Question Type: Inference
Difficulty Level: Moderate

(C) **is the best response.** Pulmonary tuberculosis is "the most common form of the disease" (lines 7–8). Since extrapulmonary tuberculosis is mentioned as "another form" of tuberculosis, it must be less common than pulmonary tuberculosis.

(D) **is the second-best response.** Response (D) is supported by the passage insofar as the author mentions that extrapulmonary tuberculosis can result in "life-threatening meningitis," while not mentioning any life-threatening results of pulmonary tuberculosis. However, just because no mention is made of the possible threat to life posed by pulmonary tuberculosis, it does not necessary follow that this form does not result in death. No information is provided to enable the reader to compare the rates of death resulting from the two forms. The author neither states nor implies that one form is more likely to result in death than the other. Thus, (D) requires an unwarranted inference.

Other Incorrect Responses

(A) contradicts the passage. "Only pulmonary and laryngeal tuberculosis are contagious through the airborne route" (lines 13–15). Thus, extrapulmonary tuberculosis (another form) cannot also be contagious in this manner.

(B) contradicts the passage; the lung is the initial site of the infection (line 18).

(E) confuses the information in the passage. Macrophages do not "disseminate" tuberculosis, as Response (E) suggests. Rather, they play a role in the body's immune response, engulfing tubercle bacilli that reach the lungs (lines 32–34).

QUESTION 3

3. **Among the following, which would the author probably agree contributes LEAST to the development or spread of tuberculosis?**

   (A) **liquefaction of caseous waste**
   (B) **tubercle bacilli**

(C) T-lymphocytes
(D) caseating granulomas
(E) unactivated macrophages

Question Type: Explicit Detail
Difficulty Level: Easier

(C) is the best response. T-lymphocytes, a type of cell, produce a chemical substance that activates macrophages, enabling the macrophages to destroy or inhibit bacilli. The spread and multiplication of bacilli seems to be the primary developmental process involved. Thus, it appear that T-lymphocytes inhibit rather than contribute to the development of the disease.

Incorrect Responses

(A) is explicitly contradicted by the passage. According to the passage, liquefaction of caseous waste is one of two factors that allow the disease to become contagious (lines 59–62). Thus, liquefaction clearly contributes to the spread of tuberculosis.

(B) is implicitly contradicted by the passage. The spread and multiplication of tubercle bacilli seem to be the primary developmental process. Other aspects of the disease process mentioned in the passage are reactions to the invasion into the lungs and subsequent multiplication of bacilli.

(D) is implicitly contradicted by the passage. Caseating granulomas (along with liquefaction of solid caseous waste) contribute to the production of tissue cavities (lines 53–54), which in turn allows bacilli to spread via airways to other parts of the body and to the outside air (lines 59–62). Thus, caseating granulomas clearly contribute to the spread of tuberculosis.

(E) is implicitly contradicted. According to the passage, the body produces an inflammatory response (DTH) which destroys bacilli-laden unactivated macrophages. This response, however, results in tissue damage, leading to liquefaction and cavity formation which in turn allow the disease to become contagious. Thus, unactivated macrophages contribute indirectly to the spread of the disease.

QUESTION 4

4. **According to the passage, lymphokynes**

   (A) **are produced by tubercle bacilli**
   (B) **produce T-lymphocytes**
   (C) **attract new macrophages from the bloodstream**
   (D) **aid in the destruction of bacilli**
   (E) **destroy unactivated macrophages**

Question Type: Explicit Detail
Difficulty Level: Easier

(D) is the best response. According to the passage, lymphokynes activate macrophages, enabling them to destroy or inhibit bacilli.

Incorrect Responses

(A) confuses the information. T-lymphocytes, not bacilli, produce lymphokynes.

(B) confuses the information in the passage. T-lymphocytes produce lymphokynes, not the other way around.

(C) confuses the information in the passage. According to the passage, it is the presence of tubercle bacilli (not lymphokynes) in the lung that attracts macrophages from the bloodstream.

(E) confuses the information in the passage. It is DTH, not lymphokynes, that destroys unactivated macrophages.

QUESTION 5

5. The passage provides information for answering all of the following questions EXCEPT:

   (A) How do tubercle bacilli escape from the body to the outside air?
   (B) In what ways does the body's immune system actually contribute to the development of tuberculosis?
   (C) How do various forms of tuberculosis manifest themselves in the body?
   (D) What is the mechanism by which the body produces macrophages?
   (E) How does the body's immune system respond to the presence of tubercle bacilli?

Question Type: Explicit Detail
Difficulty Level: Easier

(D) is the best response. Although the passage indicates that macrophages are attracted from the bloodstream, no information is provided concerning how the body actually produces macrophages.

Incorrect Responses

(A) is answered explicitly by the last sentence of the passage.

(B) is answered implicitly in the passage. The body's immune system responds to the presence of bacilli in the lung by sending macrophages to the lung to engulf and destroy the invading bacilli. However, the passage notes that this response sometimes results in (1) the logarithmic multiplication of bacilli (second paragraph) or (2) a related immune-system response (DTH) which leads to tissue damage and the spread of bacilli to other parts of the body (third paragraph).

(C) is answered (partly) in the first paragraph, which mentions some symptoms of both pulmonary (lines 9–13) and extrapulmonary tuberculosis (lines 21–22).

(E) is answered explicitly and extensively in the passage. In fact, the second and third paragraphs are devoted entirely to answering this question.

QUESTION 6

6. Which of the following best expresses the main idea of the passage?

    (A) The body's immune system both inhibits and contributes to the development of tuberculosis.

    (B) Research suggests that airborne tubercle bacilli are primarily responsible for the development of contagious tuberculosis.

    (C) The interplay and regulation of various immunological forces affecting tuberculosis remain largely uncertain.

    (D) The immune system plays a more significant role in the development of contagious tuberculosis than in that of non-contagious tuberculosis.

    (E) Immune-system responses play a more integral part in disease processes than previously believed.

Question Type: Main Idea
Difficulty Level: Moderate

(A) is the best response. While the first paragraph is introductory in nature (terms are defined and classified), the author devotes the remainder of the passage to describing how different immune responses (two are described—CMI and DTH) both inhibit and contribute to the development of tuberculosis.

Incorrect Responses

(B) may be supported by the passage, but it is off focus. The author implies that contagious tuberculosis is contracted by inhaling airborne bacilli (see, e.g., the last sentence of the passage). However, this is not the passage's focus—nowhere in the passage does the author assert that research shows airborne bacilli, not some other phenomenon, to be primarily responsible for the contraction of tuberculosis.

(C) is supported by the passage, but it is off focus. Admittedly, in the second paragraph the author states that "fundamental questions remain concerning the interplay and regulation of immunologic forces that both inhibit and actually contribute to the disease process." However, the author does not continue by raising any such questions. Instead, the discussion focuses more narrowly on the interplay of such forces. Thus, since (C) does not relate to the author's primary concern in the passage, it is not the main idea.

(D) is unsupported by the passage. The author neither states nor implies that the role of immune-system responses depends upon whether the tuberculosis is contagious or non-contagious.

(E) is too broad and is unsupported by the passage. The passage is concerned not about the disease process in general but rather about tuberculosis specifically; in this sense, (E) is too broad. Also, nowhere in the passage does the author discuss or mention any prior theories or explanations regarding the role of the immune system in the development of tuberculosis.

QUESTION 7

7. Among the following, the passage would most likely continue by

(A) identifying treatments which may help to reverse the harmful effects of immune-system responses on the development of tuberculosis

(B) defining latent tuberculosis and describing its manifestations

(C) describing the process by which extrapulmonary tuberculosis spreads through the body

(D) raising questions about the interplay of immunological processes pertaining to the development of tuberculosis

(E) examining the physiological factors that determine susceptibility to contagious tuberculosis

Question Type: Extrapolation
Difficulty Level: Challenging

(D) is the best response. The author mentions in lines 25–30 that while some immune responses relevant to tuberculosis have been identified, questions remain about immunological forces affecting tuberculosis. The author then devotes the remainder of the passage to discussing two immune-system processes that have been identified—i.e., CMI and DTH. However, the author never does identify or discuss the remaining "fundamental questions" mentioned earlier. Thus, it is reasonable that the author would continue by discussing these questions.

Incorrect Responses

(A) is wholly unsupported by the passage. Nowhere in the passage does the author either express or imply a concern with identifying any treatment for tuberculosis.

(B) is inconsistent with the focus of the passage. Latent tuberculosis refers to the infection stage (rather than the active stage) of the disease. The author mentions latent tuberculosis (line 3) only to help define active tuberculosis, which is the author's more narrow concern. No information in the passage suggests that the author might return to discuss latent tuberculosis.

(C) runs contrary to the passage. Admittedly, in the first paragraph the author does distinguish extrapulmonary tuberculosis from other forms—i.e., the pulmonary and laryngeal forms. This distinction is based upon the primary site of the infection (lines 4–6). However, Response (C) suggests that the distinction lies in the immune-system response rather than the location of the infection. Moreover, nowhere in the second or third paragraphs (where the discussion of immune-system response occurs) does the author suggest that the responses discussed therein are different from those relating to extrapulmonary tuberculosis.

(E) is unsupported by the passage. The author neither expresses nor suggests a concern with how certain physiological traits affect susceptibility to tuberculosis.

PASSAGE #3

There are two cornerstones of economic reform in the formerly-Communist states: liberalization of prices (including exchange rates) and privatization. Radical economists call for
5   immediate liberalization, with the only remaining wage regulation in the state sector, accompanied by a restrictive fiscal and monetary policy to prevent high rates of inflation. Conservative economists, on the other hand, favor gradual
10   market deregulation in view of the dangers of inflation, unemployment, and economic instability. The "gradualists" would have the government prepare enterprises for market shocks, for example, by breaking monopolies
15   before prices and foreign trade are liberalized or by limiting production of certain heavy-industry products such as coal and steel. If the gradualists have their way, however, economic reform could dissolve into the hands of bureaucrats who are
20   incapable and unwilling to face the problems that a real transition to a market economy brings.

Privatization can also be approached either gradually or rapidly. Under the gradual approach, a state bureau would decide if and
25   when an enterprise is prepared for privatization and which form is most suitable for it. Slow privatization, some experts claim, is the only way to establish true private ownership, because only those who have to pay for property rights with
30   their own money will show an interest in the enterprise and will be engaged in its management. Although this argument is not without merit, gradual privatization would, nevertheless, only prolong the core problems of inefficiency
35   and misallocation of both labor and capital.

There are also two approaches to rapid privatization. Under one, shares of an enterprise would be distributed among the enterprise's employees so that the employees would become
40   the owners of the enterprise. This socialist-reform approach discriminates in favor of workers who happen to be employed by a modern and efficient enterprise as well as by placing workers' property at great risk by requiring them to invest
45   their property in the same enterprise in which they are employed rather than permitting then to diversify their investments.

The better approach to rapid privatization involves distribution of shares in enterprises, free
50   of charge, among all the people by means of vouchers—a kind of investment money. Some critics charge that voucher holders would not be interested in how their enterprises are managed, as may be true of small corporate shareholders in
55   capitalist countries who pay little attention to

their investments until the corporation's profits fail to meet expectations, at which time these shareholders rush to sell their securities. While the resulting fall in stock prices can cause serious
60   problems for a corporation, it is this very pressure that drives private firms toward efficiency and profitability. Others who oppose voucher privatization predict that most people will sell their vouchers to foreign capitalists. These
65   skeptics ignore the capacity of individuals to consider their own future—that is, to compare the future flow of income secured by a voucher to the benefits of immediate consumption. Even if an individual should decide to sell, the aim of
70   voucher privatization is not to secure equality of property but rather equality of opportunity.

1. Which of the following does the author associate with gradual market deregulation?

    (A) a restrictive monetary policy
    (B) a policy requiring monopolistic enterprises to split into two or more enterprises
    (C) government subsidization of steel producers
    (D) state agencies' determining when enterprises should be privatized
    (E) a fall in stock prices

2. With respect to which of the following pairs of terms does the author implicitly equate the two terms in the pair with each other?

    (A) voucher privatization; gradual privatization
    (B) socialist-reform privatization; investment-money privatization
    (C) price liberalization; market deregulation
    (D) gradual privatization; gradual liberalization
    (E) rapid privatization; voucher privatization

GO ON TO THE NEXT PAGE.

3. Which of the following is LEAST accurate in characterizing the author's method of argumentation in discussing the significance of falling stock prices (lines 58–62)?

   (A) describing a paradox that supports the author's position
   (B) asserting that one drawback of an approach is outweighed by countervailing considerations
   (C) rebutting an opposing position by suggesting an alternative explanation
   (D) discrediting an opposing argument by questioning its relevance
   (E) characterizing an argument against a course of action instead as an argument in its favor

4. Which of the following is NOT mentioned in the passage as a possible adverse consequence of rapid privatization?

   (A) instability in stock prices
   (B) loss of ownership in domestic private enterprises to foreign concerns
   (C) financial devastation for employees of private enterprises
   (D) inequitable distribution of wealth among employees of various enterprises
   (E) undue prolongation of inefficiency and misallocation

5. In responding to those "skeptics" who claim that people will sell their vouchers to foreign capitalists (lines 65–68), the author implies that

   (A) foreign capitalists will not be willing to pay a fair price for the vouchers
   (B) the future flow of income is likely in many cases to exceed the present exchange value of a voucher
   (C) foreign investment in a nation's enterprises may adversely affect currency exchange rates
   (D) although the skeptics are correct, their point is irrelevant in evaluating the merits of voucher privatization
   (E) foreign capitalists are less interested in the success of voucher privatization than in making a profit

6. Which of the following would the author probably agree is the LEAST desirable outcome of economic reform in formerly-Communist countries?

   (A) effective allocation of labor
   (B) equitable distribution of property among citizens
   (C) financial security of citizens
   (D) equal opportunity for financial success among citizens
   (E) financial security of private enterprises

7. Which of the following best expresses the main idea of the passage?

   (A) The two most important principles of post-Communist economic reform are liberalization of prices and privatization.
   (B) Voucher privatization is the best approach to economic reform in the formerly-Communist nations.
   (C) Economists disagree as to whether deregulation and privatization in formerly-Communist nations should be accomplished rapidly or gradually.
   (D) A gradual approach to post-Communist economic reform is less likely to succeed than is a rapid approach.
   (E) Each proposed method of post-Communist economic reform has both its advantages and drawbacks.

STOP.

PASSAGE #3—ANSWER KEY

1. B   5. B
2. C   6. E
3. C   7. D
4. E

PASSAGE #3—ANALYSIS

QUESTION 1

1. Which of the following does the author associate with gradual market deregulation?

   (A) a restrictive monetary policy
   (B) a policy requiring monopolistic enterprises to split into two or more enterprises
   (C) government subsidization of steel producers
   (D) state agencies' determining when enterprises should be privatized
   (E) a fall in stock prices

Question Type: Explicit Detail
Difficulty Level: Easier

(B) **is the best response.** One of the possible features of gradual deregulation mentioned in the first paragraph is the breaking of monopolies by the government. (B) simply restates this possible feature.

Incorrect Responses:

(A) confuses two different areas of discussion in the passage. The passage associates a restrictive monetary policy with immediate rather than gradual deregulation.

(C) contradicts the passage. The author associates government limitation of steel production with gradual deregulation (lines 11–17). Government subsidization would, to the contrary, result in increased steel production.

(D) confuses two different areas of discussion in the passage. It is gradual privatization, not gradual deregulation, with which the author associates the feature mentioned in (D) (lines 23–26).

(E) confuses two different areas of discussion. The author associates falling stock prices (line 59) with voucher privatization, not with gradual deregulation.

QUESTION 2

2. With respect to which of the following pairs of terms does the author implicitly equate the two terms in the pair with each other?

   (A) voucher privatization; gradual privatization
   (B) socialist-reform privatization; investment-money privatization

(C) price liberalization; market deregulation
(D) gradual privatization; gradual liberalization
(E) rapid privatization; voucher privatization

Question Type: Inference
Difficulty Level: Easier

(C) **is the best response.** In the second sentence, the author indicates that one of the key features of immediate (price) liberalization is the elimination of wage regulation; thereby, the author equates, at least to an extent, price liberalization and wage regulation. Moreover, in the next sentence, the author contrasts "gradual market deregulation" to "immediate liberalization," further suggesting the interchangeability of the terms "market deregulation" and "price liberalization."

(E) **is the second-best response.** Although voucher privatization is discussed as an approach to rapid privatization, it is only one of two approaches—the other approach is socialist-reform privatization. Accordingly, it is unfair to equate the two terms listed in (E).

Other Incorrect Responses

(A) is contradicted by the passage. Voucher privatization is one of two types of rapid, not gradual, privatization.

(B) is contradicted by the passage. The third paragraph makes clear that voucher privatization and socialist-reform privatization are two separate and distinct approaches to rapid privatization. Since the passage indicates that a voucher is "a kind of investment money" (line 51), the two terms in (B) are not interchangeable.

(D) confuses two unrelated terms mentioned in the passage. Privatization and liberalization are two separate and distinct concepts. Liberalization is discussed in the first paragraph, while privatization is examined in the remaining paragraphs.

QUESTION 3

3. **Which of the following is LEAST accurate in characterizing the author's method of argumentation in discussing the significance of falling stock prices (lines 58–62)?**

    (A) describing a paradox that supports the author's position
    (B) asserting that one drawback of an approach is outweighed by countervailing considerations
    (C) rebutting an opposing position by suggesting an alternative explanation
    (D) discrediting an opposing argument by questioning its relevance
    (E) characterizing an argument against a course of action instead as an argument in its favor

Question Type: Interpretation
Difficulty Level: Challenging

(C) is the best response. Although the author does respond to what might be one undesired result of voucher privatization—falling stock prices, as well as explain the cause of falling stock prices, the author does not offer an "alternative" explanation for this phenomenon, as suggested by (C). Moreover, the author's purpose in discussing falling stock prices is not to explain their cause but rather to acknowledge that what appears to be an undesirable consequence of voucher privatization may actually help to bring about a desirable result [see (B) and (E)].

Incorrect Responses

(A) The author acknowledges falling stock prices as one potential drawback of voucher privatization in that it might cause serious problems for an enterprise. However, the author asserts that it is the fear of this very consequence that will drive enterprises to efficiency and profitability. This phenomenon can be characterized, then, as a paradox, since what appears to be negative is actually positive when viewed differently. The author uses this paradox to undermine the critics' argument, thereby supporting the author's pro-voucher position.

(B) is one way of characterizing the author's line of reasoning. The author does indeed acknowledge falling stock prices as one potential drawback of voucher privatization. Then, in the same sentence, the author goes on to assert that the fear of falling stock prices will drive enterprises to efficiency and profitability. This rebuttal, then, can be characterized as the author's attempt to introduce a countervailing (competing) consideration that is of overriding concern.

(D) is a good characterization of this discussion. The author does not disagree that voucher holders will have little interest in the management of their enterprises. The author does imply, however, that this fact is beside the point since it is the enterprises' fear of a sell-off that will drive the enterprise to efficiency and profitability, not the extent of voucher-holder involvement in management.

(E) is perhaps the best characterization among the responses of the author's line of reasoning. The author indeed acknowledges falling stock prices as one potential drawback of (argument against) voucher privatization in that it might cause serious problems for an enterprise. However, in the same sentence, the author suggests that, paradoxically, it is the fear of this very consequence that will drive enterprises to efficiency and profitability. This rebuttal, then, can be viewed as the author's attempt to recharacterize a negative feature as a positive one.

QUESTION 4

4. Which of the following is NOT mentioned in the passage as a possible adverse consequence of rapid privatization?

   (A) instability in stock prices
   (B) loss of ownership in domestic private enterprises to foreign concerns
   (C) financial devastation for employees of private enterprises
   (D) inequitable distribution of wealth among employees of various enterprises
   (E) undue prolongation of inefficiency and misallocation

Question Type: Explicit Detail
Difficulty Level: Moderate

(E) **is the best response.** The author foresees prolonged inefficiency and misallocation as a consequence of gradual, not rapid, privatization (lines 33–55).

Incorrect Responses

(A) and **(B)** are each explicitly mentioned in the last paragraph as possible consequences of voucher privatization (one of the two approaches to rapid privatization), at least according to critics of this approach.

(C) refers to the danger under the socialist-reform approach (one of two approaches respecting rapid privatization) that employees will expose themselves to undue risk if they are invested only in their employer-company (at least according to the author, who would agree with critics of rapid privatization on this point).

(D) refers to the discrimination in favor of those who happen to be employed by modern or efficient enterprises that may result under the socialist-reform approach (one of the two approaches to rapid privatization), at least according to the author, who would agree with critics of rapid privatization on this point. The shares of these employees, the criticism goes, will be more valuable than the shares of those who work for older or less-efficient firms.

QUESTION 5

5. In responding to those "skeptics" who claim that people will sell their vouchers to foreign capitalists (lines 65–68), the author implies that

   (A) foreign capitalists will not be willing to pay a fair price for the vouchers
   (B) the future flow of income is likely in many cases to exceed the present exchange value of a voucher
   (C) foreign investment in a nation's enterprises may adversely affect currency exchange rates
   (D) although the skeptics are correct, their point is irrelevant in evaluating the merits of voucher privatization
   (E) foreign capitalists are less interested in the success of voucher privatization than in making a profit

Question Type: Inference
Difficulty Level: Moderate

(B) **is the best response.** The author responds to the skeptics' claim by pointing out that people are likely to weigh the future flow of income from a voucher against the benefits of selling their vouchers now and using the proceeds for consumption. If people were not likely, at least in many cases, to hold their vouchers after weighing these two alternatives, the author would not have made this argument. Thus, the author is implying that indeed in many cases the future flow of income from a voucher will exceed the present value of the voucher.

(D) is the second-best response. Admittedly, the final sentence of the last paragraph does suggest that the author views the skeptics' argument as irrelevant; in this sense, (D) has some merit. However, in the preceding sentence, the author seems to disagree with the skeptics as to whether people will sell their vouchers to foreigners. Thus, the author does not acknowledge that the skeptics are correct.

Other Incorrect Responses

(A), (C), and (E) are unsupported by the author's response to the skeptics' claim.

QUESTION 6

6. **Which of the following would the author probably agree is the LEAST desirable outcome of economic reform in formerly-Communist countries?**

   (A) effective allocation of labor
   (B) equitable distribution of property among citizens
   (C) financial security of citizens
   (D) equal opportunity for financial success among citizens
   (E) financial security of private enterprises

Question Type: Interpretation
Difficulty Level: Moderate

(E) is the best response. The author's willingness to place a private enterprise at risk for the broader purpose of achieving a free-market system is suggested by at least two areas of discussion in the passage. In the first paragraph, the author tacitly disagrees with the gradualists who favor bracing enterprises for the shock of deregulation to help them survive the transition. In the fourth paragraph, while advocating voucher privatization, the author admits that this approach may very well result in the instability of stock prices; yet the author seems to view the insecurity caused by market pressures as "good" for private enterprises in that it will drive them to efficiency—a sort of sink-or-swim approach.

(C) is the second-best response. Response (C) is implicitly supported. One of the author's arguments against the socialist-reform approach is that employees of less profitable companies would be placed at undue financial risk. Accordingly, the author seems to value, at least to some extent, the financial security of employees (citizens). Although (C) is a less likely "objective" of economic reform than (A) or (D), the objective identified in Response (E) is clearly less "desirable" from the author's viewpoint than the objective referred to in Response (C).

Other Incorrect Responses

(A) is explicitly supported. The author identifies misallocation of labor a core problem that must be addressed if economic reform is to succeed (lines 34–35).

(B) is supported implicitly by the passage. The author argues against the socialist-reform approach to privatization on the basis that distribution of enterprise shares under this approach would discriminate against employees of less profitable enterprises—i.e., that this distribution system would be inequitable (unfair). Note that the term "equitable" means "fair," not necessarily "equal."

(D) is explicitly supported by the passage. The author states in lines 69–71 that the aim of voucher privatization (which the author advocates) is to secure equality of opportunity. The "opportunity" to which the author refers here is the freedom to determine what use of one's vouchers will be most advantageous financially.

QUESTION 7

7. Which of the following best expresses the main idea of the passage?

(A) The two most important principles of post-Communist economic reform are liberalization of prices and privatization.

(B) Voucher privatization is the best approach to economic reform in the formerly-Communist nations

(C) Economists disagree as to whether deregulation and privatization in formerly-Communist nations should be accomplished rapidly or gradually.

(D) A gradual approach to post-Communist economic reform is less likely to succeed than is a rapid approach.

(E) Each proposed method of post-Communist economic reform has both its advantages and drawbacks.

Question Type: Main Idea
Difficulty Level: Moderate

(D) is the best response. Response (D) encompasses the author's treatment of both liberalization and privatization by referring more generally to "economic reform," as well as referring to both the rapid and gradual approaches to each of these two aspects of economic reform. Just as crucial, Response (D) includes the author's position in the issue—the author favors rapid reform to gradual reform.

(C) is the second-best response. Response (C) encompasses all approaches to economic reform discussed in the passage. However, it omits the author's position on the issue and therefore is not a viable best response.

Other Incorrect Responses

(A) is too narrow in its scope. It restates the point in the first sentence of the passage which is intended to merely provide a framework for the discussion that follows.

(B) is too narrow in its scope. Voucher privatization may be the best approach to privatization, at least according to the author. However, Response (B) fails to encompass the second "cornerstone" of economic reform: liberalization (deregulation), which is the concern of the first two paragraphs.

(E) is too broad in that it incorporates ideas outside of the passage. The passage does not indicate "advantages" of either rapid or gradual deregulation and does not cite any "advantages" of the socialist-reform approach to privatization. (E) is also too narrow in the sense that it fails to reflect the author's position on the issues.

PASSAGE #4

Among the many other things it is, a portrait is always a record of the personal and artistic encounter that produced it. It is possible for artists to produce portraits of individuals who
5   have not sat for them, but the portrait that finally emerges normally betrays the restrictions under which the artist has been forced to labor. Even when an artist's portrait is simply a copy of someone else's work—as in the many portraits of
10 Queen Elizabeth I that were produced during her lifetime—the never-changing features of a monarch who refused to sit for her court painters reflect not only the putative powers of an ever-youthful queen but the remoteness of those
15 attempting to depict her as well.

Portraits are "occasional" not only in the sense that they are closely tied to particular events in the lives of their subjects but in the sense that there is usually an occasion—however brief,
20 uncomfortable, artificial, or unsatisfactory it may prove to be—in which the artist and subject directly confront each other; and thus the encounter a portrait records is most tangibly the sitting itself. The sitting may be brief or extended,
25 collegial or confrontational. Cartier-Bresson has expressed his passion for portrait photography, for instance, by characterizing it as "a duel without rules, a delicate rape." Such metaphors contrast quite sharply with Richard Avedon's
30 conception of a sitting. While Cartier-Bresson reveals himself as an interloper and opportunist, Avedon confesses—perhaps uncomfortably—to a role as diagnostician and (by implication) psychic healer: not as someone who necessarily
35 transforms his subjects, but as someone who reveals their essential nature. Both photographers appear to agree on one premise, however, which is that the fundamental dynamic in this process lies squarely in the hands of the artist.
40 A quite-different paradigm has its roots not in confrontation or consultation but in active collaboration between the artist and sitter. This very different kind of relationship was formu lated most vividly by William Hazlitt in his essay
45 entitled "On Sitting for One's Picture" (1823). To Hazlitt, the "bond of connection" between painter and sitter is most like the relationship between two lovers: "they are always thinking and talking of the same thing, in which their self love finds
50 an equal counterpart." Hazlitt fleshes out his thesis by recounting particular episodes from the career of Sir Joshua Reynolds. According to Hazlitt, Reynold's sitters, accompanied by their friends,were meant to enjoy an atmosphere that
55 was both comfortable for them and conducive to

the enterprise of the portrait painter, who was simultaneously their host and their contractual employee. In the case of artists like Reynolds—who I take to be a paradigmatic case—no funda-
60 mental difference exists between the artist's studio and all those other rooms in which the sitters spin out the days of their lives. The act of entering Reynolds' studio—this social and aesthetic encounter—did not necessarily trans-
65 form those who sat for him. Collaboration in portraiture such as Reynolds' is based on the sitter's comfort and security as well as on his or her desire to experiment with something new; and it is in this "creation of another self," as
70 Hazlitt put it, that the painter's subjects may properly see themselves for the first time.

1. Which of the following best expresses the main idea of the passage?

(A) The success of a portrait depends largely upon the relationship between artist and subject.
(B) Photographers and painters differ in their views regarding their role in portrait photography.
(C) The social aspect of portraiture sitting plays an important part in the outcome of the sitting.
(D) Portraits, more than any other art form, provide insight into the artist's social relationships.
(E) The paintings of Reynolds provide a record of his success in achieving a social bond with his subjects.

GO ON TO THE NEXT PAGE.

2. In referring to Queen Elizabeth as "ever youthful" (lines 13–14), the author implies that

    (A) she instructed her court painters to paint her portrait in a manner to make her appear younger than she actually was
    (B) all portraits of the queen available for copying were painted when she was young
    (C) she died at an early age, and so all portraits of her depicted her as a young woman
    (D) her youthful appearance belied her actual age
    (E) artists who copied her portraits believed that she was younger than she actually was

3. The author quotes Cartier-Bresson in order to

    (A) refute Avedon's conception of a portrait sitting
    (B) support the claim that portrait sitting can be a confrontational encounter
    (C) provide one perspective of the portraiture encounter
    (D) show that a portraiture encounter may be either brief or extended
    (E) distinguish a sitting for a photographic portrait from a sitting for a painted portrait

4. Which of the following best characterizes the portraiture experience as viewed by Avedon?

    (A) a collaboration
    (B) a mutual accommodation
    (C) a consultation
    (D) an uncomfortable encounter
    (E) a confrontation

5. A portrait artist operating under the Reynolds paradigm would probably disagree that

    (A) a portraiture sitting often changes the way the sitter views himself or herself
    (B) the portraiture encounter provides a means for both artist and subject to display their vanity
    (C) a successful portrait depends more upon the artist's initiative than upon the subject
    (D) the portrait sitting often heightens the sitter's self-knowledge
    (E) the success of a portrait depends largely upon whether the artist and sitter are socially compatible

6. Of the following, it would be most consistent with the information in the passage to assert that Reynolds

    (A) may have provided a transforming experience for some of his sitters
    (B) worked primarily with experienced portrait subjects
    (C) often painted portraits at his subjects' homes
    (D) was usually alone with his sitters while he painted their portraits
    (E) painted portraits primarily of friends and relatives

STOP.

PASSAGE #4—ANSWER KEY

1. C
2. B
3. C
4. C
5. C
6. A

PASSAGE #4—ANALYSIS

QUESTION 1

1. **Which of the following best expresses the main idea of the passage?**

    (A) The success of a portrait depends largely upon the relationship between artist and subject.
    (B) Photographers and painters differ in their views regarding their role in portrait photography.
    (C) The social aspect of portraiture sitting plays an important part in the outcome of the sitting.
    (D) Portraits, more than any other art form, provide insight into the artist's social relationships.
    (E) The paintings of Reynolds provide a record of his success in achieving a social bond with his subjects.

Question Type: Main Idea
Difficulty Level: Moderate

(C) is the best response. Although it is difficult to articulate a single "main idea" or thesis of this passage, the author seems to be most concerned with emphasizing that a portrait sitting is a social encounter, not just an artistic exercise, and that artists consider their relationship with their sitters to be somehow significant. Thus, Response (C) is a good statement of the author's primary point.

(A) is the second-best response. Without Response (C), Response (A) would be the best response—it embraces the passage as a whole and properly focuses on the author's primary concern with exploring the relationship between artist and sitter. However, the passage does not discuss how or whether this relationship results in a "successful" portrait; thus, (A) distorts the information in the passage.

Other Incorrect Responses

(B) is off focus and calls for an unwarranted generalization. Admittedly, the author does claim that the Reynolds paradigm (described by Hazlitt as well as by the author in the third paragraph) is "quite different" (line 40) from the two paradigms discussed in the second paragraph, and the latter does indeed involve a painter (Reynolds) while the other two paradigms involve photographers (Cartier-Bresson and Avedon). However, nowhere in the passage does the author generalize from this fact that a portrait artist's approach or view depends upon whether the artist is a painter or a photographer.

(D) distorts the information in the passage and departs from the topic at hand. Although the passage does support the notion that a portrait might reveal something about the relationship between artist and sitter, the author neither states nor implies that a portrait reveals anything about the artist's other relationships. Moreover, nowhere in the passage does the author compare portraiture with other art forms.

(E) is too narrow and refers to information not mentioned in the passage. The passage is not just about Reynolds, but about the portraiture encounter in general. Also, the author does not comment on Reynolds' "success" or about how his relationship with his sitters may have contributed to his success.

QUESTION 2

2. **In referring to Queen Elizabeth as "ever youthful" (lines 13–14), the author implies that**

   (A) she instructed her court painters to paint her portrait in a manner to make her appear younger than she actually was
   (B) all portraits of the queen available for copying were painted when she was young
   (C) she died at an early age, and so all portraits of her depicted her as a young woman
   (D) her youthful appearance belied her actual age
   (E) artists who copied her portraits believed that she was younger than she actually was

Question Type: Inference
Difficulty Level: Easier

(B) **is the best response.** According to the passage, the queen refused to sit for her court painters. The author also makes clear that the "many portraits" of her were copies of other portraits. Thus, it can reasonably be inferred that the queen was relatively young when the "master" portrait(s)—i.e., the portrait(s) from which copies were painted—was (were) painted.

Incorrect Responses

(A) runs contrary to the information in the passage which states that the queen refused to sit for her court painters.

(C) calls for an unwarranted inference. Just because all paintings of the queen depict her as a young person, it does not necessarily follow that she died when she was young.

(D) distorts the author's meaning. Considered in context of the discussion in the first paragraph, it is highly unlikely that the author's description of the queen as "ever youthful" should be taken to mean that the queen did not appear to advance in age.

(E) is nonsensical. Artists copying pictures of the queen would probably depict the queen as she appeared in the "master" portrait regardless of what age the copying artist believed the queen to be at the time.

QUESTION 3

3. The author quotes Cartier-Bresson in order to

    (A) refute Avedon's conception of a portrait sitting
    (B) support the claim that portrait sitting can be a confrontational encounter
    (C) provide one perspective of the portraiture encounter
    (D) show that a portraiture encounter may be either brief or extended
    (E) distinguish a sitting for a photographic portrait from a sitting for a painted portrait

Question Type: Purpose of Detail
Difficulty Level: Easier

(C) is the best response. In the passage, the author compares and contrasts three different perspectives of the portraiture encounter: (1) Avedon's view, (2) Cartier-Bresson's view, and (3) Reynolds' view as interpreted and reflected by Hazlitt. Response (C) properly expresses the function that the author's discussion of Cartier-Bresson (including the quote) serves in the author's overall discussion.

Incorrect Responses

(A) distorts the author's purpose as well as the meaning of the information in the passage. Although the author is explicit that Cartier-Bresson's conception is quite different from that of Avedon, the author is not concerned with "refuting" Avedon's conception—the author neither states nor implies that Avedon's conception is wrong or inaccurate in some way. The author is not arguing for one view over another, but is rather simply presenting different personal perspectives of the portraiture encounter.

(B) confuses the information in the passage. It is Avedon, not Cartier-Bresson, whose conception of the portraiture encounter is characterized as confrontational.

(D) confuses the information in the passage. The author states earlier in the paragraph that a sitting may either be "brief or extended, collegial or confrontational" (lines 24–25). The views of Cartier-Bresson and Avedon, discussed immediately thereafter, differ from each other in that Cartier-Bresson conceives his relationship with his sitters as confrontational, while Avedon views it as collegial. However, the author makes no further mention of the length of the sitting, either when describing the views of Avedon and Cartier-Bresson or in any other part of the passage.

(E) distorts the author's purpose and is unsupported by the passage. Nowhere in the passage does the author, either explicitly or implicitly, seek to distinguish between portrait photography and portrait painting.

QUESTION 4

4. Which of the following best characterizes the portraiture experience as viewed by Avedon?

(A) a collaboration
(B) a mutual accommodation
(C) a consultation
(D) an uncomfortable encounter
(E) a confrontation

Question Type: Interpretation
Difficulty Level: Moderate

(C) **is the best response.** In the first sentence of the third paragraph, the author distinguishes a "quite-different paradigm" (i.e., the case of Reynolds) from the conceptions of Cartier-Bresson and Avedon in that the Reynolds paradigm "has its roots not in confrontation or consultation but in active collaboration between artist and sitter" (lines 40–42). It is rather obvious from the quotation in the second paragraph that Cartier-Bresson conceives the encounter as "confrontational"; thus, the author seems to be characterizing an Avedon sitting as a "consultation."

(B) **is a second-best response.** Although the term "mutual accommodation" does not appear in the passage, this term suggests a relationship in which both artist and painter allow for the other's needs or desires. Such a description aligns much closer with Hazlitt's analogy of two lovers than with Avedon's view of the artist as diagnostician and psychic healer.

(D) **is a second-best response.** According to the passage, Avedon confesses "uncomfortably" to his role as diagnostician and psychic healer (lines 33–34). It does not necessarily follow, however, that Avedon finds his encounters with his sitters to be uncomfortable; in this sense, (D) distorts the information in the passage.

Other Incorrect Responses

(A) confuses the information in the passage. It is the Reynolds paradigm discussed in the third paragraph, not Avedon's view, that the author characterizes as a "collaboration" (line 65).

(E) confuses the information in the passage. It is clear from the quotation in the second paragraph that it is Cartier-Bresson (not Avedon) who conceives the encounter as "confrontational."

QUESTION 5

5. A portrait artist operating under the Reynolds paradigm would probably disagree that

(A) a portraiture sitting often changes the way the sitter views himself or herself

     (B) the portraiture encounter provides a means for both artist
         and subject to display their vanity

     (C) a successful portrait depends more upon the artist's
         initiative than upon the subject

     (D) the portrait sitting often heightens the sitter's self-
         knowledge

     (E) the success of a portrait depends largely upon whether
         the artist and sitter are socially compatible

Question Type: Interpretation
Difficulty Level: Moderate

(C) **is the best response.** The author describes a sitting under the Reynolds paradigm as a "collaboration" (line 42) which is based in part on the sitter's "desire to experiment with something new" (lines 67–68) suggesting that the sitter and artist both play active roles in the process. Response (C) runs contrary to this suggestion.

(B) **is the second-best response.** Response (B) is not as explicitly supported by the passage as the other incorrect responses. However, (B) is supported (albeit implicitly) by Hazlitt's analogy between the collaboration of artist and subject and the relationship between two lovers. Hazlitt describes both relationships as a sharing of each person's self-love (i.e., mutual displaying of each person's vanity).

Other Incorrect Responses

(A) and (D) are both supported by the last sentence of the passage which suggests that the portraiture experience provides the sitter with a new (and more accurate) view of himself or herself.

(E) is implicitly supported. Hazlitt, as well as the author, seems to emphasize the importance of putting the sitter at ease socially—the artist is host as well as contractual employee, and collaboration (under the Reynolds paradigm) depends ("is based") upon the sitter's comfort. Response (E) is thus a reasonable interpretation of the Reynolds paradigm.

QUESTION 6

6. **Of the following, it would be most consistent with the information in the passage to assert that Reynolds**

     (A) may have provided a transforming experience for some of
         his sitters

     (B) worked primarily with experienced portrait subjects

     (C) often painted portraits at his subjects' homes

     (D) was usually alone with his sitters while he painted their
         portraits

     (E) painted portraits primarily of friends and relatives

Question Type: Inference
Difficulty Level: Moderate

(A) **is the best response.** According to the passage, "[t]he act of entering Reynolds' studio" . . . "did not necessarily transform those who sat for him" (lines 63–65). This statement allows for the possibility that some sitters were transformed in some manner (although the author does not state whether this was the case).

Incorrect Responses

(B) runs contrary to the information in the passage. According to the passage, the collaboration in portraiture such as Reynolds' is based in part upon the sitter's desire to experiment with something new (line 68). It is reasonably inferable, therefore, that many of Reynolds' sitters were not experienced in this area.

(C) runs contrary to the information in the passage. In mentioning "the act of entering Reynolds' studio" (lines 62–63) and that "no fundamental difference exists between the artist's studio and all those other rooms in which the sitters spin out the days of their lives" (lines 59–62), the author strongly suggests that Reynolds' portraits were created in his own studio rather than at the homes of his subjects.

(D) is explicitly contradicted by the passage, which states that Reynolds' sitters were "accompanied by their friends" (line 54).

(E) is implicitly supported by various information in the third paragraph. Hazlitt and the author both emphasize the important role that establishing a social rapport played in the collaboration of Reynolds and his sitters. If Reynolds had limited his portrait subjects to friends and relatives, establishing a rapport would probably not have been necessary for his sitters' comfort. Also, the passage indicates that Reynold's subjects were accompanied by their friends and suggests that this was necessary to help the subjects feel at ease. However, this probably would not have been necessary if Reynolds were already a friend of his subjects.

PASSAGE #5

Non-indigenous species of plants and animals arrive by way of two general types of pathways. First, species having origins outside of the United States may enter the country and become
5 established either as free-living populations or under human cultivation—for example, in agriculture, horticulture, aquaculture, or as pets. Some cultivated species subsequently escape or are released and also become established as free-
10 living populations. Second, species of either U.S. or foreign origin and already within the United States may spread to new locales. Pathways of both types include intentional as well as unintentional species transfers. Rates of species
15 movement driven by human transformations of natural environments as well as by human mobility— through commerce, tourism, and travel—dwarf natural rates by comparison. While geographic distributions of species naturally
20 expand or contract over historical time intervals (tens to hundreds of years), species' ranges rarely expand thousands of miles or across physical barriers such as oceans or mountains.

Habitat modification can create conditions
25 favorable to the establishment of non-indigenous species. Soil disturbed in construction and agriculture is open for colonization by non-indigenous weeds, which in turn may provide habitats for the non-indigenous insects that
30 evolved with them. For example, the European viper's bugloss, a weed common along roads and railroad tracks, provides a habitat for the Eurasian lace bug. Human-generated changes in fire frequency, grazing intensity, as well as soil
35 stability and nutrient levels similarly facilitate the spread and establishment of non-indigenous plants. When human changes to natural environments span large geographical areas, they effectively create conduits for species movement
40 between previously isolated locales. The rapid spread of the Russian wheat aphid to fifteen states in just two years following its 1986 arrival has been attributed in part to the prevalence of alternative host plants that are available when
45 wheat is not. Many of these are non-indigenous grasses recommended for planting on the forty million or more acres enrolled in the U.S. Department of Agriculture Conservation Reserve Program.
50 A number of factors confound quantitative evaluation of the relative importance of various entry pathways. Time lags often occur between establishment of non-indigenous species and their detection, and tracing the pathway for a long-
55 established species is difficult. Experts estimate that non-indigenous weeds are usually detected only after having been in the country for thirty years or having spread to at least ten thousand acres. In addition, federal port inspection,
60 although a major source of information on non-indigenous species pathways, especially for agricultural pests, provides data only when such species enter via scrutinized routes. Finally, some comparisons between pathways defy
65 quantitative analysis—for example, which is more "important": the entry pathway of one very harmful species or one by which many but less harmful species enter the country?

1. According to the passage, which of the following is true about the European viper's bugloss?

(A) They serve as host plants for the Russian wheat aphid.
(B) Their natural rate of movement is comparable to that of the Eurasian lace bug.
(C) They find certain human pathways to be habitable.
(D) Their movement across physical barriers such as oceans is unlikely.
(E) Their entry into the United States went undetected for more than thirty years.

2. Which of the following statements about species movement is best supported by the information in the passage?

(A) Species movement is affected more by habitat modifications than by human mobility.
(B) Human-driven factors affect the rate at which species move more than they affect the long-term amount of such movements.
(C) Natural expansions in the geographic distribution of species account for less species movement than do natural contractions.
(D) Natural environments created by commerce, tourism, and travel contribute significantly to species movement.
(E) Movement of a species within a continent depends largely upon the geographic extent of human mobility within the continent.

GO ON TO THE NEXT PAGE.

3. According to the passage, the U.S. Department of Agriculture

   (A) contributed to the spread of the Russian wheat aphid
   (B) provides data about non-indigenous species entering the United States through scrutinized routes
   (C) has assumed the responsibility for preventing entry of non-indigenous species onto federal lands
   (D) has attempted unsuccessfully to isolate the Russian wheat aphid
   (E) favors the planting of non-indigenous grasses for the purpose of protecting certain species of insects

4. It can be inferred from the passage that all of the following influence the movement of non-indigenous species EXCEPT:

   (A) soil nutrient levels
   (B) import restrictions
   (C) popularity of aquaculture
   (D) geographic terrain
   (E) fire frequency

5. Which of the following best expresses the primary purpose of the last paragraph?

   (A) to explain why it is difficult to trace the entry pathways for long-established non-indigenous species
   (B) to describe the events usually leading to the detection of a non-indigenous species
   (C) to discuss the role that time lags and geographic expansion of non-indigenous species play in species detection
   (D) to point out the inadequacy of the federal port inspection system in detecting the entry of non-indigenous species
   (E) to identify the problems in assessing the relative significance of various entry pathways for non-indigenous species

6. Based upon the information in the passage, whether the entry pathway for a particular non-indigenous species can be determined is LEAST likely to depend upon which of the following?

   (A) whether the species is considered to be a pest
   (B) whether the species gains entry through a scrutinized route
   (C) the rate at which the species expands geographically
   (D) how long the species has been established
   (E) the size of the average member of the species

7. Which of the following is the most appropriate title for the passage?

   (A) Determining Entry Pathways for Non-Indigenous Species
   (B) The Impact of Human Activity on Species Movement
   (C) Non-Indigenous Species: Intentional vs. Unintentional Entry Pathways
   (D) Non-Indigenous Plants: Pathways for Entry
   (E) Problems in Halting the Spread of Harmful Non-Indigenous Species

STOP.

PASSAGE #5—ANSWER KEY

1. C
2. E
3. A
4. B
5. E
6. E
7. A

PASSAGE #5—ANALYSIS

QUESTION 1

1. **According to the passage, which of the following is true about the European viper's bugloss?**

   (A) They serve as host plants for the Russian wheat aphid.
   (B) Their natural rate of movement is comparable to that of the Eurasian lace bug.
   (C) They find certain human pathways to be habitable.
   (D) Their movement across physical barriers such as oceans is unlikely.
   (E) Their entry into the United States went undetected for more than thirty years.

Question Type: Explicit Detail
Difficulty Level: Moderate

(C) is the best response. According to the passage, the bugloss is common "along roads and railroad tracks"—that is, along human pathways.

(E) is the second-best response. It is possible that Statement (E) is an accurate statement. The European viper's bugloss is a type of weed, and the passage does indeed indicate that non-indigenous weeds usually go undetected for at least thirty years. However, it is unfair to infer that the European viper's bugloss was in fact one such weed.

Other Incorrect Responses

(A) confuses the information in the passage. The bugloss serves as a host plant for the Eurasian lace bug, not for the Russian wheat aphid.

(B) calls for an unwarranted inference. Although it might be inferred that human-driven movement—i.e., movement associated with road construction—of the bugloss and lace bug are comparable, no such inference can be made about their natural movement.

(D) is too broad—although their natural movement across physical barriers such as oceans is probably unlikely (based upon the information in the first paragraph), human-driven movement might very well be quite likely.

QUESTION 2

2. Which of the following statements about species movement is best supported by the information in the passage?

(A) Species movement is affected more by habitat modifications than by human mobility.

(B) Human-driven factors affect the rate at which species move more than they affect the long-term amount of such movements.

(C) Natural expansions in the geographic distribution of species account for less species movement than do natural contractions.

(D) Natural environments created by commerce, tourism, and travel contribute significantly to species movement.

(E) Movement of a species within a continent depends largely upon the geographic extent of human mobility within the continent.

Question Type: Interpretation
Difficulty Level: Moderate

(E) is the best response. Statement (E) restates the author's point in the first paragraph that rates of species movement driven by human transformation of the natural environment and by human mobility dwarf natural rates by comparison (lines 14–18).

Incorrect Responses

(A) is unsupported by the passage. Although the author compares natural species movement to human-driven movement, no such comparison is made as between human modification of habitats and human mobility.

(B) is unsupported by the passage. The author makes no attempt to compare rate (interpreted either as frequency or speed) of species movement to total amounts of movement (distance).

(C) is unsupported by the passage. The author makes no attempt to compare natural expansions to natural contractions.

(D) is nonsensical. Human mobility (commerce, tourism, and travel) do not create "natural" environments. It is human mobility itself, not the "natural environment" created by it, that contributes significantly to species movement.

QUESTION 3

3. According to the passage, the U.S. Department of Agriculture

(A) contributed to the spread of the Russian wheat aphid

(B) provides data about non-indigenous species entering the United States through scrutinized routes

       (C) has assumed the responsibility for preventing entry of
          non-indigenous species onto federal lands

       (D) has attempted unsuccessfully to isolate the Russian
          wheat aphid

       (E) favors the planting of non-indigenous grasses for the
          purpose of protecting certain species of insects

Question Type: Interpretation
Difficulty Level: Easier

(A) **is the best response.** According to the information in the second paragraph, the rapid spread of the Russian wheat aphid resulted partly from the availability of alternative host plants (non-indigenous grasses) which were recommended for planting on lands controlled by the U.S. Department of Agriculture. Thus, the Department was partly responsible for the rapid spread of the Russian wheat aphid.

(E) **is the second-best response.** Response (E) is only partly supported by the information in the passage. Although it appears that the Department intentionally planted various non-indigenous grasses, as Response (E) suggests, the author makes no mention of the reason for this.

Other Incorrect Responses

(B) confuses the information in the passage. Federal port inspection (not the U.S. Department of Agriculture) provides data about species entering through scrutinized routes.

(C) is unsupported by the passage. The author neither states nor implies that this is one of the department's duties.

(D) is unsupported by the information in the passage. The author neither states nor implies that the Department made any attempts to isolate the Russian wheat aphid either before or since the rapid spread of the species.

QUESTION 4

    4. It can be inferred from the passage that all of the following
       influence the movement of non-indigenous species EXCEPT:

       (A) soil nutrient levels
       (B) import restrictions
       (C) popularity of aquaculture
       (D) geographic terrain
       (E) fire frequency

Question Type: Explicit Detail
Difficulty Level: Moderate

(B) **is the best response.** The only discussion in the passage related to importing is the discussion in the final paragraph about the limitations of federal port inspection in detecting the entry of non-indigenous species. While common sense might suggest that import restrictions would probably affect the movement of non-indigenous plants and animals, the subject of import restrictions is not mentioned in the final paragraph or anywhere else in the passage.

(C) **is the second-best response.** Although not supported implicitly by the passage, "aquaculture" is mentioned in line 7 as a form of human cultivation which helps to establish non-indigenous species. Thus, it can be reasonably inferred that the popularity of this activity would affect the movement of certain non-indigenous species.

Other Incorrect Responses

(A) is supported explicitly by the passage. According to the passage, human-generated changes in soil nutrient levels "facilitate the spread and establishment of non-indigenous species" (lines 35–37).

(D) is supported explicitly by the passage. According to the passage, physical barriers such as mountains (i.e., natural terrain) limit species movement (lines 18–23).

(E) is supported explicitly by the passage. According to the passage, human-generated changes in fire frequency "facilitate the spread and establishment of non-indigenous species" (lines 35–37).

QUESTION 5

5. **Which of the following best expresses the primary purpose of the last paragraph?**

   (A) to explain why it is difficult to trace the entry pathways for long-established non-indigenous species
   (B) to describe the events usually leading to the detection of a non-indigenous species
   (C) to discuss the role that time lags and geographic expansion of non-indigenous species play in species detection
   (D) to point out the inadequacy of the federal port inspection system in detecting the entry of non-indigenous species
   (E) to identify the problems in assessing the relative significance of various entry pathways for non-indigenous species

Question Type: Interpretation
Difficulty Level: Moderate

(E) **is the best response.** In the first sentence of the final paragraph, the author claims that "[a] number of factors confound quantitative evaluation of the relative importance of various entry pathways." In the remainder of the paragraph, the author identifies three such problems: (1) the difficulty of early detection, (2) the inadequacy of port inspection, (3) the inherent subjectivity in determining the "importance" of a pathway.

Incorrect Responses

(A) is off focus. Although the author asserts that it is difficult to trace an entry pathway once a species is well established, the author does not explain why this is so.

(B) is off focus and is too narrow. Although the author does mention that a species is usually not detected until it spreads to at least ten-thousand acres, the author mentions this single "event" leading to detection as part of the broader point that the unlikelihood of early detection contributes to the problem of quantifying the relative importance of entry pathways.

(C) is off focus. Although the author mentions these factors, they are not "discussed" in any detail, as Response (C) suggests. Also, the primary concern of the last paragraph is not with identifying the factors affecting species detection but rather with identifying the problems in quantifying the relative importance of various entry pathways.

(D) is too narrow. The author is concerned with identifying other problems as well in determining the relative importance of various entry pathways.

QUESTION 6

6. Based upon the information in the passage, whether the entry pathway for a particular non-indigenous species can be determined is LEAST likely to depend upon which of the following?

   (A) whether the species is considered to be a pest
   (B) whether the species gains entry through a scrutinized route
   (C) the rate at which the species expands geographically
   (D) how long the species has been established
   (E) the size of the average member of the species

Question Type: Explicit Detail
Difficulty Level: Easier

(E) **is the best response.** Nowhere in the passage does the author either state or imply that the physical size of a species' members affects whether the entry pathway for the species can be determined.

(A) **is the second-best response.** Unlike Responses (B), (C) and (D), Response (A) is not supported explicitly by the passage. However, the author mentions in the final paragraph that federal port inspection is "a major source of information on non-indigenous species pathways, especially for agricultural pests." Accordingly, whether a species is an agricultural pest might have some bearing upon whether or not its entry is detected (by port inspectors).

Incorrect Responses

(B), (C), and (D) are all mentioned explicitly in the final paragraph as factors affecting how precisely the entry pathway(s) of a species can be determined.

QUESTION 7

7. Which of the following is the most appropriate title for the passage?

(A) Determining Entry Pathways for Non-Indigenous Species
(B) The Impact of Human Activity on Species Movement
(C) Non-Indigenous Species: Intentional vs. Unintentional Entry Pathways
(D) Non-Indigenous Plants: Pathways for Entry
(E) Problems in Halting the Spread of Harmful Non-Indigenous Species

Question Type: Primary Purpose
Difficulty Level: Moderate

(A) is the best response. Although (A) may not provide an ideal title for the passage, it is the best among the five responses in expressing the ideas presented in the passage as a whole—the various types of entry pathways (first paragraph), the effects of habitat modification by humans on the establishment of non-indigenous species (second paragraph), and the problems in determining the relative significance of entry pathways (final paragraph).

Incorrect Responses

(B) is too narrow. Although the title suggested in Response (B) fairly characterizes the author's concern in the second paragraph, it fails to encompass the author's chief concern with identifying the problems in determining the relative importance of various entry pathways.

(C) is off focus. Although intentional and unintentional pathways are distinguished (in the first paragraph), the remainder of the passage deals solely with unintentional entry.

(D) is too broad in one sense and too narrow in another sense. The author's specific concern is with unintentional entry pathways (not with both intentional and unintentional pathways); in this sense, then, (D) is too broad. At the same time, the passage is concerned not just with plant species but also with animal species; thus, in this sense, (D) is too narrow.

(E) distorts the passage. Although the final paragraph does identify some of the problems in obtaining information needed to prevent the establishment of non-indigenous species, the author does not focus on (or even suggest) the need to halt the spread of harmful non-indigenous species.

PASSAGE #6

The nub of the restorationist critique of preservationism is the claim that it rests on an unhealthy dualism that conceives nature and humankind as radically distinct and opposed to
5   each other. Dissatisfaction with dualism has for some time figured prominently in the unhappiness of environmentalists with mainstream industrial society, as in the writings of Carolyn Merchant and Theodore Roszak. However, the
10   writings of the restorationists themselves—particularly, William Jordan and Frederick Turner—offer little evidence to support this indictment. In their view, preservationists are imbued with the same basic mind-set as the
15   industrial mainstream, the only difference being that the latter exalts humans over nature while the former elevates nature over humans. While it is perhaps puzzling that Jordan and Turner do not see that there is no logic that requires
20   dualism as a philosophical underpinning for preservation, more puzzling is the sharpness and relentlessness of their attack on preservationists, accentuated by the fact that they offer little, if any, criticism of those who have plundered the
25   natural world.

The crucial question, however, about the restorationist outlook has to do with the degree to which the restorationist program is itself faithful to the first principle of restoration: that
30   nature and humanity are fundamentally united rather than separate. Rejecting the old domination model, which sees humans as over nature, restoration theory champions a model of community participation. Yet some of the
35   descriptions that Jordan and Turner give of what restorationists are actually up to—for example, Turner's description of humans as "the lords of creation," or Jordan's statement that "the fate and well being of the biosphere depend ultimately on
40   us and our relationship with it"—do not cohere well with the community-participation model.

Another holistic model—namely, that of nature as an organism—might be more serviceable to the restorationists. As with the community
45   model, the "organic" model pictures nature as a system of interconnected parts. A fundamental difference, however, is that in an organism the parts are wholly subservient to the life of the organism. If we could think of the biosphere as a
50   single living organism and could identify humans with the brain (or the DNA), or control center, we would have a model that more closely fits the restorationists' view.

However, to consider humans as the control
55   center of the living earth is to ascribe to them a

dominating role in nature. Is this significantly different from the old-fashioned domination model? In both systems humans hold the place of highest authority and power in the world. Also,
60   neither view recognizes any limits to the scope and range of legitimate human manipulation in the world. This does not mean that there are no constraints; only beneficial manipulation should be undertaken. But it does not mean that
65   nothing is off-limits. A further parallel is that, because the fate of the world rests on humans, they must have a clear idea of what needs to be done. There are also important differences between the two theories. For example,
70   restorationists no longer view the world in the old dominationist way as a passive and inert object. And though both assign to humans a controlling role in the world, dominationists conceive this in terms of conquest while restorationists conceive it in terms of healing.
75   Also, restorationists insist that the ideas which must serve to guide our work in the world are drawn not solely from a consideration of human needs and purposes but from an understanding of the biosphere; as a result, they are conscious
80   than dominationists of our capacity to harm nature.

1. The author's primary purpose in the passage is to

    (A) examine the similarities and differences among models for environmental philosophies
    (B) formulate a new philosophical model of the relationship between humans and their environment
    (C) critique a modern-day environmental philosophy
    (D) argue that one particular environmental philosophy is more workable than competing approaches
    (E) demonstrate the limited usefulness of models as the basis for environmental philosophies

GO ON TO THE NEXT PAGE.

2. The author of the passage would probably agree that preservationists

   (A) are not critical enough of those who have plundered the natural world
   (B) base their ideas on an unhealthy dualism
   (C) have the same basic mind-set as the industrial mainstream
   (D) have been unfairly criticized by restorationists
   (E) have been faithful to the principles upon which their ideas are based

3. Which of the following best expresses the function of the first paragraph in relation to the passage as a whole?

   (A) to establish the parameters of an ensuing debate
   (B) to identify problem areas within a school of thought, which are then explored in greater detail
   (C) to discuss secondary issues as a prelude to a more detailed examination of a primary issue
   (D) to provide an historical backdrop for a discussion of modern-day issues
   (E) to introduce opposing viewpoints, which are then evaluated.

4. In asserting that the organic model might be "more serviceable to the restorationists" (lines 43–44), the author implies that

   (A) the descriptions by Turner and Jordan of the restorationists' program conform more closely to the organic model than to the community-participation model
   (B) the organic model is more consistent than the community-participation model with the principle of restoration
   (C) the organic model is more consistent with the restorationists' agenda than with the preservationists' program
   (D) holistic models are more useful to the restorationists than is the dualist model
   (E) the organic model, unlike the community-participation model, represents nature as a system of interconnected parts

5. Which of the following models would the author most likely agree is least like the other models listed below?

   (A) domination model
   (B) holistic model
   (C) community-participation model
   (D) dualist model
   (E) organic model

6. The author's primary criticism of the restorationists is that

   (A) they fail to recognize any limits as to the scope of legitimate human manipulation of nature
   (B) they assign to humans a controlling role in the world
   (C) they reject the most workable model for the relationship between humans and nature
   (D) their critique of preservationism is not well supported
   (E) their program does not coincide with their principles

7. According to the passage, the restorationists and dominationists differ with respect to all of the following EXCEPT:

   (A) their conception of the role that humans play in the world
   (B) their level of awareness regarding the environmental consequences of human activity
   (C) their view as to what kind of constraints on human manipulation of nature are legitimate
   (D) the degree to which they view the world as a passive object
   (E) their view as to the extent to which the interests of non-human organisms should be considered in formulating environmental policy

STOP.

PASSAGE #6—ANSWER KEY

1. C   5. D
2. D   6. E
3. C   7. C
4. A

PASSAGE #6—ANALYSIS

QUESTION 1

1. The author's primary purpose in the passage is to

   (A) examine the similarities and differences among models
       for environmental philosophies
   (B) formulate a new philosophical model of the relationship
       between humans and their environment
   (C) critique a modern-day environmental philosophy
   (D) argue that one particular environmental philosophy is
       more workable than competing approaches
   (E) demonstrate the limited usefulness of models as the
       basis for environmental philosophies

Question Type: Primary Purpose
Difficulty Level: Moderate

(C) is the best response. Although the passage does digress in the last paragraph
(suggesting a possible transition to another area of discussion), the passage is
devoted mainly to a critical analysis of the restorationists' environmental
philosophy, as exemplified by Turner and Jordan.

Incorrect Responses

(A) is too narrow. Admittedly, the author does discuss (in the third and fourth
paragraphs) the similarities and differences between the organic and community-
participation models as well as between the domination and restoration models.
While response (B) would appear to encompass this discussion, (B) does not
embrace the author's larger purpose: to critique the restorationist philosophy.

(B) is too narrow and is not well supported. Admittedly, the author does introduce
(in the third paragraph) an alternative model—i.e., the organic model. However,
the author's limited purpose in introducing the organic model is to underscore
the author's broader point that the restorationists' program is inconsistent with
their principles. Moreover, the author makes no claim to having formulated the
organic model or that it is a "new" model, as (B) suggests.

(D) distorts the author's purpose. Admittedly, the author does explore the possibility
that a model other than the community-participation model might more
accurately reflect the restorationists' agenda. However, the author's point here is
that another model might be more consistent with the restorationists' program,
not that one particular model is more workable or otherwise preferable for

everyone. For all the reader knows, the author might be a mainstream industrialist who opposes all pro-environment policies.

(E) calls for an unwarranted inference as to the author's purpose. Based upon the last paragraph, the passage might conceivably continue by asserting that all environmental models are problematic and therefore of limited usefulness. However, whether the author would continue in this vein is speculative. Since the passage itself does not include such a discussion, (E) is not a viable response.

QUESTION 2

2. The author of the passage would probably agree that preservationists

    (A) are not critical enough of those who have plundered the natural world
    (B) base their ideas on an unhealthy dualism
    (C) have the same basic mind-set as the industrial mainstream
    (D) have been unfairly criticized by restorationists
    (E) have been faithful to the principles upon which their ideas are based

Question Type: Interpretation
Difficulty Level: Easier

(D) is the best response. In the first paragraph, the author asserts that a preservationist need not have a dualist view, and therefore the argument of Turner and Jordan that the preservationists are also "unhealthy" dualists is an unfair claim. Response (D) is also supported later in the first paragraph, where the author criticizes Turner and Jordan for the "sharpness and relentlessness of their attack on preservationists." The author implies that other groups (e.g., "those who have plundered the natural world") are more deserving of sharp criticism than the preservationists. In this sense as well, then, the author would probably agree that Turner and Jordan have unfairly criticized the preservationists.

Incorrect Responses

(A) confuses the information in the passage. The author suggests that it is the restorationists such as Turner and Jordan (not the preservationists) who are not critical enough of those that have plundered the natural world.

(B) and (C) confuse the author's viewpoint with the viewpoint of others mentioned in the passage. It is the restorationists, not the author, who claim that the preservationists base their ideas on an unhealthy dualism and who suffer from the same mind-set as the industrial mainstream.

(E) confuses the information in the passage and calls for speculation. First, the crucial question that the author poses (in lines 26–31) regards whether the restorationists, not the preservationists, have been faithful to their principles. Second, although the author asserts that the restorationists have not been faithful to their principle, it is unfair to infer that the preservationists have been faithful to theirs.

QUESTION 3

3. **Which of the following best expresses the function of the first paragraph in relation to the passage as a whole?**

   (A) to establish the parameters of an ensuing debate
   (B) to identify problem areas within a school of thought, which are then explored in greater detail
   (C) to discuss secondary issues as a prelude to a more detailed examination of a primary issue
   (D) to provide an historical backdrop for a discussion of modern-day issues
   (E) to introduce opposing viewpoints, which are then evaluated.

Question Type: Structure
Difficulty Level: Moderate

(C) **is the best response.** The author refers in the first sentence of the second paragraph to the "crucial question," signaling that the primary concern of the passage is to follow. Accordingly, the first paragraph introduces the topic by discussing non-crucial questions.

Incorrect Responses

(A) is wholly unsupported and runs contrary to the passage. Although the first paragraph does establish parameters insofar as it identifies the topic of the passage, in no sense does it identify which issues are subject to debate and which are not. To the contrary, the primary issue (whether the restorationists have been faithful to their own principle) is not even mentioned in the first paragraph.

(B) is only partially supported. Although in the first paragraph the author does indeed identify some problems with the restorationist critique of preservationism, rather than exploring these problems in greater detail, the author turns in subsequent paragraphs to another, more "crucial," problem.

(D) distorts the information in the passage. Although the author does include some "historical" background insofar as the environmentalists' unhappiness with mainstream industrial society (lines 6–8) is mentioned using the past tense, aside from this single reference to past events, the first paragraph speaks in terms of the present day.

(E) distorts the overall structure. The first paragraph does not really discuss opposing viewpoints but rather critiques one viewpoint: the restorationists' view of preservationism. Moreover, in subsequent paragraphs, the author makes no attempt to evaluate this viewpoint.

QUESTION 4

4. **In asserting that the organic model might be "more serviceable to the restorationists" (lines 43–44), the author implies that**

     (A) the descriptions by Turner and Jordan of the restora-
            tionists' program conform more closely to the organic
            model than to the community-participation model
     (B) the organic model Is more consistent than the
            community-participation model with the principle of
            restoration
     (C) the organic model is more consistent with the restora-
            tionists' agenda than with the preservationists' program
     (D) holistic models are more useful to the restorationists than
            is the dualist model
     (E) the organic model, unlike the community-participation model,
            represents nature as a system of interconnected parts

Question Type: Inference
Difficulty Level: Challenging

(A) **is the best response.** In the preceding sentence, the author asserts that Turner's and Jordan's descriptions of restorationist activites "do not cohere well with the community-participation model." By following this assertion with the suggestion that another model might be more serviceable, it is reasonably inferable that restorationists' activities are more consistent with this other model than with the community-participation model. The author then provides further support for this inference by pointing out a key distinction between the two models.

Incorrect Responses

(B) confuses the information in this portion of the passage. The author is concerned with which model more closely conforms to the restorationists' program, not which model better conforms to their principle.

(C) confuses the information in the passage—specifically, by bringing in irrelevant information. The author is not concerned at all in this portion of the passage with the preservationists. No attempt is made here or anywhere else in the passage to relate the organic model to the preservationists' program.

(D) is somewhat consistent with the information in the passage, but it does not respond to the question. The author does identify the organic model as one type of "holistic" model; however, the author asserts that it may be more serviceable than another holistic model (i.e., the community-participation model), not the dualist model (which is not a holistic model).

(E) is partially supported by the passage, but (E) also contradicts the passage. The author does indeed assert that the organic model represents nature as a system of interconnected parts. However, according to the author, so does the community-participation model (lines 44–46).

QUESTION 5

    5. Which of the following models would the author most likely
        agree is least like the other models listed below?

(A) domination model
(B) holistic model
(C) community-participation model
(D) dualist model
(E) organic model

Question Type: Interpretation
Difficulty Level: Easier

(D) is the best response. The author finds some point of similarity among all other models mentioned (see below). Therefore, by elimination, (D) is the best response.

Incorrect Responses

(A), (B), and (E) are not viable. The author points out (see last paragraph) several parallels between the organic model (a holistic model) and the domination model.

(C) is not a viable response, since the author points out in the third paragraph that the community-participation and organic models both picture nature as a system of interconnected parts. For this additional reason, (E) is also not viable.

QUESTION 6

6. The author's primary criticism of the restorationists is that

(A) they fail to recognize any limits as to the scope of legitimate human manipulation of nature
(B) they assign to humans a controlling role in the world
(C) they reject the most workable model for the relationship between humans and nature
(D) their critique of preservationism is not well supported
(E) their program does not coincide with their principle

Question Type: Interpretation
Difficulty Level: Moderate

(E) is the best response. The "crucial" (primary) question for the author involves the degree to which the restorationists are true to their first principle (lines 26–31). The author then claims that they are not so true in that their program "does not cohere well" with their principle (lines 40–41). Since this issue is "crucial" to the author, it is reasonable to assert that this criticism is the author's "primary" one.

(D) is the second-best response. Although the author does indeed criticize the restorationists on this count (in the first paragraph), this criticism is not the author's "primary" one, since the author raises and answers a more "crucial question" in the second paragraph.

Other Incorrect Responses

(A) and (B) are supportable statements, but they do not respond to the question. Although the author ascribes the characteristics mentioned in (A) and (B) to the restorationists (as well as to the dominationists), the author does not identify this characteristic as a point of criticism.

(C) is unsupported by the information in the passage. The author neither states nor implies that one model is more workable than others (except insofar as one model might be more appropriate than another for a particular school of thought) or which model that would be. In addition, although the passage is clear that the restorationists have embraced the community-participation model, the passage is not at all explicit that they have "rejected" any particular other model (except for the dualist model).

QUESTION 7

7. According to the passage, the restorationists and dominationists differ with respect to all of the following EXCEPT:

(A) their conception of the role that humans play in the world
(B) their level of awareness regarding the environmental consequences of human activity
(C) their view as to what kind of constraints on human manipulation of nature are legitimate
(D) the degree to which they view the world as a passive object
(E) their view as to the extent to which the interests of non-human organisms should be considered in formulating environmental policy

Question Type: Explicit Detail
Difficulty Level: Moderate

(C) **is the best response.** This view is mentioned in the last paragraph as a point of similarity rather than a point of disagreement between the two schools.

(E) **is the second-best response.** In lines 77–79, the author points out that restorationists are guided not only by "human needs and purposes but also from an understanding of the biosphere." Although (E) is not as explicit in the passage as (A), (B) or (D), it is more readily supported than (C).

Incorrect Responses

(A) is paraphrased in lines 73–75, where the author asserts that dominationists view their controlling role in the world as that of conqueror, while restorationists view it as that of healer.

(B) is paraphrased in lines 79–81: restorationists "are more conscious than dominationists of our capacity to harm nature."

(D) is explicit in the last paragraph (lines 77–79).

PASSAGE #7

The Andean *cordillera* is made up of many
interwoven mountain ranges, which include high
intermontane plateaus, basins, and valleys. The
Northern Andes contains several broad
5 ecosystems falling into four altitudinal belts. Its
northern subregion is distinguished from the rest
of the region by higher relative humidity and
greater climatic symmetry between the eastern
and western flanks of the range. The Central
10 Andes are characterized by a succession of
agricultural zones with varied climatic conditions
along the mountains' flanks and by large, high-
altitude plateaus, variously called *puna* or
altiplano, which do not occur in the Northern
15 Andes. The soil fertility of the northern *altiplano*
is generally good. The western Central Andean
ranges are relatively arid with desert-like soils,
whereas the eastern ranges are more humid and
have more diverse soils. The eastern slopes of the
20 Central Andes in many ways are similar to the
wet forests of the Northern Andes. Unlike the
Northern Andes, however, these slopes have a
dry season.

In regions of gentle topography (such as the
25 central United States or Amazon basin), regional
climatic variation can be determined from a few
widely-spaced measurements. By contrast, in the
Andean *cordillera*, with its extreme topographic
and climatic features, regional projections are
30 difficult. For example, while air temperature
generally decreases with increasing altitude,
variability of mountain topography can produce
much lower than expected air temperatures.
Nevertheless, some general climatic patterns are
35 discernible. For example, with increasing distance
south of the equator the seasonality of
precipitation increases, whereas the total annual
amount generally decreases. Humidity commonly
increases with increasing altitude, but only to
40 some intermediate altitude, above which it
declines. The variability of mountain terrain also
affects precipitation, such that conditions of
extreme wetness and aridity may exist in close
proximity. Related to this temperature gradient is
45 a pattern of greater rainfall at the valley heads,
and less rain at lower altitudes, resulting in part
from mountain rainshadow effect.

The weather patterns of the Andean *cordillera*
and Amazon basin in general reflect movements
50 of high- and low-pressure cells associated with
the Intertropical Convergence Zone, a low-
pressure trough that moves further north and
south on a seasonal basis. Precipitation is high
throughout the year in the highlands and on the
55 coast in the Northern Andes. South of central

Ecuador, at about the latitude of Guayaquil,
coastal aridity increases, culminating in the
Atacama desert of northern Chile. In the Central
Andes, highland precipitation is seasonal, and
60 amounts are approximately one half those
measured in the northern Andes. The aridity of
the Central Andean coastal zone is the result of
the drying effect of the cold Pacific Humboldt
current and the southern Pacific high-pressure
65 cell. Much of the southern portion of the Central
Andes in Bolivia is also arid. The dry season
causes soil moisture deficits and diminished
stream flow for a part of each year.

At the regional or macroscale level, vegetation
70 patterns in the Northern and Central Andes tend
to reflect climatic zones determined by latitude
and altitude. At the local or mesoscale level,
however, this correspondence becomes less
precise, as local variations in soil type, slope,
75 drainage, climate, and human intervention come
into play.

1. In the passage, the author's primary concern is to

(A) describe the climate and topography of
various regions of the Andean *cordillera*
(B) discuss the factors affecting the climate of the
Andean *cordillera*
(C) suggest various alternative explanations for
the diversity of climate among the various
regions of the Andean *cordillera*
(D) examine the effects of topography on the
climate and vegetation of the Andean
cordillera
(E) compare and contrast the climate and
topography of the Northern Andes to that
the Central Andes

2. According to the passage, which of the following
characterizes the northern part of the high-
altitude plateaus?

(A) high relative humidity
(B) fertile soil
(C) a succession of agricultural zones
(D) extremes in air temperature
(E) an arid climate

GO ON TO THE NEXT PAGE.

3. Based upon the passage, the air temperatures in the Andean *cordillera* are often "lower than expected" (line 32) probably because

(A) the Intertropical Convergence Zone creates unexpected high pressure cells
(B) the elevation varies dramatically in the mountain regions
(C) prior measurements were based upon inaccurate topographical maps
(D) the humidity varies dramatically in the mountain regions
(E) precipitation increases nearer to the equator

4. Which of the following statements finds LEAST support from the passage?

(A) The northern subregion of the Northern Andes is more humid than the western subregion of the Central Andes.
(B) The soil in the northern subregion of the Central Andes is more fertile than the soil in the western subregion of the Central Andes.
(C) The eastern subregion of the Central Andes is more humid than the western subregion of the Central Andes.
(D) The highlands of the Northern Andes receive more precipitation than the highlands of the Central Andes.
(E) The coastal subregion of the Central Andes is less arid than the southern subregion of the Central Andes.

5. According to the passage, all of the following affect the climate of the Central Andes *cordillera* EXCEPT:

(A) the Intertropical Convergence Zone
(B) the rainshadow effect
(C) the southern Pacific high-pressure cell
(D) the symmetry of the mountain ranges
(E) the Pacific Humboldt current

6. Which of the following statements about vegetation patterns in the Andean *cordillera* is most strongly supported by the passage?

(A) Local vegetation patterns are determined by the same factors as regional vegetation patterns.
(B) Vegetation patterns vary more widely at the macroscale level than at the mesoscale level.
(C) Vegetation patterns are affected by more factors at the mesoscale level than at the local level.
(D) Human intervention has a greater effect than either altitude or latitude upon vegetation patterns.
(E) Some factors affecting vegetation patterns have only a local impact, whereas others have a broader impact.

7. Among the following, the passage would most logically continue by

(A) describing the climate and topography of portions of the Andean *cordillera* other than the Northern and Central regions
(B) discussing how high- and low-pressure systems affect the climate of the Amazon
(C) exploring how proximity to the equator affects vegetation in the Andes *cordillera*
(D) identifying problems in determining the relation between soil type and vegetation in the Andean *cordillera*
(E) examining the effects of vegetation patterns on the topography of the Andean *cordillera*

STOP.

PASSAGE #7—ANSWER KEY

1.	B	5.	D
2.	B	6.	E
3.	B	7.	C
4.	E		

PASSAGE #7—ANALYSIS

QUESTION 1

1. In the passage, the author's primary concern is to

   (A) describe the climate and topography of various regions of the Andean *cordillera*

   (B) discuss the factors affecting the climate of the Andean *cordillera*

   (C) suggest various alternative explanations for the diversity of climate among the various regions of the Andean *cordillera*

   (D) examine the effects of topography on the climate and vegetation of the Andean *cordillera*

   (E) compare and contrast the climate and topography of the Northern Andes to that the Central Andes

Question Type: Primary Purpose
Difficulty Level: Moderate

(B) is the best response. The bulk of the passage—the entire second and third paragraphs—is concerned with examining the factors affecting the climate of various portions of the Andean *cordillera*. The first paragraph provides a framework for this discussion by describing the climate and topography of the various regions.

Incorrect Responses

(A) is too narrow. Response (A) indicates the author's purpose in the first paragraph only, omitting the discussion of the factors influencing climate.

(C) distorts the passage. Nowhere does the passage state or imply that competing explanations or theories exist to account for climatic differences among the different regions of the Andean *cordillera*. Also, the author is just as concerned with identifying the similarities among the regions as with discussing their differences.

(D) is off focus in two respects. First, although the author is concerned with the effects of topography on climate, topography is only one of several such factors discussed in the passage. Second, the effect of topography on vegetation is only briefly suggested in the final paragraph; since this topic is not explored in any detail, it is not fair to say that it is of primary concern to the author.

(E) is too narrow. Although the author does indeed discuss the similarities and differences in climate and topography between the two regions, the author is just as concerned (and probably more concerned) with the factors which affect the climate in both regions.

QUESTION 2

2. According to the passage, which of the following characterizes the northern part of the high-altitude plateaus?

    (A) high relative humidity
    (B) fertile soil
    (C) a succession of agricultural zones
    (D) extremes in air temperature
    (E) an arid climate

Question Type: Explicit Detail
Difficulty Level: Easier

(B) is the best response. The high-altitude plateaus are called *altiplano* (line 14). The passage states explicitly that the soil fertility in the northern *altiplano* is generally good (lines 15–16).

Incorrect Responses

(A) confuses the information in the first paragraph. High relative humidity is mentioned as a feature of the Northern Andes and of the eastern portion of the Central Andes but not of the northern plateaus.

(C) confuses the information in the first paragraph. Successive agricultural zones are mentioned as a characteristic of the Central Andes in general, not of any portion of the Central Andes in particular.

(D) confuses the information in the first and second paragraphs. Variations in air temperature are not discussed until the second paragraph and are not associated explicitly with any particular region of the Andes.

(E) confuses the information in the first and last paragraphs. An arid climate is mentioned as a characteristic of the western, coastal, and southern portions of the Central Andes but not specifically with the *altiplano* (plateaus).

QUESTION 3

3. Based upon the passage, the air temperatures in the Andean *cordillera* are often "lower than expected" (line 32) probably because

    (A) the Intertropical Convergence Zone creates unexpected high pressure cells
    (B) the elevation varies dramatically in the mountain regions

(C) prior measurements were based upon inaccurate
    topographical maps
(D) the humidity varies dramatically in the mountain regions
(E) precipitation increases nearer to the equator

Question Type: Inference
Difficulty Level: Easier

(B) **is the best response.** The passage points out that while air temperature generally decreases as altitude increases, "variability of mountain topography"—i.e., dramatic changes in elevation—makes it difficult to determine temperature in any given spot from widely-spaced measurements. It can be reasonably inferred from this information that an unexpected temperature would probably be the result of unexpected altitude.

(C) **is a second-best response.** Statement (C) in itself is supported (at least in part) by the passage insofar as the author implies that in measuring altitude in mountainous regions, "widely-spaced measurements" do not provide an accurate report for areas between the measured points. However, nowhere in the passage is the reliability of older maps compared with that of newer maps.

(D) **is a second-best response.** Statement (D) in itself is supported by the passage insofar as the author indicates a correlation between humidity and altitude (lines 38–39). However, the passage makes no correlation between humidity and air temperature. Thus, (D) calls for an unwarranted inference. Moreover, (D) does not respond to the question.

Other Incorrect Responses

(A) confuses the information in the passage. The topic of air pressure (discussed in the third paragraph) is unrelated to the question, which deals with information in the second paragraph.

(E) does not respond to the question. The relevant portion of the passage is not concerned with precipitation. Moreover, although Statement (E) might be inferred from the information in the third paragraph, the passage makes no correlation between air temperature and precipitation.

QUESTION 4

4. Which of the following statements finds LEAST support from
   the passage?

   (A) The northern subregion of the Northern Andes is more
       humid than the western subregion of the Central
       Andes.
   (B) The soil in the northern subregion of the Central Andes is
       more fertile than the soil in the western subregion of
       the Central Andes.
   (C) The eastern subregion of the Central Andes is more humid
       than the western subregion of the Central Andes.

(D) **The highlands of the Northern Andes receive more
      precipitation than the highlands of the Central Andes.**
(E) **The coastal subregion of the Central Andes is less arid
      than the southern subregion of the Central Andes.**

Question Type: Inference
Difficulty Level: Moderate

(E) is the best response. The author refers in lines 61–62 to the "aridity of the
Central Andean coastal zone" as well as indicating (in lines 65–66) that "[m]uch
of the southern portion of the Central Andes in Bolivia is also arid." However,
nowhere does the author compare the two regions in this respect.

(B) is the second-best response. The author describes the soil fertility in the northern
altiplano as "relatively good" (line 15). Although the author does not specify in
which subregion(s) the *altiplano* lie, the description in the passage suggests that
they run in a north-south direction through the different regions. Thus, the
"northern" *altiplano* are probably located in the northern subregion. By contrast,
the passage describes the soil in the western subregion as "desert-like."

Other Incorrect Responses

(A) is well-supported. The northern portion of the Northern Andes is characterized
by "higher relative humidity" than other subregions (line 7), and the author
mentions its "wet forests" in line 21. By contrast, the western portion of the
Central Andes is described as "relatively arid with desert-like soils" (line 17).

(C) is explicitly supported in the passage: the author describes the western portion of
the Central Andes as "relatively arid" compared to the humidity of the eastern
subregion (line 17).

(D) is explicitly supported by the passage. In lines 58–61, the author states that the
precipitation in the Central Andes measures approximately half of that in the
Northern Andes.

QUESTION 5

5. **According to the passage, all of the following affect the
   climate of the Central Andes *cordillera* EXCEPT:**

   (A) **the Intertropical Convergence Zone**
   (B) **the rainshadow effect**
   (C) **the southern Pacific high-pressure cell**
   (D) **the symmetry of the mountain ranges**
   (E) **the Pacific Humboldt current**

Question Type: Explicit Detail
Difficulty Level: Easier

(D) is the best response. The only discussion of mountain symmetry is in the first
paragraph, which mentions the symmetry in climate between the east and west

flanks of the Northern Andes mountains. No mention is made anywhere in the passage of any symmetry with respect to the Central Andes mountains.

Incorrect Responses

(A), (B), (C) and (E) are all mentioned in the passage as factors affecting the climate of the Central Andes *cordillera*.

QUESTION 6

6. Which of the following statements about vegetation patterns in the Andean *cordillera* is most strongly supported by the passage?

    (A) Local vegetation patterns are determined by the same factors as regional vegetation patterns.
    (B) Vegetation patterns vary more widely at the macroscale level than at the mesoscale level.
    (C) Vegetation patterns are affected by more factors at the mesoscale level than at the local level.
    (D) Human intervention has a greater effect than either altitude or latitude upon vegetation patterns.
    (E) Some factors affecting vegetation patterns have only a local impact, whereas others have a broader impact.

Question Type: Interpretation
Difficulty Level: Moderate

(E) is the best response. This question focuses on the information in the last paragraph. The author first notes that vegetation patterns correspond generally with climate (as determined primarily by latitude and altitude). Accordingly, altitude and latitude affect vegetation patterns throughout the region. Then, in the final sentence the author points out that, in spite of the general correspondence between climate and vegetation, local patterns may not correspond so precisely with climate, due to a number of local factors. Response (E) accurately reflects the information in the final paragraph.

Incorrect Responses

(A) runs contrary to the information in the last paragraph. Regional patterns do not depend upon local variations; thus, fewer factors come into play in identifying these broader patterns.

(B) runs contrary to the information in the last paragraph. Regional patterns are broad patterns that do not take into account local variations (due to local factors). Thus, regional patterns will not vary to the extent that local patterns might.

(C) confuses the terms used by the author. The author equates "mesoscale" with "local." Accordingly, Response (C) makes no sense.

(D) is an exaggeration. Although the author identifies human intervention as one factor that might distort the effect of climate (altitude and latitude) upon vegetation patterns, the author neither states nor implies that the impact of human intervention is greater than that of climate (altitude and latitude).

QUESTION 7

7. Among the following, the passage would most logically continue by

(A) describing the climate and topography of portions of the Andean *cordillera* other than the Northern and Central regions

(B) discussing how high- and low-pressure systems affect the climate of the Amazon

(C) exploring how proximity to the equator affects vegetation in the Andes *cordillera*

(D) identifying problems in determining the relation between soil type and vegetation in the Andean *cordillera*

(E) examining the effects of vegetation patterns on the topography of the Andean *cordillera*

Question Type: Extrapolation
Difficulty Level: Moderate

(C) is the best response. In the final paragraph, the author asserts that altitude as well as latitude (proximity to the equator) determine climatic zones as reflected by vegetation patterns. Accordingly, a more detailed discussion about why different forms of vegetation appear at different latitudes is a logical continuation.

(D) is the second-best response. Response (D) is consistent with the content of the final paragraph, and thus is a better response than either (A) or (B). Moreover, the author does suggest a relationship between soil type and vegetation (presumably, soil type determines what forms of vegetation will thrive). However, the final paragraph neither indicates nor suggests any potential "problems" in determining such a relationship.

Other Incorrect Responses

(A) ignores the direction of the final paragraph. Additionally, nowhere in the passage does the author suggest that regions other than the Northern and Central regions will be or should be examined.

(B) ignores the direction of the final paragraph, returning instead to the Amazon which was mentioned only in passing in the second and third paragraphs. Nowhere in the passage does the author suggest that a more detailed discussion of the Amazon climate will follow.

(E) appears at first glance to be a viable response since it includes the same subject matter (i.e., vegetation) as the final paragraph. However, (E) is a bit nonsensical—it is unlikely that vegetation would have much of an effect upon topography; even if it did, nothing in the final paragraph indicates that this is the direction the discussion is likely to turn.

PASSAGE #8

In recent years, the life insurance industry has abandoned its emphasis on death benefits in favor of a "living benefits" focus. In 1970, 59% of company premium income came from life
5   insurance and only 10% from annuities; today, 29% of company premium income comes from life insurance, while nearly half comes from annuities. The transition isn't rooted in a single cause, but in varied market forces converging
10 simultaneously.

Its genesis coincided with the release of the 1978 Federal Trade Commission report that unfairly criticized the rate of return paid on the inside buildup of a life policy. For the first time,
15 the spotlight focused on the life product as an investment rather than as a risk protector. Consumer groups soon spread the message. Then came double-digit inflation and soaring interest rates, bringing with them new competition for the
20 life insurance premium dollar from other members of the financial services industry. Traditional life insurance policies were being drained of cash values by policy owners who could earn 15% to 20% interest on policy loans placed in money-
25 market investments. To stem the cash outflow, interest-sensitive products were developed.

Meanwhile, the population was aging. For the baby boomers—the 70 million Americans born between 1946 and 1961—retirement became an
30 increasing concern. Skeptical about the government's reliability in general and of the Social Security trust fund in particular, most retirement-minded individuals took matters into their own hands and made retirement funding a
35 top concern. There were other contributing demographic factors as well: the declining proportion of young married adults, the increase in childless couples and of individuals living alone, and the growing diversity in the American
40 population—specifically, the influx of racial and ethnic groups having different beliefs about security, death, and family responsibility. Finally, more individuals became covered by group insurance through their employer or a
45 professional association, while the number of people not solely dependent upon a spouse's income increased almost correspondingly.

Classifying families into five income segments, life insurance ownership is increasing in the two
50 highest segments and declining in the three lowest segments. Approximately seven in ten households in the highest segment own individual life insurance, compared to four in ten in the lowest segment. However, households with
55 incomes of more than $75,000 a year account for

only 10% of all U.S. households, certainly not a large enough segment to support the entire industry. Others within the financial services industry—such as banks—are sure to fill the
60 void. Thus, despite the short-term advantages of serving the highest income classes (the average premium paid in the highest segment is more than five times greater than in the lowest segment), the current trend could end the life
65 insurance industry's days as a big business and transform it into a cottage industry. It is difficult today to portray life insurance as the protector of widows and children or to justify the continued tax advantages of investment-oriented life prod-
70 ucts to politicians. To retain the non-taxability of inside buildup and to curb additional government regulation, the life insurance industry must again become the principal financial advisor to the middle- and lower-income markets, which in
75 turn will require either work-site and direct-response marketing or a return to single-needs selling.

1. The author's primary concern in the passage is to

(A) identify the historical causes of the current decline in life insurance as a risk-protection device
(B) argue for the necessity of action to prevent further erosion of the life insurance industry
(C) convince the reader that tax reform is required in order to reverse a current trend in the life insurance industry
(D) evaluate alternative proposals for reforming the life insurance industry
(E) present statistical evidence to support the claim that life insurance is no longer a competitive investment vehicle

GO ON TO THE NEXT PAGE.

2. It can be inferred from the information in the passage that annuities

(A) are attributable primarily to the new emphasis on living benefits
(B) account for most premium income for life insurance companies
(C) are a more popular form of life insurance today than in 1970
(D) account for ten percent of all premium income for life insurance companies today
(E) provide living benefits rather than death benefits

3. The author considers the 1978 Federal Trade Commission Report to be unfair most probably because it

(A) failed to adequately account for the benefits associated with risk protection
(B) inaccurately reported the rate of return on the inside buildup of a life policy
(C) captured the attention of consumer groups
(D) contributed to the ensuing double-digit inflation
(E) failed to consider the relative returns of other types of investments

4. The author mentions all of the following possible ways for the life industry to reverse the current trend EXCEPT:

(A) developing work-site marketing programs
(B) introducing products that are sensitive to interest rates
(C) establishing an advisory relationship with the lower- and middle-income markets
(D) instituting a direct-response marketing program
(E) offering products that fill a single insurance need

5. According to the passage, all of the following demographic factors contributed to the declining popularity of life insurance for risk protection EXCEPT:

(A) an increase in the number of individuals living alone
(B) the baby-boom phenomenon
(C) the declining birth rate
(D) the declining percentage of young adults who are married
(E) the increasing diversity of attitudes toward death

6. Based upon the passage, the number of people entirely dependent upon a spouse's income has

(A) increased, but not as much as the number of people covered by employers' group insurance or by professional associations
(B) increased, although the proportion of such people in relation to the overall population has decreased
(C) decreased, but not as much as the number of people covered by employers' group insurance or by professional associations
(D) decreased almost as much as the number of people not covered by employers' group insurance or by professional associations
(E) decreased, although the number of such people as a percentage of the number of people covered by employers' group insurance or by professional associations has increased

7. Which of the following statements is best supported by the passage?

(A) Ten percent of U.S. households account for more than fifty percent of the total number of premium dollars.
(B) Seven of ten households with income of more than $75,000 per year own life insurance.
(C) Four out of ten households with income not exceeding $75,000 per year own life insurance.
(D) Life insurance ownership among households in the highest of five income segments is thirty percent greater than among those in the lowest of five income segments.
(E) Life insurance ownership among the two highest income segments is increasing at a faster rate than the rate of decline in life insurance ownership among the three lowest income segments.

8. Among the following, the passage above would be most likely to appear in a

(A) publication of a consumer-advocacy organization
(B) transcript from a U.S. Senate subcommittee hearing on tax reform
(C) life insurance industry trade magazine
(D) professional journal for economists
(E) report of the Federal Trade Commission

STOP.

PASSAGE #8—ANSWER KEY

1.	B	5.	C
2.	E	6.	D
3.	A	7.	D
4.	B	8.	C

PASSAGE #8—ANALYSIS

QUESTION 1

1. The author's primary concern in the passage is to

   (A) identify the historical causes of the current decline in life insurance as a risk-protection device
   (B) argue for the necessity of action to prevent further erosion of the life insurance industry
   (C) convince the reader that tax reform is required in order to reverse a current trend in the life insurance industry
   (D) evaluate alternative proposals for reforming the life insurance industry
   (E) present statistical evidence to support the claim that life insurance is no longer a competitive investment vehicle

Question Type: Primary Purpose
Difficulty Level: Moderate

(B) is the best response. After (and not until) reading the final paragraph, the reader should realize that the statistics and other facts mentioned in the preceding paragraphs were intended by the author to support the argument that reform measures are required to reverse the current undesirable decline of the life insurance industry. Although the author explicitly argues for reform only in the last paragraph, suggesting that (B) might be a bit too narrow in its focus to be a viable best response, (B) is nevertheless the best of the five choices.

Incorrect Responses

(A) is too narrow in that it fails to encompass the author's broader purpose—i.e., arguing for reform in the life insurance industry.

(C) distorts the information in the passage and is too narrow in focus. The author is not in favor of additional tax reform but rather argues against any additional tax reform that might adversely affect the life industry. Moreover, the author argues for far broader reforms (see the last paragraph).

(D) is wholly unsupported by the passage. Nowhere in the passage does the author weigh advantages or disadvantages of two or more proposals.

(E) is off focus. Although statement (E) may be an accurate statement based upon the information in the passage, the author is not concerned with emphasizing the drawbacks of life insurance as an investment vehicle.

QUESTION 2

2. It can be inferred from the information in the passage that annuities

   (A) are attributable primarily to the new emphasis on living benefits
   (B) account for most premium income for life insurance companies
   (C) are a more popular form of life insurance today than in 1970
   (D) account for ten percent of all premium income for life insurance companies today
   (E) provide living benefits rather than death benefits

Question Type: Inference
Difficulty Level: Moderate

(E) **is the best response.** Lines 1–3 distinguish between death benefits and living benefits. The next sentence contrasts life insurance with annuities, implicitly equating life insurance with death benefits and annuities with living benefits.

Incorrect Responses

(A) calls for an unwarranted inference. Although the author suggests a correlation between living benefits and annuities, no causal connection is implied.

(B) is contradicted by the statistical data in the first paragraph. "Nearly half" [not "most," as (B) asserts] of premium income comes from annuities.

(C) calls for an inference that runs contrary to the information in the first paragraph. The passage implies that annuities are something distinct and different from life insurance; however, (C) suggests that annuities are a form of life insurance.

(D) confuses the statistical data in the first paragraph—life insurance premiums, not annuities, provide 10% of all premium income for life insurance companies today.

QUESTION 3

3. The author considers the 1978 Federal Trade Commission Report to be unfair most probably because it

   (A) failed to adequately account for the benefits associated with risk protection
   (B) inaccurately reported the rate of return on the inside buildup of a life policy
   (C) captured the attention of consumer groups
   (D) contributed to the ensuing double-digit inflation
   (E) failed to consider the relative returns of other types of investments

Question Type: Inference
Difficulty Level: Moderate

(A) **is the best response.** The next sentence (lines 14–16) reveals how the author considers the report to be "unfair." Although not explicit from reading lines

14–16, it is reasonably inferable that the unfairness refers to the report's sole focus on life insurance as an investment while ignoring the death-benefits feature.

Incorrect Responses

(B) calls for an unwarranted inference. The author neither states nor implies that the report was inaccurate in this respect.

(C) may be a true statement, but it does not respond to the question. The fact that the report may have caught the attention of consumer groups is not unfair in itself.

(D) is unsupported by the passage. The author neither states nor suggests any cause-and-effect relationship between the report and the rate of inflation.

(E) is unsupported by the information in the passage. The author neither states nor suggests that the report omitted to discuss other types of investments.

QUESTION 4

4. The author mentions all of the following possible ways for the life industry to reverse the current trend EXCEPT:

   (A) developing work-site marketing programs
   (B) introducing products that are sensitive to interest rates
   (C) establishing an advisory relationship with the lower- and middle-income markets
   (D) instituting a direct-response marketing program
   (E) offering products that fill a single insurance need

Question Type: Explicit Detail
Difficulty Level: Easier

(B) **is the best response.** Response (B) confuses the information in the passage. It was in response to the exodus from life insurance to money market instruments that the life insurance industry developed "interest-sensitive products" (line 26). Question 4, however, focuses on the reforms suggested in the final paragraph.

Incorrect Responses

(A), (C), (D) and (E) are all mentioned explicitly (either word-for-word or paraphrased) in the last paragraph as possible means to reverse the current decline of the life insurance industry.

QUESTION 5

5. According to the passage, all of the following demographic factors contributed to the declining popularity of life insurance for risk protection EXCEPT:

   (A) an increase in the number of individuals living alone
   (B) the baby-boom phenomenon

   (C) the declining birth rate
   (D) the declining percentage of young adults who are married
   (E) the increasing diversity of attitudes toward death

Question Type: Explicit Detail
Difficulty Level: Moderate

(C) is the best response. Although the pertinent part of the passage (the third paragraph) mentions an increase in childless couples (lines 38–39) as a contributing demographic factor, such an increase does not necessarily imply a declining birth rate (for example, an increase in the birth rate among single mothers may have exceeded any decline in births among couples).

Incorrect Responses

(A), (B), (D) and (E) are all listed in the third paragraph as demographic factors contributing to the declining popularity of life insurance for risk protection.

QUESTION 6

   6. **Based upon the passage, the number of people entirely dependent upon a spouse's income has**

   (A) increased, but not as much as the number of people covered by employers' group insurance or by professional associations
   (B) increased, although the proportion of such people in relation to the overall population has decreased
   (C) decreased, but not as much as the number of people covered by employers' group insurance or by professional associations
   (D) decreased almost as much as the number of people not covered by employers' group insurance or by professional associations
   (E) decreased, although the number of such people as a percentage of the number of people covered by employers' group insurance or by professional associations has increased

Question Type: Interpretation
Difficulty Level: Challenging

(D) is the best response. According to the passage, the number of people not solely dependent upon a spouse's income has increased "almost correspondingly" with the number of people covered either by employer group insurance or by a professional association (lines 42–44). Response (D) restates this point in the negative.

Incorrect Responses

(A) and (B) both confuse the statistical data presented in the passage. Specifically, both responses confuse an increase in the number of people not solely dependent upon a spouse's income (lines 45–47) with a decrease—i.e., with the number of people entirely (solely) dependent on a spouse's income.

(C) is partially right, but partially wrong. According to the passage, the number of people entirely dependent on a spouse's income has indeed decreased. However, the number of people covered by employer group insurance or by professional associations has (according to the passage) increased, not decreased.

(E) is partially right, but partially unsupported. (E) is partially right in the same way as (D): the number of people entirely dependent on a spouse's income has indeed decreased (according to the passage). However, the author does not attempt to compare the number of such people as a percentage of the number of people covered by employers' group insurance or by professional associations.

QUESTION 7

7. Which of the following statements is best supported by the passage?

(A) Ten percent of U.S. households account for more than fifty percent of the total number of premium dollars.

(B) Seven of ten households with income of more than $75,000 per year own life insurance.

(C) Four out of ten households with income not exceeding $75,000 per year own life insurance.

(D) Life insurance ownership among households in the highest of five income segments is thirty percent greater than among those in the lowest of five income segments.

(E) Life insurance ownership among the two highest income segments is increasing at a faster rate than the rate of decline in life insurance ownership among the three lowest income segments.

Question Type: Interpretation
Difficulty Level: Moderate

(D) **is the best response.** Response (D) restates the statistical information presented in lines 51–54. The difference between 70% (the percentage of those households in the two highest income segments that own life insurance) and 40% (the percentage of those households in the three lowest income segments that own life insurance) is 30%.

Incorrect Responses

(A) is unsupported by the information in the passage. The passage states that 10% of U.S. households earn more than $75,000 per year. The passage, however, does not indicate the percentage of premium dollars accounted for by this segment.

(B) calls for an unwarranted inference. It cannot be inferred that the 10% of U.S. households that earn more than $75,000 are the same group that constitute the top two income segments referred to earlier in the paragraph.

(C) calls for an unwarranted inference. (C) simply restates (B) in a negative fashion, and thus is incorrect for the same reason.

(E) calls for an unwarranted inference. The passage indicates that life insurance ownership is increasing in the two highest segments while decreasing in the three lowest segments. However, the passage provides no information concerning the rate of these changes (i.e., how fast these percentage figures are changing).

QUESTION 8

8. **Among the following, the passage above would be most likely to appear in a**

   (A) **publication of a consumer-advocacy organization**
   (B) **transcript from a U.S. Senate subcommittee hearing on tax reform**
   (C) **life insurance industry trade magazine**
   (D) **professional journal for economists**
   (E) **report of the Federal Trade Commission**

Question Type: Extrapolation
Difficulty Level: Easier

(C) is the best response. The author seems to represent the life insurance industry's interests—by arguing, for example, that the Federal Trade Commission Report was "unfair," and by recommending specific steps which might help the life insurance industry to improve its competitive position in the financial marketplace. Response (C) is, therefore, consistent with the point of view conveyed in the passage.

(B) is the second-best response. It is conceivable that the passage is excerpted from the testimony of a life insurance industry spokesperson before a Congressional committee whose function is to determine the impact of tax reforms on the financial-services industry. Such a scenario is consistent with the author's point of view. However, (C) is also consistent with the author's point of view. Moreover, unlike (C), (B) fails to account for the author's marketing recommendations in the last paragraph, which are unrelated to tax issues and probably inappropriate for a hearing on tax reform. Thus, (C) is a better response than (B).

Other Incorrect Responses

(A) and (E) both run contrary to the author's apparent point of view. The author discusses the Federal Trade Commission's Report and the involvement of consumer groups as if they were partly to blame for the life insurance industry's current problems. (A) and (E) are quite inconsistent with this point of view.

(D) is unsupported by the author's apparent point of view. An economist would probably be more interested in the role that inflation and interest rates played in the decline in popularity of life insurance as a means of risk protection. However, the author mentions these factors only in passing, focusing more on demographic trends and specific marketing ideas for the life insurance industry.

PASSAGE #9

The origin of the attempt to distinguish early from modern music and to establish the canons of performance practice for each lies in the eighteenth century. In the first half of that

5   century, when Telemann and Bach ran the collegium musicum in Leipzig, Germany, they performed their own and other modern music. In the German universities of the early twentieth century, however, the reconstituted collegium

10 musicum devoted itself to performing music from the centuries before the beginning of the "standard repertory," by which was understood music from before the time of Bach and Handel.

Alongside this modern collegium musicum,
15 German musicologists developed the historical subdiscipline known as "performance practice," which included the deciphering of obsolete musical notation and its transcription into modern notation, the study of obsolete instru-
20 ments, and—most important because all musical notation is incomplete—the reestablishment of lost oral traditions associated with those forgotten repertories. The cutoff date for this study was understood to be around 1750, the year of Bach's
25 death. The reason for this demarcation was that the music of Bach, Handel, Telemann, and their contemporaries did call for obsolete instruments and voices and unannotated performing tradi-tions (for instance, the spontaneous realization of
30 vocal and instrumental melodic ornamentation as well as chordal accompaniments of the so-called basso continuo). Furthermore, with a few excep-tions, late baroque music had ceased to be performed for nearly a century, with the result
35 that the orally transmitted performing traditions associated with it were forgotten. In contrast, the notation in the music of Haydn and Mozart from the second half of the eighteenth century was more complete than in the earlier styles, and the
40 instruments seemed familiar, so no "special" knowledge appeared necessary. Also, the music of Haydn and Mozart, having never ceased to be performed, had maintained some kind of oral tradition of performance practice.
45 Beginning around 1960, however, the early musicians—the performers of early music—began to encroach upon the music of Haydn, Mozart, and Beethoven. Why? Scholars studying perfor-mance practice had discovered that the living oral
50 traditions associated with the Viennese classics frequently could not be traced back to the eighteenth century and that there were nearly as many performance mysteries to solve for music after 1750 as in earlier repertories. Furthermore,
55 more and more young singers and instrumen-

talists became attracted to early music, and as many of them graduated from student and amateur status to become fully professional, the technical level of early-music performances took a
60 giant leap forward.

As professional early-music groups, building on these developments, began gradually to expand their repertories to include later music, the angry cries from the mainstream could be
65 heard on five continents. The differences between the two camps extended beyond the already fascinating question of which instruments to use and how (or whether) to ornament, to the much more critical matter of style and delivery: Was it
70 to be the smooth legato, continuous vibrato, and powerful tone of the mainstream, or the more rhetorical, quirky, discontinuous delivery of the early-music movement? At the heart of their disagreement is the issue of whether historical
75 knowledge about performing traditions is a prerequisite for proper interpretation of music or whether it merely creates an obstacle to inspired musical tradition.

1. It can be inferred that the "standard repertory" mentioned in lines 11–12 might have included music

    (A) composed before 1700
    (B) of the early twentieth century
    (C) written by the performance-practice composers
    (D) written before the time of Handel
    (E) that called for the use of obsolete instruments

2. According to the passage, German musicologists of the early twentieth century limited performance practice to pre-1750 works because:

    (A) special knowledge was generally not required to decipher pre-1750 music
    (B) unannotated performing traditions had been maintained for later works
    (C) generally speaking, only music written before 1750 had ceased to be performed
    (D) the annotation for earlier works was generally less complete than for the works of Bach and Handel
    (E) music written prior to 1750 was considered obsolete

GO ON TO THE NEXT PAGE.

3. The author mentions the improved technical level of early-music performances (line 59) in order to

   (A) call into question the fairness of the mainstream's objections to the expansion of performance practice to include later works
   (B) explain why an increasing number of young musicians were being attracted to early music
   (C) refute the mainstream's claim that historical knowledge about performing traditions creates an obstacle to inspired musical tradition
   (D) explain the expansion of performance practice to include later works of music
   (E) support the argument that the Viennese classics were more difficult to perform than earlier works

4. The author refers to modern performance practice as a "subdiscipline" (line 16) probably because it

   (A) was not sanctioned by the mainstream
   (B) required more discipline than performing the standard repertory.
   (C) focused on particular aspects of the music being performed at the German universities
   (D) involved deciphering obsolete musical notation
   (E) involved performing the works that were being transcribed at the universities

5. According to the passage, performance practice in the early twentieth century involved all of the following EXCEPT:

   (A) deciphering outdated music notation
   (B) varying the delivery of music to suit the tastes of the particular audience
   (C) determining which musical instrument to use
   (D) reestablishing unannotated performing traditions
   (E) transcribing older music into modern notation

6. Which of the following statements, if true, would best support the author's explanation for the encroachment by the early-musicians upon the music of Mozart, Haydn, and Beethoven?

   (A) The mainstream approved of the manner in which the early-musicians treated the music of Bach and Handel.
   (B) Unannotated performing traditions associated with these composers were distinct from those associated with pre-1750 works.
   (C) Most instrumentalist are attracted to early music because of the opportunities to play obsolete instruments.
   (D) The music of these composers is notated more completely than is the music of Bach and Handel.
   (E) The early-musicians and the mainstream both prefer the same style and delivery of music.

7. Which of the following statements is best supported by the passage?

   (A) The scope of performance practice expanded significantly during the latter half of the twentieth century.
   (B) Twentieth-century musicologists interpret early music differently than did musicologists of the eighteenth century.
   (C) Attempts to distinguish between early and modern music date back to the early eighteenth century.
   (D) The works of Mozart are now considered by the mainstream to be "early music."
   (E) Although the definition of early music has changed over the last century, the canons of performance practice have remained relatively unchanged.

8. Which of the following is the most appropriate title for the passage?

   (A) Performance Practice: The Legacy of the German Collegium Musicum
   (B) How Far Should Early Music Extend?
   (C) Unannotated Performing Traditions of the Eighteenth and Twentieth Centuries
   (D) Performance Practice and New Interpretations of the Viennese Classics
   (E) Competing Views Regarding the Necessity of Historical Knowledge for Inspired Musical Tradition

STOP.

PASSAGE #9—ANSWER KEY

1. E
2. B
3. D
4. C
5. B
6. B
7. A
8. B

PASSAGE #9—ANALYSIS

QUESTION 1

1. It can be inferred that the "standard repertory" mentioned in lines 11–12 might have included music

    (A) composed before 1700
    (B) of the early twentieth century
    (C) written by the performance-practice composers
    (D) written before the time of Handel
    (E) that called for the use of obsolete instruments

Question Type: Inference
Difficulty Level: Moderate

(E) is the best response. It is reasonably inferable from the first paragraph as a whole that the "standard repertory" mentioned in lines 11–12 refers to the music of Bach and Telemann as well as to other ("modern") music from their time (first half of the eighteenth century). In the second paragraph, the author mentions that the music of Bach, Telemann, and their contemporaries called for obsolete instruments (line 19). Thus, the standard repertory might have included music that called for the use of obsolete instruments, as Response (E) indicates.

Incorrect Responses

(A) runs contrary to the information in the passage. The "standard repertory" refers to the music of Bach, Telemann, and other composers of the first half of the eighteenth century. Thus, it probably did not include music written prior to 1700.

(B) confuses the information in the passage. As noted above, the "standard repertory" refers to the music of Bach, Telemann, and other composers of the first half of the eighteenth century. Thus, it could not have included music written during the twentieth century.

(C) is nonsensical. "Performance practice" refers not to a group of composers but rather to a subdiscipline formed by German musicologists who deciphered and interpreted early works.

(D) runs contrary to the information in the passage. The passage suggests that Handel was a contemporary of Bach. Thus, the standard repertory included works written during, not before, Handel's time.

QUESTION 2

2. According to the passage, German musicologists of the early twentieth century limited performance practice to pre-1750 works because:

(A) special knowledge was generally not required to decipher pre-1750 music

(B) unannotated performing traditions had been maintained for later works

(C) generally speaking, only music written before 1750 had ceased to be performed

(D) the annotation for earlier works was generally less complete than for the works of Bach and Handel

(E) music written prior to 1750 was considered obsolete

Question Type: Explicit Detail
Difficulty Level: Moderate

(B) is the best response. According to the passage, the German musicologists did not study the music of Mozart and Haydn (post-1750 music) because, among other reasons, their music, "having never ceased to be performed, had maintained some kind of oral tradition of performance practice" (lines 42–45). Response (B) restates this point.

Incorrect Responses

(A) runs contrary to the information in the passage. The author states that later works were not included in the musicologists' studies because, among other reasons, the notation was more complete and the instruments seemed familiar, "so no 'special' knowledge appeared necessary" (lines 41–44). This statement implies, of course, that special knowledge was required to decipher pre-1750 music.

(C) distorts the information in the passage. Although the unannotated oral traditions may have ceased, the author neither states nor implies that the basic works of pre-1750 composers were no longer being performed.

(D) confuses the information in the passage. The works of Bach and Handel were included in the musicologists' early-music studies. The cutoff date for the study was 1750, the year of Bach's death. Whether notation of works prior to those of Bach or Handel were less complete than notation of works by Bach or Handel is not the issue.

(E) distorts the information in the passage. The author refers to older musical notation, not the music itself, as obsolete (lines 17–18).

QUESTION 3

3. The author mentions the improved technical level of early-music performances (line 59) in order to

(A) call into question the fairness of the mainstream's objections to the expansion of performance practice to include later works

(B) explain why an increasing number of young musicians were being attracted to early music

(C) refute the mainstream's claim that historical knowledge about performing traditions creates an obstacle to inspired musical tradition

(D) explain the expansion of performance practice to include later works of music

(E) support the argument that the Viennese classics were more difficult to perform than earlier works

Question Type: Purpose of Detail
Difficulty Level: Moderate

(D) **is the best response.** At the beginning of the third paragraph, the author states that, beginning around 1960, early-musicians began to encroach upon the works of Haydn, Mozart, and Beethoven. The remainder of the third paragraph is devoted to explaining the reasons for this encroachment. One of the contributing reasons given is that the technical level of early-music performances had improved.

(E) **is the second-best response.** According to the author, improvements in the technical skills of early musicians somehow contributed to the encroachment by early musicians upon the music of Mozart, Haydn, and Beethoven. However, the author does not spell out the precise causal connection. Although it might be inferred that these works were more difficult to perform than earlier works, the author does not make this point explicitly; thus, Response (E) exaggerates the author's purpose in mentioning this detail. The author mentions the improved technical level of the performances not so much to make a narrow point about how difficult the music was to perform, but rather to explain the reasons for the encroachment upon this music by the early-musicians.

Other Incorrect Responses

(A) is wholly unsupported by the passage. In the final paragraph, the author does mention that the mainstream objected to the early-musicians' encroachment upon later works. However, the author neither defends the early-musicians nor in any other way suggests that these objections were unfair.

(B) confuses cause and effect. It was because more young musicians were being attracted to early music that the technical level of early-music performances began to improve, not the other way around.

(C) confuses the information in the passage. Response (C) refers to information included in the final sentence of the passage and is irrelevant to the question posed.

QUESTION 4

4. The author refers to modern performance practice as a "subdiscipline" (line 16) probably because it

   (A) was not sanctioned by the mainstream
   (B) required more discipline than performing the standard repertory.
   (C) focused on particular aspects of the music being performed at the German universities
   (D) involved deciphering obsolete musical notation
   (E) involved performing the works that were being transcribed at the universities

Question Type: Interpretation
Difficulty Level: Easier

(C) **is the best response.** Performance practice, according to the passage, was developed alongside the modern (early twentieth-century) collegium musicum, which was part of the German university. While the modern collegium musicum performed music from before the time of Bach and Handel, the field of performance practice studied certain aspects (e.g., choice of instruments, deciphering notation) of music from the same time period.

(D) **is the second-best response.** The fact that performance practice involves the specific task of deciphering musical notation is indeed relevant to why it is called a "subdiscipline"—it involves a narrow area of concern within a broader field of study. However, performance practice includes other concerns as well (most notably, the reestablishment of unannotated performing traditions). Thus, it is termed a "subdiscipline" not just because it involves deciphering musical notation but, more generally, because all of its concerns are also encompassed by a more broadly-defined field of study or discipline. Thus, Response (D) is too narrow.

Other Incorrect Responses

(A) does not respond to the question. In itself, Statement (B) finds some support in the passage. The mainstream's objections to the expansion of early music to include later works (see the last paragraph) might be interpreted as disapproval. Even so, this discussion in the final paragraph of the passage is irrelevant to why performance practice is referred to as a "subdiscipline."

(B) is nonsensical. In the context of the passage, the term "discipline" refers to an area or field of study, and so "subdiscipline" refers to a component or more specific area within a broader field of study. An entirely different meaning of the word "discipline" is suggested by Response (B).

(E) confuses the information in the passage. Musicologists involved in the narrow subdiscipline of performance practice transcribed the works performed by musicians at the universities, not the other way around.

QUESTION 5

5. According to the passage, performance practice in the early twentieth century involved all of the following EXCEPT:

   (A) deciphering outdated music notation
   (B) varying the delivery of music to suit the tastes of the particular audience
   (C) determining which musical instrument to use
   (D) reestablishing unannotated performing traditions
   (E) transcribing older music into modern notation

Question Type: Explicit Detail
Difficulty Level: Easier

(B) is the best response. Although performance practice did indeed involve varying the performance of a work of music from one time to the next (by including spontaneous vocal and instrumental ornamentation), the passage neither states nor implies that how the delivery of music varied from time to time depended upon the particular tastes of the audience. Thus, (B) is unsupported by the passage.

(C) is the second-best response. Response (C) is not supported by the information in the passage as explicitly as (A), (D) or (E). The author does not state explicitly that performance practice involved determining which musical instrument to use. However, the passage does indicate that early music often called for the use of obsolete instruments and that one of the issues separating the mainstream and the early-musicians was "the fascinating question of which instrument to use" (line 67). Thus, it is reasonably inferable that performance practice involved determining whether modern instruments or earlier (obsolete) instruments were appropriate for a particular piece of music.

Other Incorrect Responses

(A) and (E) are explicitly supported in the second paragraph, where the author states that performance practice "included the deciphering of obsolete musical notation and its transcription into modern notation" (lines 17–19).

(D) is explicitly supported in the second paragraph. The author asserts that the most important concern of performance practice is the "reestablishment of lost oral traditions" (lines 21–22). The author then describes these lost oral traditions as the use of obsolete instruments and voices and unannotated performing traditions.

QUESTION 6

6. Which of the following statements, if true, would best support the author's explanation for the encroachment by the early-musicians upon the music of Mozart, Haydn, and Beethoven?

(A) The mainstream approved of the manner in which the early-musicians treated the music of Bach and Handel.

(B) Unannotated performing traditions associated with these composers were distinct from those associated with pre-1750 works.

(C) Most instrumentalist are attracted to early music because of the opportunities to play obsolete instruments.

(D) The music of these composers is notated more completely than is the music of Bach and Handel.

(E) The early-musicians and the mainstream both prefer the same style and delivery of music.

Question Type: Logical Reasoning
Difficulty Level: Challenging

(B) is the best response. According to the passage, one reason for the encroachment was that some of the oral traditions associated with the Viennese classics (the works of Mozart, Haydn, and Beethoven) could not be traced back to the eighteenth century. Response (B) supports this point by providing specific evidence that this was indeed the case.

Incorrect Responses

(A) is irrelevant. No information in the passage supports the notion that the mainstreams' approval or disapproval of how early-musicians treated other works would have been relevant to the early-musicians' encroachment upon the music of Mozart, Haydn, and Beethoven.

(C) is not responsive to the question. If Statement (C) were true, and if the music of Mozart, Haydn, and Beethoven did indeed call for the use of obsolete instruments, then this may help to explain why the early-musicians encroached upon the music of Mozart, Haydn, and Beethoven. However, Statement (C) would not support the author's explanation but rather provide an additional explanation; thus, in this respect, (C) is irrelevant.

(D) would actually undermine (weaken) the author's explanation. Early-musicians are interested in exploring unannotated performance traditions. Music that is fully annotated does not allow for such exploration. Thus, if Statement (D) were true, the early-musicians would not be interested in the music of Mozart, Haydn, and Beethoven.

(E) is irrelevant. Even if true, Statement (E) would not support the author's explanation but rather provide an additional explanation; thus, (E) is irrelevant.

QUESTION 7

7. **Which of the following statements is best supported by the passage?**

   (A) The scope of performance practice expanded significantly during the latter half of the twentieth century.
   (B) Twentieth-century musicologists interpret early music differently than did musicologists of the eighteenth century.
   (C) Attempts to distinguish between early and modern music date back to the early eighteenth century.
   (D) The works of Mozart are now considered by the mainstream to be "early music."
   (E) Although the definition of early music has changed over the last century, the canons of performance practice have remained relatively unchanged.

Question Type: Interpretation
Difficulty Level: Easier

(A) is the best response. According to the passage, beginning around 1960 (i.e., in the latter half of the century), early-musicians began to expand the scope of performance practice to include works by major composers of a later period. Response (B) paraphrases this rather explicit point.

Incorrect Responses

(B) is wholly unsupported by the passage. Although the scope of the music explored by twentieth-century musicologists may be greater than that of earlier musicologists, the author neither states nor implies that modern musicologists interpret early music differently than did their predecessors.

(C) distorts and runs contrary to the information in the passage. The first sentence of the passage indicates that the origin of the attempt to distinguish early from modern music lies in the eighteenth century. However, this sentence does not indicate that the attempt itself began during this time period. In fact, the passage makes no mention of any such attempt prior to the early twentieth century.

(D) is unsupported and actually runs contrary to the passage. Nowhere does the author indicate that the definition of early music would, for the mainstream, embrace the music of Mozart. To the contrary, the mainstream would probably not oppose this notion, since the mainstream objected to the early-musicians' encroachment upon Mozart's music.

(E) is partially accurate, but it is self-contradictory. The definition of early music has indeed changed during the twentieth century to include later works. It is not clear from the information in the passage exactly what all of the canons (rules) of performance practice are. However, one of the canons relates to the scope of music included within this subdiscipline, and the passage makes clear that this scope has indeed changed during the twentieth century. In this sense, then, the second clause of Statement (E) contradicts the first clause.

QUESTION 8

8. Which of the following is the most appropriate title for the passage?

   (A) Performance Practice: The Legacy of the German
        Collegium Musicum
   (B) How Far Should Early Music Extend?
   (C) Unannotated Performing Traditions of the Eighteenth and
        Twentieth Centuries
   (D) Performance Practice and New Interpretations of the
        Viennese Classics
   (E) Competing Views Regarding the Necessity of Historical
        Knowledge for Inspired Musical Tradition

Question Type: Primary Purpose
Difficulty Level: Moderate

(B) is the best response. The author's primary concern in the passage is to trace the scope of works included in performance practice from the early twentieth century to the latter half of the century. The author identifies and explains the reasons for the trend of including later works within the scope of so-called "early music" (second and third paragraphs), then refers (in the final paragraph) to a controversy surrounding this trend. Response (B) reflects the author's primary concern as well as embracing the controversy.

Incorrect Responses

(A) is too broad. While the author does establish that performance practice originated in the German Collegium Musicum, the author's primary concerns are more specific—to explain why the scope of works included in this discipline have expanded and to identify a controversy concerning this expansion.

(C) is off focus. The author does describe (in the second paragraph) some of the unannotated performing traditions of concern to early-musicians but does not discuss such traditions in much detail. The author is more concerned with explaining the expansion in the scope of works included in performance practice.

(D) is off focus. While the third paragraph of the passage does point out that new discoveries led to new interpretations of the music of Mozart, Haydn, and Beethoven, this is in no sense the author's primary concern in the passage. The author does not mention what these new discoveries were, nor does the author describe any new interpretations of these works.

(E) is off focus. The author mentions the competing views to which Response (E) refers for the first time in the final sentence of the passage. Thus, while this title might possibly be appropriate for a continuation of the passage, it is not the focus of the passage itself.

PASSAGE #10

Diseases associated with aging in women are difficult to correlate explicitly with estrogen deficiency because aging and genetics are important influences in the development of such
5 diseases. A number of studies, however, indicate a profound effect of estrogen deficiency in syndromes such as cardiovascular disease (including atherosclerosis and stroke) and osteoporosis—the loss and increasing fragility of
10 bone in aging individuals.

Available evidence attests to the apparent role of estrogen in the protection against cardio-vascular disease although it does not delineate the precise mechanisms involved. The incidence
15 of cardiovascular disease in women increases markedly after menopause with each year of estrogen reduction. Women who have had a bilateral oophorectomy have a substantially greater risk of cardiovascular disease than do
20 women with intact ovaries. Evidence clearly shows that high levels of high-density lipoprotein cholesterol and low levels of low-density lipoprotein cholesterol are protective against the development of atherosclerosis and that
25 menopause (both natural and surgical) is associated with changes in these levels.

As for osteoporosis, the amount of bone in the elderly skeleton—a key determinant in its susceptibility to fractures—is believed to be a
30 function of two major factors. The first is the peak amount of bone mass attained, determined to a large extent by genetic inheritance. The marked effect of gender is obvious—elderly men experience only one-half as many hip fractures
35 per capita as elderly women. Also, however, African-American women have a lower incidence of osteoporotic fractures than Caucasian women. Other important variables include diet, exposure to sunlight, and physical activity. The second
40 major factor is the rate of bone loss after peak bone mass has been attained. While many of the variables that affect peak bone mass also affect rates of bone loss, additional factors influencing bone loss include physiological stresses such as
45 pregnancy and lactation. It is hormonal status, however, reflected primarily by estrogen and progesterone levels, that may exert the greatest effect on rates of decline in skeletal mass.

Because accelerated bone loss is a frequent
50 occurrence during perimenopause, the change in ovarian function is believed to be pivotal in the pathogenesis of post-menopausal osteoporosis. In one study, the level of bone density in a group of 50-year-old women who had had their ovaries
55 removed twenty years earlier was shown to be comparable to that reported in a group of 70-year-old women who had experienced natural menopause twenty years earlier or contemporane-ously with the oophorectomized group. Another
60 study showed that women who have been hysterectomized are more likely to develop osteoporosis than women who experience a natural menopause. Evidence of the pivotal role of ovarian function is not limited to correlative
65 studies. It has been shown that while premeno-pausal women over the age of thirty may lose less than one percent of their bone tissue yearly, such losses may reach 3 to 5 percent per year for the first five to ten years of menopause. More-
70 over, recent research has identified estrogen receptors not only in the uterus, hypothalamus, pituitary, and breast, but also in bone.

1. Which of the following findings from a hypo-thetical study, if true, would most seriously undermine the author's claim about the relationship between menopause and cardio-vascular disease?

(A) Natural, but not surgical, menopause was found to result in increased levels of low-density lipoprotein.

(B) Surgical, but not natural, menopause was found to result in decreased levels of high-density lipoprotein.

(C) An increase in estrogen was found to result in decreased levels of low-density lipoprotein.

(D) A decrease in estrogen was found to result in increased levels of high-density lipoprotein.

(E) A decrease in estrogen was found to have no effect on the levels of low-density lipoprotein.

GO ON TO THE NEXT PAGE.

2. Which of the following conclusions is best supported by the study mentioned in lines 53–59?

   (A) Surgical menopause is more likely than natural menopause to result in cardiovascular disease.
   (B) The role of natural menopause in age-related diseases is not as great as suggested by evidence provided earlier in the passage.
   (C) Age is not the key factor in the development of osteoporosis among post-menopausal women.
   (D) The rate of bone-tissue loss accelerates during menopause.
   (E) Fifty-year-old women are just as likely to suffer from osteoporosis as seventy-year-old women.

3. Based upon the passage, which of the following is LEAST clearly a factor affecting the rate of decline in bone mass?

   (A) gender
   (B) exposure to sunlight
   (C) progesterone levels
   (D) age
   (E) estrogen levels

4. In discussing the "marked effect of gender" (line 33), the author assumes all of the following EXCEPT:

   (A) The difference in incidence of hip fractures is not due instead to different rates of bone loss.
   (B) The incidence of hip fractures among elderly men as compared to elderly women is representative of the total number of bone fractures among elderly men as compared to elderly women.
   (C) Elderly women are not more accident-prone than elderly men.
   (D) The population upon which the cited statistic is based includes both African-Americans and Caucasians.
   (E) Men achieve peak bone mass at the same age as women.

5. It can be inferred from the passage that the peak amount of bone mass in women

   (A) is not affected by either pregnancy or lactation
   (B) is determined primarily by diet
   (C) depends partly upon hormonal status
   (D) may play a role in determining the rate of decrease in estrogen and progesterone levels
   (E) is not dependent upon genetic makeup

6. Which of the following statements is best supported by the passage?

   (A) The rate at which Caucasian women lose bone mass is greater than that of African-American women.
   (B) Estrogen reduction is the most significant cause of cardiovascular disease among women.
   (C) A bilateral oophorectomy reduces the risk of cardiovascular disease.
   (D) Bone mass in men remains fairly constant with age.
   (E) African-American women have a higher peak amount of bone mass than Caucasian women.

7. Which of the following best expresses the main idea of the passage?

   (A) Recent research supports the claim that bone tissue is a receptor of estrogen.
   (B) Osteoporosis is the leading cause of estrogen deficiency in post-menopausal women.
   (C) A decrease in estrogen is perhaps the primary cause of osteoporosis among post-menopausal women.
   (D) More research is needed to determine the relationship between estrogen production and certain diseases associated with aging.
   (E) Osteoporosis and cardiovascular disease in women are related to decreasing amounts of estrogen.

STOP.

PASSAGE #10—ANSWER KEY

1. D   4. E   6. E
2. C   5. A   7. E
3. B

PASSAGE #10—ANALYSIS

QUESTION 1

1. Which of the following findings from a hypothetical study, if true, would most seriously undermine the author's claim about the relationship between menopause and cardiovascular disease?

   (A) Natural, but not surgical, menopause was found to result in increased levels of low-density lipoprotein.
   (B) Surgical, but not natural, menopause was found to result in decreased levels of high-density lipoprotein.
   (C) An increase in estrogen was found to result in decreased levels of low-density lipoprotein.
   (D) A decrease in estrogen was found to result in increased levels of high-density lipoprotein.
   (E) A decrease in estrogen was found to have no effect on the levels of low-density lipoprotein.

Question Type: Logical Reasoning
Difficulty Level: Moderate

(D) is the best response. According to the passage, high levels of high-density lipoprotein protect against atherosclerosis. If a decrease in estrogen amounts were to result in an increase in high-density lipoprotein, then the risk of atherosclerosis would decline upon menopause. However, just the opposite is true.

(E) is the second-best response. (E) tends to weaken the author's claim; in two respects, however, it does not weaken the claim to as great an extent as (D). First, it ignores the effects that a decrease in estrogen might have upon levels of high-density lipoprotein. Second, it would more seriously undermine the author's claim if the decrease in estrogen to which (E) refers resulted in increased levels of low-density lipoprotein rather than having no effect on such levels.

Other Incorrect Responses

(A) does tend to weaken the author's argument that the risk of atherosclerosis increases upon menopause (due to decreasing estrogen production). However, since it excludes surgical (non-natural) menopause, Statement (A) does not undermine the author's argument to as great an extent as Response (D).

(B) does tend, like Statement (A), to weaken the author's argument that the risk of atherosclerosis increases upon menopause (due to decreasing estrogen production). However, since it excludes natural menopause, Statement (B) does not undermine the author's argument to as great an extent as Response (D).

(C) if true would actually strengthen the author's claim. Since low levels of low-density lipoprotein offer protection against atherosclerosis, a further decrease in such levels would further decrease such risk. Increased levels of estrogen would also be consistent with a decline in the risk of atherosclerosis.

QUESTION 2

2. **Which of the following conclusions is best supported by the study mentioned in lines 53–59?**

   (A) **Surgical menopause is more likely than natural menopause to result in cardiovascular disease.**
   (B) **The role of natural menopause in age-related diseases is not as great as suggested by evidence provided earlier in the passage.**
   (C) **Age is not the key factor in the development of osteoporosis among post-menopausal women.**
   (D) **The rate of bone-tissue loss accelerates during menopause.**
   (E) **Fifty-year-old women are just as likely to suffer from osteoporosis as seventy-year-old women.**

Question Type: Inference
Difficulty Level: Moderate

(C) is the best response. The study showed that bone density was comparable among 50- and 70-year-old women. Since these women all had ovaries removed or began to experience natural menopause at the same time (not at the same age), the study supports the claim that age is not the key factor in bone density among older women.

(E) is the second-best response. Statement (E) appears to be consistent with the results of the study. However, it overgeneralizes from the study by including all 50-year-old women, including those 50-year-old women who experienced menopause naturally and later in life than the 50-year-old women in the study.

Other Incorrect Responses

(A) confuses the information in the passage. Whether or not Statement (C) is supported by the information in the passage, the study to which the question refers involves osteoporosis, not cardiovascular disease.

(B) runs contrary to the passage. The study to which (B) refers shows that menopause (natural or otherwise) plays an even greater role than age in bone density. Also, (B) is too broad a response to the question—the question refers to a study of osteoporosis (bone density), while (B) generalizes about all diseases associated with aging.

(D) may be an accurate statement, but it does not respond to the question. The study to which the question refers does not address changes in the rate of bone loss.

QUESTION 3

3. **Based upon the passage, which of the following is LEAST clearly a factor affecting the rate of decline in bone mass?**

> **(A)** gender
> **(B)** exposure to sunlight
> **(C)** progesterone levels
> **(D)** age
> **(E)** estrogen levels

Question Type: Explicit Detail
Difficulty Level: Moderate

(B) **is the best response.** Exposure to sunlight was mentioned as one factor determining peak bone mass. Although the passage states that "many of the factors that affect the attainment of peak bone mass also affect rates of bone loss," it is unwarranted to infer that exposure to sunlight is one such factor.

(D) **is the second-best response.** The notion that age is a factor in the rate of decline in bone mass seems to run contrary to the passage, particularly to the last paragraph, which suggests that menopause (natural or otherwise), not age in itself, triggers an increase in the rate of decline in bone mass. Notwithstanding these findings, age is indeed a factor in the rate of decline in bone mass, since women do not generally experience natural menopause until mid-life.

Other Incorrect Responses

(A) is mentioned as an "obvious" factor in line 33.

(C) and (E) are explicitly mentioned as exerting "the greatest effect on rates of decline in skeletal mass" (lines 46–48).

QUESTION 4

> 4. In discussing the "marked effect of gender" (line 33), the author assumes all of the following EXCEPT:
>
> **(A)** The difference in incidence of hip fractures is not due instead to different rates of bone loss.
> **(B)** The incidence of hip fractures among elderly men as compared to elderly women is representative of the total number of bone fractures among elderly men as compared to elderly women.
> **(C)** Elderly women are not more accident-prone than elderly men.
> **(D)** The population upon which the cited statistic is based includes both African-Americans and Caucasians.
> **(E)** Men achieve peak bone mass at the same age as women.

Question Type: Logical Reasoning
Difficulty Level: Challenging

(E) **is the best response.** As long as the population upon which the cited statistic was based excluded those who had not yet achieved peak bone mass, it does not make a difference whether the men in the group achieved their peak bone mass at a different age than the women.

Incorrect Responses

(A), (B), (C) and (D) must all be assumed by the author to confidently conclude that gender has a marked effect on osteoporosis:

(A) The author concludes that the difference in hip-fracture incidence between men and women is due to a disparity in peak bone mass between the sexes. Theoretically, the difference might instead be due to different rates of bone loss.

(B) The author cites only one type of fracture (hip fractures) to support the conclusion. Theoretically, however, men might actually incur just as many such fractures as women, as might be the case if hip fractures constitute only a small percentage of the total osteoporotic fractures.

(C) Theoretically, clumsiness or lack of coordination rather than bone fragility might cause most hip fractures. If so, no conclusion about the relative fragility of bones in men and women could be fairly drawn from the statistic cited by the author.

(D) A fair comparison of osteoporotic fractures based upon gender should take into account a person's race or ethnic origin, especially considering the fact that a woman's peak bone mass depends upon her ethnic origin (as suggested by the next sentence in the passage).

QUESTION 5

5. It can be inferred from the passage that the peak amount of bone mass in women

    (A) is not affected by either pregnancy or lactation
    (B) is determined primarily by diet
    (C) depends partly upon hormonal status
    (D) may play a role in determining the rate of decrease in estrogen and progesterone levels
    (E) is not dependent upon genetic makeup

Question Type: Inference
Difficulty Level: Easier

(A) is the best response. In lines 37–39, the author lists various factors affecting peak bone mass, then asserts that many of these factors also affect the rate of bone loss. In mentioning pregnancy and lactation as "additional factors" affecting bone loss, the author implies that these two factors do not also affect peak bone mass.

Incorrect Responses

(B) calls for an unwarranted inference. The author mentions diet as one of several "important" factors affecting bone mass but not as the most important factor.

(C) confuses the information in the passage. While the author states that hormonal status may exert the greatest effect on rates of decline in skeletal mass (lines 45–48), the rate of decline in skeletal mass and peak bone mass are two different factors.

(D) confuses cause and effect, as well as confusing peak bone mass and bone loss. The passage indicates explicitly that hormonal status (reflected in part by estrogen levels) is the key determinant in the rate of bone loss, not the other way around, as suggested by (D). Also, estrogen levels are related to the rate of bone loss, not to peak bone mass.

(E) is contradicted by the information in the passage. According to the passage, "peak bone mass is determined largely by genetic inheritance" (lines 31–32).

QUESTION 6

6. **Which of the following statements is best supported by the passage?**

    (A) **The rate at which Caucasian women lose bone mass is greater than that of African-American women.**

    (B) **Estrogen reduction is the most significant cause of cardiovascular disease among women.**

    (C) **A bilateral oophorectomy reduces the risk of cardiovascular disease.**

    (D) **Bone mass in men remains fairly constant with age.**

    (E) **African-American women have a higher peak amount of bone mass than Caucasian women.**

Question Type: Inference
Difficulty Level: Moderate

(E) **is the best response.** The author cites two statistics to support the claim that peak bone mass is determined to a large extent by genetic inheritance. One compares men and women in terms of incidence of hip fractures; the other compares African-American women to Caucasian women in terms of osteoporotic fractures. By using the second comparison to support the claim that peak bone mass is determined in part by genetic inheritance, the author must be implying that peak bone mass of African-American women is greater than that of Caucasian women.

Incorrect Responses

(A) confuses the information in the passage and calls for an unwarranted inference. The author compares African-American women to Caucasian women in terms of peak bone mass, not in terms of the rate of bone loss. It is unfair to draw any conclusions about their relative rates of bone loss from the fact that African-American women have a greater peak bone mass than Caucasian women.

(B) calls for an unwarranted inference. Although the information in the second paragraph clearly supports the notion that declining levels of estrogen contribute to the risk of cardiovascular disease, the author neither states nor implies that it is the single most significant factor.

(C) contradicts the information in the passage, which states explicitly that "[w]omen who have had a bilateral oophorectomy have a substantially greater risk of cardiovascular disease than do women with intact ovaries."

(D) calls for an unwarranted inference. The author neither states nor implies that bone mass in men remains fairly constant after reaching a peak amount. The only conclusion about men that can be properly drawn from the passage is that their peak bone mass is greater than that of women.

QUESTION 7

7. Which of the following best expresses the main idea of the passage?

(A) Recent research supports the claim that bone tissue is a receptor of estrogen.

(B) Osteoporosis is the leading cause of estrogen deficiency in post-menopausal women.

(C) A decrease in estrogen is perhaps the primary cause of osteoporosis among post-menopausal women.

(D) More research is needed to determine the relationship between estrogen production and certain diseases associated with aging.

(E) Osteoporosis and cardiovascular disease in women are related to decreasing amounts of estrogen.

Question Type: Main Idea
Difficulty Level: Moderate

(E) **is the best response.** Statement (E) encompasses both broad areas of discussion—cardiovascular disease and osteoporosis as well as embracing the author's primary concern with showing that estrogen levels play a role in the development of both types of diseases.

(C) **is the second-best response.** Statement (C) expresses the author's main point in the third and fourth paragraphs. However, it entirely ignores the discussion of cardiovascular disease and thus is too narrow in scope to be a viable response.

Other Incorrect Responses

(A) is far too narrow. (A) focuses on the last sentence of the passage, which merely provides additional evidence that estrogen levels are related to osteoporosis.

(B) confuses cause and effect and is too narrow. According to the passage, estrogen deficiency contributes to the development of osteoporosis, not the other way around. (B) also ignores the discussion of cardiovascular disease.

(D) distorts the author's overall purpose, which is to point out the relationship between estrogen levels and two types of age-related diseases. Nowhere in the passage does the author suggest that more research is needed to determine the relationship between estrogen production and certain diseases associated with aging. In order for (D) to be a viable response, the author would have to comment on either the sufficiency, adequacy, or accuracy of the data presented.

PASSAGE #11

In recent years, the People's Republic of China has been one of the fastest growing economies of the world. Its gross national product has increased at an average annual rate of 12.8
5   percent over the last three years and is projected to increase at an average annual rate of eight to nine percent during the next decade. Foreign trade as a percentage of China's gross national product rose from about ten percent in the late
10 1970s to thirty-eight percent in 1992.

This dynamic growth can be attributed to several factors. Trade between the United States and China resumed in 1972, after a twenty-year hiatus, following the signing of the Shanghai
15 Communique at the conclusion of Nixon's historic trip to China. Trade has developed rapidly since normalization of diplomatic relations in 1979; two-way trade increased from 2.3 billion dollars in 1979 to 33.1 billion dollars in
20 1992. Economic growth is also attributable largely to China's policies of economic reform. The pace of reform quickened in the wake of senior leader Deng Xiaoping's call in early 1992 for more growth, greater openness, and stepped-up reform.
25 Deng's policies were endorsed that year by the Fourteenth Congress of the Chinese Communist Party, by the Eighth National People's Congress in 1993, and again in 1993 by the Third Plenum of the Chinese Communists Party's Fourteenth
30 Central Committee. The Third Plenum adopted several new reform initiatives aimed at transforming the Chinese economy into a market system; priority areas for reform included state-owned enterprises, banking and taxation, foreign
35 trade, social security, and economic structure.

These bold reform measures will no doubt result in many promising business opportunities, especially in the areas of energy, telecommunications, and transportation. The United States is
40 likely to be a primary beneficiary of Chinese economic reform. The Chinese have a high regard for American products and are encouraging American companies to enter the Chinese market. Potential for United Stated exports to China was
45 enhanced by two particular agreements between these countries in 1992. The first regards the protection of intellectual-property rights by which the Chinese government pledged to significantly upgrade its intellectual-property regime. The
50 second is a market-access agreement which calls for the Chinese government to substantially reduce nontariff import barriers, especially in product categories of great interest to United States firms. Notwithstanding these develop-
55 ments, the issue of annual renewal of China's

current Most Favored Nation status is and will continue to be of primary significance to United States firms.

Chinese leadership continues to stress eco-
60 nomic development as the country's primary objective, paying little attention officially to political reform. What are the possible intra-national political consequences of the government's current agenda? Certain regions are
65 experiencing a greater economic boom than others. Guangdong province, for example, has benefitted from neighboring Hong Kong's freewheeling capitalistic economy, and the movement of Hong Kong's manufacturing sector
70 into the province has created what is probably the most dynamic economy in the world. Such anomalies in economic development are likely to create unrest in the less prosperous areas. Political instability might also result if current
75 inflationary trends become uncontrollable. Further, the question of leadership succession remains unresolved, a situation that might generate political unrest. On the whole, however, as long as economic expansion continues and
80 spreads to the internal regions, political unrest should remain relatively dormant.

1. According to the passage, foreign trade as a percentage of China's gross national product

    (A) increased at an average annual rate of 12.8 percent over the last three years
    (B) is projected to increase at an average annual rate of eight to nine percent during the next decade
    (C) increased from 2.3 percent in 1979 to 33.1 percent in 1992
    (D) increased by more than twenty-five percent in less than twenty years
    (E) increased in the wake of Deng's call for greater openness with other countries

GO ON TO THE NEXT PAGE.

2. It can be reasonably inferred from the passage that the amount of trade between the United States and China

    (A) was greater during the period immediately preceding 1952 than during the years immediately following 1952
    (B) decreased from 1972 to 1979, then increased from 1979 to 1992
    (C) decreased during the years immediately preceding the Shanghai Communique
    (D) increased after the Eighth National People's Congress
    (E) remained relatively unchanged until normalization of diplomatic relations between the two countries in 1979

3. The passage mentions all of the following as factors contributing to China's economic growth EXCEPT:

    (A) renewed political relations between China and the United States
    (B) the policies of Deng Xiaoping
    (C) particular initiatives of the Third Plenum
    (D) a decrease in the number of state-owned enterprises
    (E) endorsements made by the Eighth Annual People's Congress

4. The author discusses Guangdong province primarily in order to

    (A) illustrate a political phenomenon
    (B) discount an economic theory
    (C) support a prediction
    (D) help define an historical trend
    (E) rebut an opposing viewpoint

5. Which of the following best expresses the main idea of the last paragraph in the passage?

    (A) Unless accompanied by political reforms, economic growth and reform in China may result in political instability.
    (B) In order to ensure future economic growth, China must continue to trade with the United States.
    (C) China's recent economic growth is the result of both improving political relations with the United States and reforms in economic policy.
    (D) While positive political developments have been largely responsible for China's recent economic growth, continued unfettered growth may ironically have adverse political consequences in the future.
    (E) The potential for United States exports to China, although great, may be adversely affected in the future by both economic and political factors.

6. All of the following factors positively affecting business opportunities for the United States in China are mentioned in the passage EXCEPT:

    (A) consumer sentiment in China toward American products
    (B) China's laws regarding intellectual property
    (C) China's current policies regarding tariffs on imported products
    (D) product areas of primary interest among United States firms
    (E) China's Most Favored Nation Status

7. Which of the following would be the most appropriate title for the passage?

    (A) Is Political Unrest Inevitable in Light of China's Current Economic Agenda?
    (B) A Prescription for Economic Reform In China
    (C) Trade Relations Between the United States and China: Historical Perspective and Future Outlook
    (D) The Booming Economy of China: Economic and Political Implications
    (E) China: One of the World's Fastest Growing Economies

STOP.

PASSAGE #11—ANSWER KEY

1. D
2. A
3. D
4. C
5. A
6. C
7. D

PASSAGE #11—ANALYSIS

QUESTION 1

1. According to the passage, foreign trade as a percentage of China's gross national product

   (A) increased at an average annual rate of 12.8 percent over the last three years
   (B) is projected to increase at an average annual rate of eight to nine percent during the next decade
   (C) increased from 2.3 percent in 1979 to 33.1 percent in 1992
   (D) increased by more than twenty-five percent in less than twenty years
   (E) increased in the wake of Deng's call for greater openness with other countries

Question Type: Explicit Detail
Difficulty Level: Easier

(D) is the best response. In the first paragraph, the author states explicitly that foreign trade as a percentage of China's gross national product rose from about ten percent in the late 1970s to thirty-eight percent in 1992.

Incorrect Responses

(A) and (B) both refer to China's gross national product as a whole rather than to foreign trade as a percentage of the gross national product.

(C) refers to the increase in trade between China and the United States from 1979 to 1992, not to foreign trade as a percentage of China's gross national product and confuses percentage figures with dollar amounts.

(E) is neither explicitly stated in the passage nor well supported by the passage. Although Deng's call for greater openness (line 24) may have resulted in increased foreign trade, the passage does not suggest that such an increase exceeded the percentage increase in China's gross national product as a whole.

QUESTION 2

2. It can be reasonably inferred from the passage that the amount of trade between the United States and China

   (A) was greater during the period immediately preceding 1952 than during the years immediately following 1952
   (B) decreased from 1972 to 1979, then increased from 1979 to 1992
   (C) decreased during the years immediately preceding the Shanghai Communique
   (D) increased after the Eighth National People's Congress
   (E) remained relatively unchanged until normalization of diplomatic relations between the two countries in 1979

Question Type: Explicit Detail
Difficulty Level: Moderate

(A) is the best response. In mentioning a twenty-year hiatus (break) in trade between the United States and China (lines 13–14), the author implies that the two countries were engaged in trade just prior to the beginning of that twenty-year period. Since the twenty-year period ended in 1972, it began in 1952.

Incorrect Responses

(B) is partly accurate, but is unsupported in part by the passage. Although the passage is explicit that trade between the two countries increased between 1979 and 1992 (lines 18–20), the passage does not address whether trade increased or decreased between 1972 and 1979; the passage merely indicates that trade "resumed" in 1972; in fact, an increase in trade would seem far more likely during the years immediately after the end of the hiatus than a decrease. Thus, (B) is not fully supported nor is it inferable from the passage.

(C) is unsupported; the time period (C) refers to is the hiatus period before 1972. The passage suggests neither an increase nor a decrease in trade during that period.

(D) is unsupported. The Eighth National People's Congress met in 1993; nowhere in the passage does the author state or imply that trade between the United States and China increased following this event.

(E) runs contrary to the passage, since a significant change in the amount of trade occurred immediately following the Shanghai Communique in 1972.

QUESTION 3

3. The passage mentions all of the following as factors contributing to China's economic growth EXCEPT:

   (A) renewed political relations between China and the United States

(B) the policies of Deng Xiaoping
(C) particular initiatives of the Third Plenum
(D) a decrease in the number of state-owned enterprises
(E) endorsements made by the Eighth Annual People's
       Congress

Question Type: Explicit Detail
Difficulty Level: Easier

(D) is the best response. Although, according to the passage, The Third Plenum adopted initiatives aimed in part at reforming state-owned enterprises (lines 30–35), the passage does not support the assertion that any such reforms occurred or that such reforms actually included a reduction in the number of such enterprises.

Incorrect Responses

(A), (B), (C) and (E) are all mentioned explicitly in the second paragraph following the author's assertion at the beginning of that paragraph that the Chinese economy's "dynamic growth can be attributed to several factors." Accordingly, (A), (B), (C) and (E) are all clearly such factors and are thus incorrect responses.

QUESTION 4

4. The author discusses Guangdong province primarily in order to

       (A) illustrate a political phenomenon
       (B) discount an economic theory
       (C) support a prediction
       (D) help define an historical trend
       (E) rebut an opposing viewpoint

Question Type: Purpose of Detail
Difficulty Level: Moderate

(C) is the best response. In pointing out the prosperity of Guangdong province, the author seeks to point out the disparity in economic development among various regions within China and asserts that such disparity may result in political unrest in the less prosperous areas (lines 72–73). Thus, the prosperity of Guangdong is evidence in support of the author's prediction of political unrest.

(A) is a second-best response. Although the author mentions Guangdong as an example (illustration) of how certain regions are experiencing a greater boom than others, the "boom" that the author refers to is really an economic rather than a political phenomenon. Also, the author's primary purpose in mentioning Guangdong is broader than merely to provide an illustration or an example. Thus, (A) both distorts the information in the passage and is too narrow.

(D) is a second-best response. Although the author is arguably identifying a "trend" in China toward unfettered economic growth, the author's broader purpose in mentioning Guangdong is to forecast possible political consequences of an economic phenomenon. Thus, (D) is off focus and is too narrow.

Other Incorrect Responses

(B) is unsupported. The author neither presents nor discounts any economic theory.

(E) is unsupported. The passage does not present any viewpoint other than the author's own.

QUESTION 5

5. **Which of the following best expresses the main idea of the last paragraph in the passage?**

    (A) **Unless accompanied by political reforms, economic growth and reform in China may result in political instability.**
    (B) **In order to ensure future economic growth, China must continue to trade with the United States.**
    (C) **China's recent economic growth is the result of both improving political relations with the United States and reforms in economic policy.**
    (D) **While positive political developments have been largely responsible for China's recent economic growth, continued unfettered growth may ironically have adverse political consequences in the future.**
    (E) **The potential for United States exports to China, although great, may be adversely affected in the future by both economic and political factors.**

Question Type: Interpretation
Difficulty Level: Moderate

(A) is the best response. In the last paragraph, the author deals exclusively with the possible political consequences of economic reform without political reform, presenting three possible scenarios that may result in political instability.

(D) is the second-best response. Although (D) does encompass the broad point of the last paragraph, (D) goes too far. Statement (D) is broad enough to encompass nearly the entire passage, including both the factors affecting China's economic growth in the past (second paragraph) and those which may affect its growth in the future (third and fourth paragraphs).

Other Incorrect Responses

(B) is off focus and calls for an unwarranted inference. The author discusses the significance of China's trading relationship with the United States in the second and third paragraphs, not in the last paragraph. Furthermore, (B) calls for an unwarranted inference—just because economic growth in the past has resulted in part from improved diplomatic and trade relations with the United States, it does not necessarily follow that continued trade between these two countries is necessary for China's economic growth in the future.

(C) is true but does not respond to the question. Based upon the information in the second and third paragraphs, Statement (C) is an accurate statement. However, since it is not restated or argued further at all in the last paragraph, (C) does not respond to the question.

(E) is off focus. Although Statement (E) may be accurate based upon the last sentence of the third paragraph, the last paragraph is concerned with the internal political consequences of China's policies, not with relations between countries.

QUESTION 6

6. **All of the following factors positively affecting business opportunities for the United States in China are mentioned in the passage EXCEPT:**

   (A) **consumer sentiment in China toward American products**
   (B) **China's laws regarding intellectual property**
   (C) **China's current policies regarding tariffs on imported products**
   (D) **product areas of primary interest among United States firms**
   (E) **China's Most Favored Nation Status**

Question Type: Explicit Detail
Difficulty Level: Moderate

(C) **is the best response.** Although the passage mentions the reduction of nontariff import barriers, tariffs are not mentioned.

Incorrect Responses

(A), (B), (D) and (E) are all mentioned explicitly in the third paragraph as reasons why the United States is likely to be a primary beneficiary of Chinese economic reform.

QUESTION 7

7. **Which of the following would be the most appropriate title for the passage?**

   (A) **Is Political Unrest Inevitable in Light of China's Current Economic Agenda?**
   (B) **A Prescription for Economic Reform In China**
   (C) **Trade Relations Between the United States and China: Historical Perspective and Future Outlook**
   (D) **The Booming Economy of China: Economic and Political Implications**
   (E) **China: One of the World's Fastest Growing Economies**

Question Type: Main Idea
Difficulty Level: Challenging

(D) is the best response. The first part of the title encompasses the first and second paragraphs insofar as these paragraphs describe and explain the current economic boom in China. The second part of the title embraces the third and fourth paragraphs—the third paragraph addresses how the boom will impact the economies of other countries (the United States, in particular), while the fourth paragraph considers the internal political implications of the boom.

Incorrect Responses

(A) is too narrow. Although (A) fairly captures the thrust of the final paragraph, it fails to encompass the historical events contributing to the high current growth rate of the Chinese economy.

(B) is off focus. It suggests that the author is outlining a plan or series of steps (either the author's own or someone else's) necessary to accomplish economic reform in China. Although the passage alludes (in the second paragraph) to a plan devised by the Third Plenum, the author does not elaborate on this plan.

(C) is too narrow. Although the author does discuss (in the second and third paragraphs) the United States' trade history and outlook vis-a-vis China, the author is concerned just as much, and perhaps more so, with China's internal economic reforms and their possible internal political consequences. (C) fails to encompass this concern.

(E) is far too narrow. Although (C) arguably encompasses the information presented in the first two paragraphs, it ignores the author's attention in the third paragraph to the impact of economic reform on international business as well as ignoring the author's concern in the last paragraph for the impact of economic reform on the Chinese political landscape.

PASSAGE #12

In 1930, the centenary of Christina Rossetti's birth, Virginia Woolf reviewed a new biography of her, in which she identified the Victorian poetess as one of Shakespeare's more recent
5   sisters whose life had been reclusively Victorian but whose achievement as an artist was enduring. Rossetti's potent sensual imagery—the richest since Keats—compelled Edmond Gosse, perhaps the most influential critic and bibliophile in late
10   Victorian England, to observe that Christina Rossetti "does not shrink from strong delineation of the pleasures of life even when denouncing them." In the face of Rossetti's virtual canonization by critics at the end of the nineteenth
15   century, Woolf ignores her apparent conservatism, instead seeing in her something of curiosity value and a model of artistic purity and integrity for women writers. What Woolf remembers Rossetti for are her four volumes of explosively
20   original poems loaded with vivid images and dense emotional energy.

"A Birthday," for instance, is no typical Victorian poem and is certainly unlike predictable works of the era's best known women poets.
25   Rossetti's most famous poem, "Goblin Market," bridges the generic space between simplistic fairy tale and complex adult allegory (at once Christian, psychological, and profeminist). Like many of Rossetti's works, it is extraordinary in its
30   originality and unorthodox in its form. Its subject matter is radical and therefore risky for a Victorian poetess because it implies castigations of an economic (and even marital) marketplace dominated by men, whose motives are, at best,
35   suspect. Its Christian allusions are obvious but grounded in opulent images whose lushness borders on the erotic. From Rossetti's work emerge not only emotional force, artistic polish, frequently-ironic playfulness, and intellectual
40   vigor but also an intriguing, enigmatic quality. "Winter: My Secret," for example, combines these traits along with a very high (and un-Victorian) level of poetic self-consciousness.

"How does one reconcile the aesthetic
45   sensuality of Rossetti's poetry with her repressed, ascetic lifestyle?" Woolf wondered (as have many critics after her). That Rossetti did indeed withhold a "secret" both from those intimate with her and from posterity is an argument found at
50   the center of Lona Packer's 1963 biography of Rossetti. While Packer believed Rossetti's to be a secret of the heart, her thesis has been disproved through the discovery of approximately seventeen hundred letters by Rossetti which reinforce
55   the conventional image of her as pious, scrupu-

lously abstinent, and semi-reclusive. The passions expressed in her love poems, if not entirely the products of fantasy or literary tradition, seem to have been largely repressed in real life.
60   Yet those poems, read properly, do expose the "secret" at the heart of both Rossetti's life and art: a willingness to forego worldly pleasures in favor of an aestheticized Christian version of transcendent fulfillment in the heavenly afterlife. Her
65   sonnet "The World," therefore, becomes pivotal in understanding Rossetti's literary project as a whole—including her rhymes for children, her fairy tale narratives, her love poems, her bleak verses of spiritual desolation and death-longing,
70   as well as her books of devotional commentary. The world, for Rossetti, is a fallen place. Her work is pervasively designed to force upon readers an acute sensitivity to this inescapable Christian truth. The beauty of her poetry must be
75   seen therefore as an artistic strategy, a means toward a moral end.

1. Based upon the information in the passage, Virginia Woolf would most likely agree that Rossetti's work

    (A) exposes a secret about Rossetti's life
    (B) describes yet at the same time denounces life's pleasures
    (C) has an enigmatic quality
    (D) affirms that Rossetti was pious and reclusive
    (E) serves as a model of artistic integrity

2. The author refers to all of the following qualities that emerge from Rossetti's work EXCEPT:

    (A) lush imagery
    (B) ironic playfulness
    (C) stark realism
    (D) unorthodox form
    (E) intellectual vigor

GO ON TO THE NEXT PAGE.

3. The author implies that Rossetti's style was similar to that of

    (A) Keats
    (B) Shakespeare
    (C) Gosse
    (D) Woolf
    (E) Packer

4. Which of the following statements is most reasonably inferable from the passage?

    (A) "Winter: My Secret" is Rossetti's best-known poem.
    (B) Rossetti was not among the best-known poets during her era.
    (C) The accounts of Rossetti's life contained in Packer's biography of Rossetti differ from those included in Woolf's biography of Rossetti.
    (D) Rossetti's display of poetic self-consciousness drew criticism from her contemporaries.
    (E) "Goblin Market" was published later than "A Birthday."

5. The passage mentions all of the following types of works by Rossetti EXCEPT:

    (A) the love poem
    (B) the sonnet
    (C) the one-stanza canzone
    (D) the children's rhyme
    (E) the devotional commentary

6. The author discusses Packer's thesis and its flaws in order to

    (A) contrast the sensuality of Rossetti's poetry with the relative starkness of her devotional commentary
    (B) reveal the secret to which Rossetti alludes in "Winter: My Secret"
    (C) call into question the authenticity of recently discovered letters written by Rossetti
    (D) compare Woolf's understanding of Rossetti with a recent, more enlightened view
    (E) provide a foundation for the author's own theory about Rossetti's life and work

7. The author implies that Rossetti's "The World"

    (A) combines several genres of poetry in a single work
    (B) was Rossetti's last major work
    (C) is the most helpful expression of Rossetti's motives
    (D) was Rossetti's longest work
    (E) reflects Rossetti's shift away from her earlier feminist viewpoint

8. Which of the following best expresses the main idea of the passage?

    (A) Newly-discovered evidence suggests that Rossetti's works were misinterpreted by earlier critics and scholars.
    (B) Rossetti can be compared to Shakespeare both in her private life and in the enduring quality of her work.
    (C) Victorian poetry can be properly interpreted only by considering the personal life of the particular poet
    (D) The apparent inconsistency between Rossetti's personal life and literary work are explained by Rossetti's poems themselves.
    (E) Rossetti's artistic integrity served as a model for later women poets.

STOP.

PASSAGE #12—ANSWER KEY

1. E   5. C
2. C   6. E
3. A   7. C
4. B   8. D

PASSAGE #12—ANALYSIS

QUESTION 1

1. Based upon the information in the passage, Virginia Woolf
   would most likely agree that Rossetti's work

   (A) exposes a secret about Rossetti's life
   (B) describes yet at the same time denounces life's pleasures
   (C) has an enigmatic quality
   (D) affirms that Rossetti was pious and reclusive
   (E) serves as a model of artistic integrity

Question Type: Explicit Detail
Difficulty Level: Easier

(E) is the best response. In lines 17–18, the author states that Woolf saw in Rossetti "a model of artistic purity and integrity for women writers."

Incorrect Responses

(A) and (C) confuse the opinions of Woolf with those of the author. The author does indeed discuss, in the third and fourth paragraphs, how some of Rossetti's works revealed a secret about her life and art. Also, in line 40 the author does claim that from Rossetti's work emerges (among other qualities) "an enigmatic quality." However, these are the author's opinions, not those of Woolf.

(B) confuses the opinion of Woolf with that of Edmond Gosse. It was Gosse, not Woolf, who commented that Rosetti "does not shrink from a strong delineation of the pleasures in life even when denouncing them" (lines 11–13).

(D) confuses the information in the passage. In the third paragraph, the author discusses how Rossetti's recently discovered letters confirm that she was pious, scrupulously abstinent, and semi-reclusive. These are not Woolf's impressions of Rossetti's work but rather the author's analysis of Rossetti's personal letters.

QUESTION 2

2. The author refers to all of the following qualities that emerge
   from Rossetti's work EXCEPT:

   (A) lush imagery
   (B) ironic playfulness
   (C) stark realism

(D) unorthodox form
(E) intellectual vigor

Question Type: Explicit Detail
Difficulty Level: Easier

(C) is the best response. In describing Rossetti's work, the author never uses the words "stark" or "realism," nor does the author describe her work in any way that might be re-expressed by either of these terms.

(D) is the second-best response. The author refers to the form of Rossetti's works in reference specifically to "Goblin Market," claiming that in its unorthodox form "Goblin Market" is like many of Rossetti's works. In this way, the author identifies "unorthodox form" as one quality that emerges from Rossetti's work.

Other Incorrect Responses

(A), (B) and (E) are all mentioned explicitly in the second paragraph (lines 35–40) as qualities that emerge from Rossetti's work.

QUESTION 3

3. **The author implies that Rossetti's style was similar to that of**

(A) **Keats**
(B) **Shakespeare**
(C) **Gosse**
(D) **Woolf**
(E) **Packer**

Question Type: Inference
Difficulty Level: Easier

(A) is the best response. The author claims that Rossetti's potent sensual imagery was "the richest since Keats" (line 8). Thus, it can be inferred that Rossetti's style was similar to that of Keats in that both writers used potent sensual imagery.

(B) is the second-best response. (B) distorts the comparison in the passage between Rossetti and Shakespeare. It was Woolf who compared Rossetti to Shakespeare; also, the similarities Woolf noted between the two writers regarded their personal lives and the enduring quality of their works, not their writing styles.

Other Incorrect Responses

(C), (D) and (E) are all discussed in the passage as critics of Rossetti. Their writing styles are wholly irrelevant to and are not discussed at all in the passage.

QUESTION 4

4. **Which of the following statements is most reasonably inferable from the passage?**

(A) "Winter: My Secret" is Rossetti's best-known poem.
(B) Rossetti was not among the best-known poets during her era.
(C) The accounts of Rossetti's life contained in Packer's biography of Rossetti differ from those included in Woolf's biography of Rossetti.
(D) Rossetti's display of poetic self-consciousness drew criticism from her contemporaries.
(E) "Goblin Market" was published later than "A Birthday."

Question Type: Inference
Difficulty Level: Moderate

(B)   is the best response. In the first sentence of the second paragraph, the author states that " 'A Birthday' is no typical Victorian poem and is certainly unlike predictable works of the era's best-known women poets." It is reasonably inferable that Rossetti was not among the era's best-known women poets, at least during her time.

Incorrect Responses

(A)   is contradicted by the passage. The author states that "Market Goblin" is Rossetti's most famous poem (line 25).

(B)   confuses the information in the passage. Woolf reviewed but did not write a biography of Rossetti.

(D)   distorts the information in the passage. The author does indicate that in "Winter: My Secret," Rossetti displayed a high level of poetic self-consciousness (lines 41–43). However, the author neither states nor implies that Rossetti drew criticism during her lifetime as a result. To the contrary, the fact that she was virtually canonized by critics at the end of the nineteenth century (lines 13–15) suggests her work was the object of very little negative criticism from her contemporaries.

(E)   distorts the information in the passage. Although the author discusses "Goblin Market" after "My Birthday," the author neither states nor implies which work was written earlier.

QUESTION 5

5. The passage mentions all of the following types of works by Rossetti EXCEPT:

(A) the love poem
(B) the sonnet
(C) the one-stanza canzone
(D) the children's rhyme
(E) the devotional commentary

Question Type: Explicit Detail
Difficulty Level: Easier

(C) is the best response. The passage makes no mention of this literary form.

Incorrect Responses

(A), (B), (D) and (E) are all mentioned explicitly in the last paragraph as different types of works by Rossetti.

QUESTION 6

6. The author discusses Packer's thesis and its flaws in order to

   (A) contrast the sensuality of Rossetti's poetry with the relative starkness of her devotional commentary
   (B) reveal the secret to which Rossetti alludes in "Winter: My Secret"
   (C) call into question the authenticity of recently discovered letters written by Rossetti
   (D) compare Woolf's understanding of Rossetti with a recent, more enlightened view
   (E) provide a foundation for the author's own theory about Rossetti's life and work

Question Type: Purpose of Detail
Difficulty Level: Challenging

(E) is the best response. The author's threshold purpose in discussing Packer's biography is to affirm that Rossetti's style of writing was not a reflection of her personal lifestyle. Having dismissed the theory that Rossetti was keeping secrets about her life, the author goes on (in the final paragraph) to offer a better explanation for the apparent contradiction between Rossetti's lifestyle and the emotional, sensual style of her poetry.

Incorrect Responses

(A) distorts the information in the passage. First, the passage does not indicate that Rossetti's devotional commentary was in the form of prose rather than poetry. Second, nowhere in the passage does the author compare or contrast Rossetti's devotional commentary with her other works.

(B) distorts and actually runs contrary to the author's purpose. The author discusses Packer's biography to affirm that Rossetti's style of writing was not a reflection of her personal lifestyle—in other words, that she was not keeping secrets about her life. In this sense, Response (B) actually runs contrary to the author's purpose.

(C) distorts the information in the third paragraph. The author does not raise the issue of whether these letters were actually written by Rossetti. In fact, insofar as the author mentions these letters to disprove Packer's thesis, the author seems to affirm that the letters are indeed authentic.

(D) distorts and actually runs contrary to the information in the passage. The author compares Woolf's view only with that of Gosse, who actually preceded Woolf; in this sense, then, Response (D) distorts the information in the passage. Second,

Packer's thesis does not reflect a more enlightened view; to the contrary, the author points out that Packer's thesis has been disproved.

QUESTION 7

7. The author implies that Rossetti's "The World"

    (A) combines several genres of poetry in a single work
    (B) was Rossetti's last major work
    (C) is the most helpful expression of Rossetti's motives
    (D) was Rossetti's longest work
    (E) reflects Rossetti's shift away from her earlier feminist
             viewpoint

Question Type: Inference
Difficulty Level: Moderate

(C) **is the best response.** In the final paragraph, the author states that "The World" is "pivotal in understanding Rossetti's literary project as a whole." Based upon the remainder of the final paragraph, the author seems to understand Rossetti's "literary project as a whole" as an attempt to convey an inescapable Christian truth to her readers (see lines 71–74). It is reasonably inferable, then, that "The World" provides significant insight into Rossetti's motives.

Incorrect Responses

(A) is contradicted by the passage. The author identifies "The World" as a sonnet (one type of poetry), never suggesting that it might incorporate other types of poetry as well.

(B) calls for speculation. Although "The World" is the last of Rossetti's works discussed in the passage, it does not necessarily follow that it was Rossetti's last major work.

(D) calls for speculation. The author neither states nor implies that "The World" is Rossetti's longest work; indeed, nowhere in the passage does the author mention the length of any of Rossetti's works.

(E) distorts the information in the passage. The author suggests that "The World" is pivotal in understanding Rossetti's general literary agenda: to convey an inescapable Christian truth to her readers. However, the author neither states nor implies that Rossetti's motives in writing "The World" or her viewpoint at the time she wrote it departed from earlier motives or viewpoints.

QUESTION 8

8. Which of the following best expresses the main idea of the
    passage?

    (A) Newly-discovered evidence suggests that Rossetti's works
             were misinterpreted by earlier critics and scholars.

    (B) **Rossetti can be compared to Shakespeare both in her private life and in the enduring quality of her work.**

    (C) **Victorian poetry can be properly interpreted only by considering the personal life of the particular poet.**

    (D) **The apparent inconsistency between Rossetti's personal life and literary work are explained by Rossetti's poems themselves.**

    (E) **Rossetti's artistic integrity served as a model for later women poets.**

Question Type: Main Idea
Difficulty Level: Moderate

(D) **is the best response.** The author's primary concern in the first two paragraphs is to point out that Rossetti's work conflicts with her apparently-conservative personal life. The author's own impressions of Rossetti's work are corroborated by those of Woolf and Gosse. The third paragraph begins by asking how to reconcile this apparent conflict (the newly discovered letters discussed in the third paragraph only reinforce the inconsistency between her personal life and literary work). In the last paragraph, the author attempts to explain the inconsistency by examining Rossetti's love poems (particularly, her sonnet "The World").

(A) **is the second-best response.** The newly-discovered personal letters disprove Packer's thesis that Rossetti may have had personal affairs of the heart that she kept secret. Thus, Packer (and possibly Woolf) may have misinterpreted Rossetti's works by assuming that Rossetti wrote from personal experience. However, the author does not make this point explicit in the passage. Moreover, this point is far too narrow. It ignores the author's own explanation (in the final paragraph) for the apparent inconsistency between Rossetti's personal life and her work.

Other Incorrect Responses

(B) is off focus. Admittedly, in the first paragraph the author does point out that Woolf compared Rossetti to Shakespeare in both of these respects. However, the author makes no further attempt to explain or describe these similarities. Moreover, the point made in Response (B) is Woolf's point, not the author's.

(C) distorts the author's argument and is too broad. First, in the last paragraph the author seems to claim that, through a proper reading of Rossetti's love poems, one can understand the ironic, enigmatic, contradictory nature of her work (in turn explaining the inconsistency between Rossetti's personal life and work). In this sense Response (C) distorts and actually runs contrary to the author's argument. Second, the passage concerns only Rossetti, not Victorian poetry or poetry in general, as (C) suggests; in this sense, then, (C) is too broad.

(E) is off focus. While the author does point out in the first paragraph that Woolf viewed Rossetti's work as a model for women writers, this is Woolf's point, not the author's. Moreover, the author does not elaborate on this point—there is no further discussion of particular women writers who might have seen Rossetti as a model for their own work.

LONGER PASSAGES (for the MCAT)
BEGIN ON THE NEXT PAGE

MCAT passages are 650–700 words in length and are accompanied by 6–8 questions each. Try to LIMIT YOUR TIME TO 10 MINUTES for each of the following three passages (#13, #14, and #15).

NOTE TO GRE, LSAT, AND GMAT STUDENTS:
Although the next three passages are a bit longer than those appearing on your exam, go ahead and try them—MCAT passages are comparable in style and difficulty level to those appearing on the GRE, LSAT, and GMAT. Just remember that you won't allot as much time to the passages that appear on your exam.

PASSAGE #13

Although accounts differ as to which of two men—Hiawatha or Degandawida—played a more significant role in founding the Iroquois League of Indian nations, it is generally agreed among
(5) anthropologists and historians that the principles on which the League was founded were formulated by Degandawida, while Hiawatha served as his advocate. Because the League proposed by Degandawida was a radical step in an unfamiliar
(10) direction for the warring and fiercely-autonomous Iroquois nations, acceptance required that the League be tied to familiar Iroquois customs and institutions.

Degandawida's philosophy that warring nations could lay down their arms and become partners was
(15) embraced by the Iroquois only by his associating this notion with the Iroquois custom by which the families of slain warriors adopted war prisoners into the tribe to prevent the tribe's male population from dwindling. Degandawida also used unquestioned
(20) social institutions as symbols. He compared the League to the traditional Iroquois clan in which several families share a "Longhouse," likening the Great Council, comprised of representatives from each member nation, to the ever-burning Council Fire
(25) of the Longhouse. To ease the Iroquois' fear of losing national identity, Degandawida assigned a meaning-ful League title as well as specific duties to each nation. The powerful Mohawks, for example, were given the title "Keepers of the Eastern Door" and
(30) were given a council veto, while the Onondagas, who were centrally-positioned geographically, were made "Fire Keepers" or perpetual hosts. Degandawida also replicated the power structure of the traditional Iroquois clan. Each of the five Iroquois nations was
(35) comprised of matriarchal totemic clans in which, although the clan's chiefs were men, the heads of the clan were women. A chief's children were considered members of his wife's clan. Degandawida determined that the heads of each nation should select their
(40) League representatives, thereby effectively precluding the possibility of League representatives passing their power on to their sons as well as decreasing the likelihood that a pro-war representative would be appointed.
(45) Unification of the Iroquois nations lasted for over two hundred years, until the American Revolution of 1776 when disagreement as to whether they should become involved in the war divided the Iroquois. Due to the success of the revolutionaries and the
(50) encroachment upon Iroquois lands that followed, many Iroquois resettled in Canada while those who remained behind lost the respect they had enjoyed among other Indian nations. The introduction of distilled spirits resulted in widespread alcoholism,
(55) leading in turn to the rapid decline of both the culture and the population. The influence of the Quakers impeded, yet in another sense contributed to, this decline. By establishing schools for the Iroquois and by introducing them to modern technology for
(60) agriculture and husbandry, the Quakers instilled in the Iroquois some hope for the future yet undermined the Iroquois' sense of national identity.

Ironically, it was the alcoholic half-brother of Seneca Cornplanter, perhaps the most outspoken
(65) proponent among the Iroquois for assimilation of white customs and institutions, who can be credited with reviving the Iroquois culture. Inspired by a near-death vision in 1799, Handsome Lake, a former member of the Great Council, established a new
(70) religion among the Iroquois that tied the more useful aspects of Christianity to traditional Indian beliefs and customs. Within a year, Handsome Lake had converted most of the Iroquois to his religion and had assumed an unprecedented position of power in the
(75) tribe. His teachings became firmly entrenched among the Iroquois and sparked reunification and renewed confidence, while also helping to end rampant alcoholism. The influence of Handsome Lake is still evident today; many modern-day Iroquois belong to
(80) both the religion of Handsome Lake and to one or another Christian sect. However, due in part to this dualism and in part to an absence of hierarchy, organization, or even a name, the extent of his influence upon modern-day Iroquois culture is not readily determinable.

1. The passage refers to all of the following ways by which Degandawida persuaded the Iroquois to join his League of Indian Nations EXCEPT:

    (A) drawing an analogy between the Longhouse and the League
    (B) assigning each member nation its own specific duties
    (C) devising a system of representation that avoided family dynasties
    (D) likening the notion that enemies could become allies to the adoption of war prisoners
    (E) allowing each nation a council veto in matters affecting all nations

2. In stating that the heads of the nations should select council representatives, thereby "decreasing the likelihood that a pro-war representative would be appointed" (lines 42–44), the author implies that

  (A) women were more likely to select peace-loving representatives than were men
  (B) heads of the nations were less likely to select pro-war representatives than were heads of the individual totemic clams
  (C) war was more likely where power was passed down by a chief to his children
  (D) a chief's children were more likely to favor war than were other members of the totemic clan
  (E) children of clan heads were less likely to favor war than were the chief's children

3. Which of the following best characterizes the structure of the passage as a whole?

  (A) A theory is presented and then applied to two related historical phenomena.
  (B) Two historical figures are introduced; then the nature and extent of their influence are compared.
  (C) The inception of an historical phenomenon is examined; then the subsequent life of the phenomenon is traced.
  (D) Competing views respecting an historical phenomenon are presented and then evaluated based upon empirical evidence.
  (E) An historical event is recounted; then possible explanations for the event are presented.

4. The passage mentions all of the following events as contributing to the decline of the Iroquois culture EXCEPT:

  (A) new educational opportunities for the Iroquois people
  (B) divisive power struggles among the leaders of the Iroquois nations
  (C) introduction of new farming technologies
  (D) territorial threats against the Iroquois nations
  (E) discord among the nations regarding their role in the American Revolution

5. Among the following reasons, it is most likely that the author considers Handsome Lake's leading a revival of the Iroquois culture to be "ironic" (line 63) because

  (A) he was a former member of the Great Council
  (B) he was not a full-blooded relative of Seneca Cornplanter
  (C) he was related by blood to a chief proponent of assimilation
  (D) he was alcoholic
  (E) his religious beliefs conflicted with traditional Iroquois beliefs

6. Assuming that the reasons asserted in the passage for the decline of the Iroquois culture are historically representative of the decline of cultural minorities, which of the following developments would most likely contribute to the demise of a modern-day ethnic minority?

  (A) a bilingual education program in which children who are members of the minority group learn to read and write in both their traditional language and the language prevalent in the present culture
  (B) a tax credit for residential-property owners who lease their property to members of the minority group
  (C) increased efforts by local government to eradicate the availability of illegal drugs
  (D) a government-sponsored program to assist minority-owned businesses in using computer technology to improve efficiency
  (E) the declaration of a national holiday commemorating a past war in which the minority group played an active role

7. Based upon the information in the passage, the author would agree that Degandawida and Handsome Lake most resembled each other in which of the following respects?

  (A) They combined traditional Iroquois religious beliefs and the most useful aspects of Christianity.
  (B) They drew upon their knowledge of Iroquois customs and traditions to persuade the Iroquois people.
  (C) Their policies were aimed at uniting the Iroquois people against the white settlers.
  (D) Their efforts resulted in peace among the formerly feuding Iroquois factions.
  (E) Their teachings were largely responsible for a decline of alcoholism among the Iroquois population.

STOP.

PASSAGE #13—ANSWER KEY

1. E
2. A
3. C
4. B
5. C
6. D
7. B

PASSAGE #13—ANALYSIS

QUESTION 1

1. **The passage refers to all of the following ways by which Degandawida persuaded the Iroquois to join his League of Indian Nations EXCEPT:**

    (A) drawing an analogy between the Longhouse and the League
    (B) assigning each member nation its own specific duties
    (C) devising a system of representation that avoided family dynasties
    (D) likening the notion that enemies could become allies to the adoption of war prisoners
    (E) allowing each nation a council veto in matters affecting all nations

Question Type: Explicit Detail
Difficulty Level: Moderate

(E) **is the best response.** The last sentence in the first paragraph suggests that the second paragraph will discuss ways in which Degandawida tied the League to familiar Iroquois customs and institutions to gain acceptance of his League. (E) is the only response that is not supported explicitly by the information in the second paragraph. Although the Mohawks were given a council veto in order to acknowledge their power, the passage does not indicate that any other nations were given veto power.

Incorrect Responses

(A) is well supported by the second paragraph. According to the passage, Degandawida drew an analogy between traditional institutions—the Longhouse and Council Fire—and the concepts of the League and the Great Council to help the Iroquois appreciate the League's meaning and significance (lines 20–25).

(B) is well supported by the second paragraph. According to the passage, each nation was assigned specific duties in order to ease its fear of losing national identity (lines 26–28).

(C) is well supported by the second paragraph. A system for selecting representatives by which the heads of the clans—i.e., the chiefs' wives—were to make the selections effectively precluded the possibility of representatives passing down their power to their sons (lines 38–42).

(D) is well supported by the second paragraph. Degandawida compared the custom of adopting war prisoners into the captor's tribe to the peace-making process in order to persuade the Iroquois that long-standing enemies could lay down their arms and become brothers (lines 15–19).

QUESTION 2

2. In stating that the heads of the nations should select council representatives, thereby "decreasing the likelihood that a pro-war representative would be appointed (lines 42–44)," the author implies that

(A) women were more likely to select peace-loving representatives than were men

(B) heads of the nations were less likely to select pro-war representatives than were heads of the individual totemic clams

(C) war was more likely where power was passed down by a chief to his children

(D) a chief's children were more likely to favor war than were other members of the totemic clan

(E) children of clan heads were less likely to favor war than were the chief's children

Question Type: Inference
Difficulty Level: Challenging

(A) **is the best response.** The passage states that the heads of each nation (i.e., the clan heads) were women, while the chiefs were men; the passage goes on to state that, according to Degandawida, the clan heads (women) rather than the chiefs (men) should select League representatives because the likelihood that a pro-war representative would be appointed would be decreased thereby. Among the five responses, the only response that is inferable from this information is that Degandawida believed the men to be more pro-war than the women—i.e., Statement (A).

(D) **is a second-best response.** Statement (D) is of the same nature substantively as Statement (A). Qualitatively, however, (D) calls for an unwarranted inference. The passage does imply a connection between a chief's passing power down to his children and the children's propensity for war, but only insofar as men (e.g., chiefs) are more likely to choose pro-war representatives than are women [see Response (A)]. However, the additional inference that a chief's children are more likely to favor war than all other clan members is unwarranted based upon the information in the passage. Although the passage supports the idea that women are less likely than men to select pro-war representatives, the passage does not suggest that, of the male population in a clan, a chief's children have the greatest propensity for war.

(E)   is a second-best response. Statement (E) is defective in much the same way as (D). The passage does imply a connection between a chief's passing power down to his children and the children's propensity for war, but only insofar as men (e.g., chiefs) are more likely to choose pro-war representatives than are women [see Response (A)]. (D) suggests a comparison (in terms of propensity for war) between the chiefs' children and the children of the clan heads. However, the passage does not support the inference that children of a clan head will be less likely than any other member of the clan to want war.

Other Incorrect Responses

(B)   is unsupported and distorts the information in the passage. The author makes no comparison in terms of the propensity for war between clan heads and nation heads because a nation's heads and the heads of that nation's clans were one and the same. Statement (B) suggests, however, that a nation's heads are different people from the clan heads.

(C)   confuses the information presented in the pertinent part of the passage. The author does not make a connection between family dynasties and the propensity for war.

QUESTION 3

3.   Which of the following best characterizes the structure of the passage as a whole?

(A)   A theory is presented and then applied to two related historical phenomena.

(B)   Two historical figures are introduced; then the nature and extent of their influence are compared.

(C)   The inception of an historical phenomenon is examined; then the subsequent life of the phenomenon is traced.

(D)   Competing views respecting an historical phenomenon are presented and then evaluated based upon empirical evidence.

(E)   An historical event is recounted; then possible explanations for the event are presented.

Question Type: Primary Purpose
Difficulty Level: Moderate

(C)   is the best response. The first and second paragraphs are concerned with the inception of the Iroquois League, while the third and fourth paragraphs outline the subsequent history of the League from its decline through its subsequent resurgence under Handsome Lake. Statement (C) recapitulates this overall structure.

(A) **is the second-best response.** It could be argued that the author is presenting a "theory" as to how the Iroquois were swayed by Degandawida and later by Handsome Lake and that the "two related historical phenomena" mentioned in Statement (A) refer to the inception of the League (under Degandawida) and its revival (under Handsome Lake). However, the author presents the information as historical facts rather than as theories—that is, the passage merely recounts historical events rather than seeking to explain them by way of a more fundamental theory. Moreover, Statement (A) omits the discussion in the third paragraph concerning the decline of the Iroquois culture; in this sense, then, (A) is too narrow.

Other Incorrect Responses

(B) distorts the overall view of the passage. Although two historical figures—Degandawida and Hiawatha—are indeed introduced in the first paragraph, the author makes no attempt to trace Hiawatha's influence or to compare the influence of these two men. An argument can be made that Statement (B) refers to Degandawida and Handsome Lake (not to Degandawida and Hiawatha) since the passage does examine the influence of both of these men. However, no attempt is made to compare their influence. Also, although Handsome Lake is not mentioned until the last paragraph, Statement (B) suggests that the two historical figures are introduced early in the passage.

(D) is unsupported. Nowhere in the passage are "competing views" presented or evaluated.

(E) is far too narrow and is unsupported. The passage does provide some explanation for the three phases (inception, decline, and revival) of the Iroquois history, but is the "historical event" to which Statement (E) refers the inception of the League, its decline, or its resurgence? Since the passage discusses all three, (E) is far too narrow to reflect the overall structure of the passage.

QUESTION 4

4. **The passage mentions all of the following events as contributing to the decline of the Iroquois culture EXCEPT:**

   (A) **new educational opportunities for the Iroquois people**
   (B) **divisive power struggles among the leaders of the Iroquois nations**
   (C) **introduction of new farming technologies**
   (D) **territorial threats against the Iroquois nations**
   (E) **discord among the nations regarding their role in the American Revolution**

Question Type: Explicit Detail
Difficulty Level: Easier

(B) **is the best response.** Nowhere in this paragraph does the author mention any power struggles among the leaders of the Iroquois nations. Although the third paragraph does refer to a dispute among the Iroquois leaders, the dispute regarded the role that the Iroquois should play in the American Revolution [Response (E)].

Incorrect Responses

(A), (C), (D) and (E) are all explicitly mentioned in the third paragraph as factors contributing to the decline of the Iroquois culture.

QUESTION 5

5. Among the following reasons, it is most likely that the author considers Handsome Lake's leading a revival of the Iroquois culture to be "ironic" (line 63) because

   (A) he was a former member of the Great Council
   (B) he was not a full-blooded relative of Seneca Cornplanter
   (C) he was related by blood to a chief proponent of assimilation
   (D) he was alcoholic
   (E) his religious beliefs conflicted with traditional Iroquois beliefs

Question Type: Interpretation
Difficulty Level: Easier

(C) **is the best response.** The passage states that Cornplanter was an outspoken proponent of assimilation and that Handsome Lake was related to Cornplanter as a half-brother. The fact that Lake was responsible for the Iroquois reasserting their national identity is ironic, then, in light of Lake's blood relationship to Cornplanter.

Incorrect Responses

(A), (B) and (D) are all accurate statements, based upon the information in the passage. However, they do not respond to the question.

(E) runs contrary to the information in the passage and fails to respond to the question. Lake emphasized the similarities between Christianity and his brand of Iroquois religion; the passage does not deal with the differences between Christianity and the Iroquois' traditional beliefs. Moreover, even if (E) were supported by the passage, it is not the irony to which the author refers.

QUESTION 6

6. Assuming that the reasons asserted in the passage for the decline of the Iroquois culture are historically representative of the decline of cultural minorities, which of the following

developments would most likely contribute to the demise of a modern-day ethnic minority?

(A) a bilingual education program in which children who are members of the minority group learn to read and write in both their traditional language and the language prevalent in the present culture

(B) a tax credit for residential-property owners who lease their property to members of the minority group

(C) increased efforts by local government to eradicate the availability of illegal drugs

(D) a government-sponsored program to assist minority-owned businesses in using computer technology to improve efficiency

(E) the declaration of a national holiday commemorating a past war in which the minority group played an active role

Question Type: Extrapolation
Difficulty Level: Challenging

(D) is the best response. According to the passage, the Quaker's introduction of new technology to the Iroquois was partly responsible for the decline of the Iroquois culture in that it contributed to their loss of national identity. (D) presents a similar situation.

(A) is the second-best response. Insofar as the children referred to in scenario (A) learn the language of the prevailing culture, assimilation and a resulting loss of ethnic identity might tend to occur. However, this sense of identity might be reinforced by their learning to read and write in their traditional language as well. Therefore, (A) is not as likely to lead to the demise of the minority group as (D), at least based upon the Iroquois' experience as discussed in the passage.

Other Incorrect Responses

(B) is too vague and is not supported. Whether a government incentive to provide housing for members of the minority group actually undermines the group's sense of ethnic identity would probably depend upon whether the incentives result in integration or segregation. Moreover, since the passage does not address whether the Iroquois became geographically integrated (assimilated), scenario (B) is insupportable.

(C) would probably carry the opposite result from that called for in the question. The scenario posed in (C) would actually contribute to the minority group's retaining its ethnic identity, at least based upon the information in the passage. According to the passage, the introduction of spirits to the Iroquois population led to rampant alcoholism, which in turn contributed to the culture's decline. Similarly, widespread drug abuse might have a similar effect today. Accordingly, any effort to curb such abuse—e.g., scenario (C)—would tend to impede a decline rather than contribute to it.

(E) like (C) would carry a result opposite from that called for in the question; (E) is also unsupported. Any ceremony or holiday calling attention to the ethnic population as a distinct group and helping to bring the population together as a group under a shared experience would tend to reinforce a sense of identity. Moreover, the passage does not refer to any developments during the time of the Iroquois decline that might be similar in any way to scenario (C); accordingly, (C) is unsupported.

QUESTION 7

7. Based upon the information in the passage, the author would agree that Degandawida and Handsome Lake most resembled each other in which of the following respects?

(A) They combined traditional Iroquois religious beliefs and the most useful aspects of Christianity.

(B) They drew upon their knowledge of Iroquois customs and traditions to persuade the Iroquois people.

(C) Their policies were aimed at uniting the Iroquois people against the white settlers.

(D) Their efforts resulted in peace among the formerly feuding Iroquois factions.

(E) Their teachings were largely responsible for a decline of alcoholism among the Iroquois population.

Question Type: Interpretation
Difficulty Level: Easier

(B) **is the best response.** Both men had a thorough understanding of Iroquois traditions. Degandawida used Iroquois traditions as symbols to convey concepts and as models for the structure of his League, all with the goal of persuading the nations to join his League. Similarly, Handsome Lake's use of traditional religious beliefs helped convert the Iroquois people to his new religion.

(D) **is the second-best response.** Statement (D) is only partly supported by the passage. Although Degandawida's efforts did result in a new and lasting peace among the Iroquois, the author does not make a similar claim with respect to Handsome Lake. Admittedly, the passage does mention a dispute among the Iroquois as to their proper role in the American Revolution. However, it is unwarranted to infer from this fact that the Iroquois factions were feuding amongst themselves just prior to Lake or that Lake's influence was responsible for some sort of new peace.

Other Incorrect Responses

(A) is not supported. Although the author explicitly mentions that Handsome Lake combined Christianity and the traditional Iroquois religion, there is no indication in the passage of any similar efforts by Degandawida.

(C) is not supported. Although the policies of both men were indeed aimed at uniting the Iroquois, the author does not suggest that either man's efforts were directed toward establishing an opposing force against the white settlers.

(E) is not supported. Although the passage does explicitly acknowledge Lake's influence in the decline of alcoholism among the Iroquois, no similar influence is mentioned with respect to Degandawida.

PASSAGE #14

While disease is omnipresent and prior to social organization, communal life creates special hazards. While the organization of society can reduce the dangers of disease, trade and urbanization, with their
(5) consequent problems of sanitation and pollution, can also exacerbate such dangers. Epidemiological phenomena can be seen most starkly in the coloni-zation of the New World by Europeans. As is well known, European settlement wreaked havoc on the
(10) native population by exposing it to Old World diseases. Even within the white settlements of North America, however, it was urbanization (without adequate sanitation) accompanied by international trade that brought forth repeated epidemics of yellow
(15) fever and cholera, and, later, the enduring epidemic of tuberculosis. Even in the mid-twentieth century, during the brief calm between the polio and AIDS epidemics when communicable disease seemed anachronistic, epidemic health risks associated with
(20) carcinogens from polluted air threatened the industrialized world.

To the economist, efforts to combat these risks are at least partially public goods. The benefits from public goods are indivisible among beneficiaries. A
(25) sole private purchaser of health care would give others in society a "free ride" with respect to the benefits obtained. For example, one's vaccination protects another from infection. Conversely, the costs of failing to pay for such goods may be borne by
(30) others. To market theorists, such goods are legitimate objects of governmental intervention in the market. While the theory of public goods helps explain aspects of public health law and assists in fitting it into modern economic theory, it omits a critical point.
(35) Ill health is not a mere byproduct of economic activity. It is an inevitable concomitant of human existence. As a result, wherever there is human society, there will be public health. Every society has to face the risks of disease. And because it must,
(40) every society searches to make disease, like mortality, comprehensible within the context of the society's own particular culture, theology, or science. In this sense, health care is public not only because its benefits are indivisible and threats to it arise from
(45) factors outside of the individual but also because communal life gives individuals the cultural context in which to understand it.

Governments typically have assumed an active role with respect to health care, acting as if their role
(50) were obligatory. How governments have fulfilled that duty has varied throughout time and across societies, according not only to the wealth and scientific sophistication of the culture but also to its funda-mental values—because health is defined in part by a
(55) community's belief system, public health measures

will necessarily reflect cultural norms and values. In highly religious societies, the preservation and regulation of health is intermingled with theological considerations. In our more secular era, governments
(60) rely on less theistic approaches, such as investment in medical research.

Those who criticize the United States government today for not providing health care to all citizens equate the provision of health care with insurance
(65) coverage for the costs of medical expenses. By this standard, seventeenth- and eighteenth-century America lacked any significant conception of public health law. However, despite the general paucity of bureaucratic organization in pre-industrial America,
(70) the vast extent of health regulation and provision stands out as remarkable. Of course the public role in the protection and regulation of eighteenth-century health was carried out in ways quite different from those today. Organizations responsible for health
(75) regulation were less stable than modern bureaucra-cies, tending to appear in crises and wither away in periods of calm. The focus was on epidemics which were seen as unnatural and warranting a response, not to the many endemic and chronic conditions
(80) which were accepted as part and parcel of daily life. Additionally, and not surprisingly, religious influence was significant, especially in the seventeenth century. Finally, in an era which lacked sharp demarcations between private and governmental bodies, many
(85) public responsibilities were carried out by what we would now consider private associations. Neverthe-less, the extent of public health regulation long before the dawn of the welfare state is remarkable and suggests that the founding generation's assumptions
(90) about the relationship between government and health were more complex than is commonly assumed.

1. In the passage, the author's primary purpose is to:

(A) present and evaluate different views regarding the proper role of government in the provision of health care

(B) argue for the expansion of the United States government's role regarding the provision of health care

(C) trace the historical development of the United States government's role in the provision of health care

(D) discuss the societal causes of epidemic disease and propose a policy for addressing those causes

(E) examine and explain the reasons for the different ways in which governments have fulfilled their perceived obligation with respect to health care

2. The author mentions all of the following as causes of epidemiological phenomena EXCEPT:

   (A) inadequate preventive health care
   (B) international trade
   (C) urbanization
   (D) inadequate sanitation
   (E) pollution

3. Based upon the information in the passage, the author would agree that health care is inherently a public concern for all of the following reasons EXCEPT:

   (A) The benefits of health care are indivisible among its beneficiaries.
   (B) The health of an individual person is affected in part by societal factors.
   (C) Governments have typically acted as if they have a duty to provide health care.
   (D) Disease is fully comprehended only within the context of one's particular culture.
   (E) The costs of one person's failing to pay for health care is often borne by others.

4. Which of the following best characterizes the market theorists' argument for public health care as viewed by the author of the passage?

   (A) theoretically sound
   (B) empirically unsupported
   (C) politically biased
   (D) cogent but inadequate
   (E) irrelevant in today's cultural environment

5. Among the following statements about the United States government's role in the provision of health care, which finds the least support in the passage?

   (A) The government today addresses health concerns that formerly were not considered serious enough to warrant government involvement.
   (B) What were once public health-care functions are now served by the private sector.
   (C) Philosophical considerations play a less significant role today in the formulation of public health-care policies than in previous centuries.
   (D) Public health care today is guided largely by secular rather than religious values.
   (E) Modern public health-care agencies are typically established not as temporary measures but rather as permanent establishments.

6. Which of the following best expresses the author's point of contention with "those who criticize the United States government for not providing health care to all citizens" (lines 62–63)?

   (A) Their standard for measuring such provision is too narrow.
   (B) They underestimate the role that insurance plays in the provision of health care today.
   (C) They fail to recognize that government plays a more significant role today in health care than in previous eras.
   (D) They misunderstand the intent of the founding generation with respect to the proper role of the government in the area of health care.
   (E) They lack any significant conception of public health law.

7. Which of the following best expresses the main point of the last paragraph in the passage?

   (A) The government's role in health care has not expanded over time to the extent that many critics have asserted.
   (B) The government should limit its involvement in health care to epidemiological problems.
   (C) Health problems plaguing pre-industrial America resulted largely from inadequate public health care.
   (D) History suggests that the United States government has properly played a significant role in provision of health care.
   (E) Private insurance is an inadequate solution to the problem of health care.

STOP.

PASSAGE #14—ANSWER KEY

1.	A	3.	C	5.	C	7.	D
2.	A	4.	D	6.	A		

PASSAGE #14—ANALYSIS

QUESTION 1

1. In the passage, the author's primary purpose is to:

   (A) present and evaluate different views regarding the proper
       role of government in the provision of health care
   (B) argue for the expansion of the United States government's
       role regarding the provision of health care
   (C) trace the historical development of the United States
       government's role in the provision of health care
   (D) discuss the societal causes of epidemic disease and propose
       a policy for addressing those causes
   (E) examine and explain the reasons for the different ways in
       which governments have fulfilled their perceived obligation
       with respect to health care

Question Type: Primary Purpose
Difficulty Level: Moderate

(A) is the best response. In the passage, the author presents and critiques (i.e.,
evaluates) both the economists' point of view (second paragraph) and the view of
modern-day critics of the government (fourth paragraph) regarding the proper
role of government in health care. Admittedly, Response (A) does not embrace
the entire passage—it does not encompass the discussion in the third paragraph
regarding the extent and manner in which governments have historically
provided health care, nor does it encompass the author's suggestion at the close
of the passage regarding the founding generation's probable intent as to the
proper role of government in health care. However, in the context of this short
passage, these two areas of discussion are not of primary concern to the author.

Incorrect Responses

(B) is unsupported. Although the author takes the position that government should
play a significant role in health care, nowhere does the author go so far as to
suggest that the United States government's role in health care today is too small.
Although, in the last paragraph, the author rebuts the critics' argument that
government is not providing health care to all citizens, the author does not go so
far as to assert that the government's present role should be expanded.

(C) is too narrow. Although the last paragraph discusses some of the changes regarding the U.S. government's role in health care over the last three centuries, the
author's broader concern is to point out that the government has always played a
significant role in this area because health care is inherently a public concern.

(D) is unsupported. Although epidemic diseases are inherently associated with communal life, the author argues more broadly that health care is inherently a public concern and should be addressed by government. Also, the author does not offer a prescription for dealing with the underlying causes of epidemics; thus, the second portion of (D) is off focus and is unsupported.

(E) is too narrow. This response encompasses the discussion in the third paragraph only. This paragraph does examine some of the ways in which governments have fulfilled their perceived role in health care and does indeed explain why different governments have offered different solutions to health-care problems. However, this discussion is peripheral to the author's primary argument that health care is inherently public and that government should therefore play a role in health care.

QUESTION 2

2. The author mentions all of the following as causes of epidemiological phenomena EXCEPT:

   (A) inadequate preventive health care
   (B) international trade
   (C) urbanization
   (D) inadequate sanitation
   (E) pollution

Question Type: Explicit Detail
Difficulty Level: Easier

(A) is the best response. Causes of epidemiological phenomena are discussed only in the first paragraph. Preventive health care is not mentioned.

Incorrect Responses

(B), (C), (D) and (E) are all mentioned explicitly in the first paragraph as contributing causes of epidemiological phenomena.

QUESTION 3

3. Based upon the information in the passage, the author would agree that health care is inherently a public concern for all of the following reasons EXCEPT:

   (A) The benefits of health care are indivisible among its beneficiaries.
   (B) The health of an individual person is affected in part by societal factors.
   (C) Governments have typically acted as if they have a duty to provide health care.
   (D) Disease is fully comprehended only within the context of one's particular culture.
   (E) The costs of one person's failing to pay for health care is often borne by others.

Question Type: Explicit Detail
Difficulty Level: Challenging

(C) **is the best response.** Although (C) may be a true statement (see lines 48–50), it does not respond to the question. The fact that governments have typically acted as if they had a health-care obligation is not mentioned by the author as a reason why health care is inherently a public concern, but rather as empirical evidence that health care is inherently a public concern.

Incorrect Responses

(A), (B) and **(E)** restate arguments made by market theorists (second paragraph) in favor of the inherently-public nature of health care. Although the author asserts that the market theorists' explanation is inadequate ("misses a critical point"), the author nevertheless expresses some agreement with their explanation ("the theory of public goods helps explain aspects of public health law...").

(D) expresses the author's sociological argument, contained in the latter portion of the second paragraph (lines 35–42), for the inherently-public nature of health care.

QUESTION 4

4. **Which of the following best characterizes the market theorists' argument for public health care as viewed by the author of the passage?**
   (A) theoretically sound
   (B) empirically unsupported
   (C) politically biased
   (D) cogent but inadequate
   (E) irrelevant in today's cultural environment

Question Type: Author's Attitude
Difficulty Level: Easier

(D) **is the best response.** This question deals with the author's evaluation of the market theory of public goods (lines 30–34). The author views the theory as cogent (valid; appealing to reason) in that it "help[s] to explain an aspect of modern public health law." At the same time, however, the author views the theory as inadequate in that "it omits a critical point."

(A) **is the second-best response.** In acknowledging that the market theory of public goods "help[s] to explain an aspect of modern public health law and assists in fitting it into modern economic theory," the author is suggesting that the theory is a sound one. Accordingly, Response (A) is incomplete, since it fails to acknowledge the author's criticism of the theory.

Other Incorrect Responses

(B) and **(E)** both run contrary to the author's evaluation of the public-goods theory.

(C) is unsupported. The author never suggests that the market theorists are biased.

QUESTION 5

5. Among the following statements about the United States government's role in the provision of health care, which finds the least support in the passage?

(A) The government today addresses health concerns that formerly were not considered serious enough to warrant government involvement.

(B) What were once public health-care functions are now served by the private sector.

(C) Philosophical considerations play a less significant role today in the formulation of public health-care policies than in previous centuries.

(D) Public health care today is guided largely by secular rather than religious values.

(E) Modern public health-care agencies are typically established not as temporary measures but rather as permanent establishments.

Question Type: Explicit Detail
Difficulty Level: Challenging

(C) **is the best response.** Statement (C) is unsupported; nowhere does the author suggest that the government polices today regarding health care are guided less by philosophical considerations than in previous eras. The term "philosophical" should not be equated with the term "religious" (otherwise, (C) and (D) would be essentially the same responses).

(A) **is the second-best response.** Support for (A) is less explicit than for any other incorrect answer choice. Nevertheless, (A) finds support from the author's point in lines 78–80 that many non-epidemic diseases were not formerly addressed by the government because they were considered part and parcel of daily life. It can be reasonably inferred from this excerpt that epidemic diseases were considered a greater threat (i.e., more serious), thereby warranting government's attention.

Other Incorrect Responses

(B) restates the author's assertion in lines 84–86 that "many public responsibilities were carried out by what we would now consider private associations."

(D) is readily inferable from the last paragraph. The author asserts that the public role in health care is carried out in different ways today than in prior centuries. The author then points out in lines 81–82 that "religious influence was significant, especially in the seventeenth century." It is reasonably inferable, then, that religion does not play a significant role today in public health care decisions.

(E) restates the author's point in lines 74–76 that government health-care organizations in previous eras were less stable than modern bureaucracies.

QUESTION 6

6. **Which of the following best expresses the author's point of contention with "those who criticize the United States government for not providing health care to all citizens" (lines 62–63)?**

(A) Their standard for measuring such provision is too narrow.
(B) They underestimate the role that insurance plays in the provision of health care today.
(C) They fail to recognize that government plays a more significant role today in health care than in previous eras.
(D) They misunderstand the intent of the founding generation with respect to the proper role of the government in the area of health care.
(E) They lack any significant conception of public health law.

Question Type: Interpretation
Difficulty Level: Moderate

(A) **is the best response.** According to the author, the critics equate the degree (extent) of health-care provision with insurance coverage. The author contends that by this standard of measurement, public health care during the eighteenth century was practically non-existent. In fact, however, the government played a significant role in health care during that century in ways other than providing insurance to its citizens. Thus, the critics' standard for measuring the extent of the government's role in health care is far too narrow in that it ignores all of the other possible ways in which government can play a role in health care.

Incorrect Responses

(B) is unsupported. Nowhere does the author state or imply that insurance plays a larger role in health care than the critics contend; also, Statement (B) makes no distinction between private and public insurance.

(C) is not well supported. Based upon the information in the last paragraph, it appears that the United States government has played a significant role in health care throughout history; the author does not contend that the government's role in health care is greater today than in previous eras (implicitly, some of the evidence in the last paragraph supports this contention, while other evidence undermines it). Moreover, even if (C) were strongly supported by the passage, the statement is nevertheless not the author's point of contention with the critics.

(D) is unsupported and does not respond to the question. The author makes no attempt to evaluate the critics' understanding of the founding generation's intent. Even if Statement (D) were supported by the passage, the statement is nevertheless not the author's point of contention with the critics.

(E) confuses the details in the last paragraph. It was America that, by the critics' standards, "lacked any significant conception of public health law." Statement (E) asserts, however, that the critics were the ones that lacked such conception.

QUESTION 7

7. Which of the following best expresses the main point of the last paragraph in the passage?

(A) The government's role in health care has not expanded over time to the extent that many critics have asserted.

(B) The government should limit its involvement in health care to epidemiological problems.

(C) Health problems plaguing pre-industrial America resulted largely from inadequate public health care.

(D) History suggests that the United States government has properly played a significant role in provision of health care.

(E) Private insurance is an inadequate solution to the problem of health care.

Question Type: Interpretation
Difficulty Level: Moderate

(D) is the best response. In the last paragraph, the author rebuts the critics' argument that government is not providing health care to all citizens and implies, at the close of the passage, that the founding generation probably intended that government play a significant ("complex") role in health care.

Incorrect Responses

(A) is unsupported and runs contrary to the passage. The evidence in the last paragraph is conflicting as to whether the government's role has in fact expanded over time, and the author does not really address this issue. Also, according to the passage, the critics assert that the government plays too small a role in health care; thus, (A) actually tends to run contrary to the critics' contention.

(B) is unsupported, calling for an unwarranted inference. Although acknowledging that the government in fact has expanded its health concerns from epidemics to chronic and endemic disorders, the author does not take a position on whether such expansion is desirable or proper.

(C) is wholly unsupported. Although the first paragraph of the passage does identify the fundamental causes of certain epidemics occurring in the United States (during the twentieth as well as previous centuries), the author makes no attempt in the last paragraph to further identify the health problems of pre-industrial America or their causes.

(E) distorts the main idea of the last paragraph (as expressed above). Although Statement (E) is consistent with the author's implicit argument that the government should play a significant role in health care, it fails to express the broader point which the author seeks to make in the final paragraph.

PASSAGE #15

Scientists have long made two claims about their discipline: that it requires freedom to flourish and progress and that it is inherently international, transcending the divisions of national and political
(5)   boundaries. These are related claims since the internationalism of science lies partly in the freedom to communicate openly with all of one's scientific colleagues, wherever they may live. Though these ideals have not always been attained, especially in the area
(10)   of international scientific relations, they have served as normative assumptions for most scientists.

Before this, challenges to these assumptions came primarily from religious quarters—such as Galileo's trial by the Catholic Church and the controversy
(15)   surrounding Darwin's *Descent of Man*. But in this century, they have come largely from political and ideological pressures growing out of the increasing importance of science to social and national life. The close link between science and national governments,
(20)   largely spurred by scientific contributions to warfare and defense in World War I and even more decisively in World War II, facilitated large and expensive projects, such as the particle-accelerator and space programs, that would have been difficult to fund
(25)   through private sources. But the connection also channelled the direction of scientific research increasingly toward military defense; scientific knowledge had become closely linked with national security and could no longer be so freely communicated to all
(30)   scientific colleagues without any restrictions.

One of the most interesting and complex challenges to science's normative assumptions involves the diverse developments related to science that have arisen in Russia since the Bolshevik
(35)   Revolution of 1917. The new Soviet state based itself on science in a way no previous government ever had. Yet Soviet scientists occupied an ambiguous position from the beginning, for while the government encouraged and generally supported
(40)   scientific research, it simultaneously imposed significant restrictions on science and scientists.

The Soviets strongly emphasized planned science, sparking criticism from many Western scientists who charged that planned science could not be free since
(45)   the choice of investigation had been taken from the researcher and that without such freedom science could not progress. A strong nationalistic emphasis on science led at times to the dismissal of all non-Russian scientific work as irrelevant to Soviet science.
(50)   One leading Soviet philosopher wrote, in 1940, that "it is impossible to speak of a world science as something single, whole and continuous." A 1973 article in *Literatunaya Gazeta*, a Soviet publication, insisted that: "World science is based upon national
(55)   schools, so the weakening of one or another national

school inevitably leads to stagnation in the development of world science." Scientific internationalism was further challenged in a more profound way by the assertion that there are two kinds of science—a
(60)   socialist science and a capitalistic, or bourgeois, science—each developing out of the particular economic organization of the society in which it arises. According to the Soviet regime, socialist science must be consistent with, and in fact grows out
(65)   of the Marxism-Leninism political ideology. Soviet scientists were exhorted to build a genuinely socialist science rather than to conduct an impartial search for nature's truths.

Toward these ends, the Soviet regime curtailed
(70)   many of the freedoms considered essential for the advancement of science. Where scientific work conflicted with political criteria, the work was often disrupted. During the Stalinist purges of the 1930s, many Soviet scientists simply disappeared. In the
(75)   1970s, Soviet scientists who were part of the refusenik movement lost their jobs, were barred from access to scientific resources, were shunned by colleagues, and were even imprisoned. The government even sought to erase their previous contributions by removing
(80)   their books and articles from libraries and by excising citations to their work from the scientific literature. Some scientific theories or fields, such as relativity, and genetics, were criticized, or even abolished, because they deviated from Marxism-Leninism.

(85)   Of course, hindrances to scientific freedom and scientific internationalism in this century are not limited to the Soviet Union. In the 1930s a nationalistic science promoted in Nazi Germany proclaimed the existence of a *Deutsche Physik*, which
(90)   the Nazis distinguished from "Jewish physics." More recently, scientists in South American countries, especially Argentina, were fired from their positions or arrested for political reasons. But the Soviet Union constitutes the longest-lived instance of a seemingly
(95)   contradictory situation which couples a strong dependence on, and support for, science with stringent restrictions on that very scientific activity.

1. Which of the following is NOT mentioned as a Soviet attempt to impinge upon scientific freedom?

   (A) a strong emphasis on planned science
   (B) governmental interference with scientific research
   (C) charges respecting the relevance of scientific research performed in other countries
   (D) criticism of scientific inquiry relating to theories that conflicted with the Soviet regime's political ideology
   (E) dissemination of the notion of two types of science: socialist and naturalist.

2. In stating that scientific knowledge had become close-ly linked with national security and could no longer be freely communicated, the author implies that

   (A) expensive research projects such as the particle accelerator and space programs apply tech-nology that can also be applied toward projects relating to national security

   (B) governments have subordinated the ideal of scientific freedom to national security interests

   (C) without free access to new scientific knowledge, scientists in different countries are less able to communicate with one another

   (D) governments should de-emphasize scientific projects related to military defense and empha-size instead research that can be shared freely within the international scientific community

   (E) government funding of scientific research undermines the ideal of scientific freedom to a greater extent than does private funding

3. The author quotes an article from *Literatunaya Gazeta* (line 53) most probably in order to:

   (A) illustrate the general sentiment among members of the international scientific community during the time period

   (B) underscore the Soviet emphasis on the notion of a national science

   (C) show the disparity of views within the Soviet intellectual community regarding the proper role of science

   (D) underscore the point that only those notions about science that conformed to the Marxist-Leninist ideal were sanctioned by the Soviet government

   (E) support the author's assertion that the Marxist-Leninist impact on Soviet scientific freedom continued through the decade of the 1970s

4. Which of the following statements is LEAST supported by the passage?

   (A) Intervention by the Soviet government in scientific research reached its zenith during the Stalinist era of the 1930s.

   (B) Soviet attempts to suppress scientific freedom during the 1970s resembled those made by the Argentinean government.

   (C) Like the Soviet regime, the Nazi regime promot-ed the notion of a national science and attempted to distinguish it from other science.

   (D) Western scientists opposed the notion of planned science on the grounds that it restricts the scientist's freedom.

   (E) The notion of "world science" runs contrary to the Nazi's *Deutsche Physik*.

5. Which of the following best characterizes the "ambiguous position" (lines 37–38) in which Soviet scientists were placed during the decades that followed the Bolshevik Revolution?

   (A) The Soviet government demanded that their research result in scientific progress, although funding was insufficient to accomplish this goal.

   (B) They were exhorted to strive toward scientific advancements, while at the same time the freedoms necessary to make such advancements were restricted.

   (C) While required to direct their research entirely toward military defense, most advancements in this field were being made by non-Soviet scientists with whom the Soviet scientists were prohibited contact.

   (D) They were encouraged to collaborate with Soviet colleagues but were prohibited from any discourse with scientists from other countries.

   (E) The Soviet government failed to identify those areas of research that it deemed most worth-while, but punished those scientists with whose work it was not satisfied.

6. Which of the following does the author identify as a fundamental cause of twentieth-century challenges to scientific freedom?

   (A) the increasing role that science has played in national life

   (B) religious intolerance, particularly in the Soviet Union and in Nazi Germany

   (C) the Bolshevik Revolution of 1917 and the Marxism-Leninism political ideology

   (D) increasing disloyalty on the part of scientists to their governments

   (E) proliferation of nuclear weapons throughout the world

7. The author's primary purpose in the passage is to

   (A) examine the events leading up to the suppression of the Soviet refusenik movement of the 1970s

   (B) define and dispel the notion of a national science as promulgated by the post-revolution Soviet regime

   (C) describe specific attempts by the modern Soviet regime to suppress scientific freedom

   (D) examine the major twentieth-century challenges to the normative assumptions that science requires freedom and that it is inherently international

   (E) point out the similarities and distinctions between scientific freedom and scientific inter-nationalism in the context of the Soviet Union

STOP.

PASSAGE #15—ANSWER KEY

1. E
2. B
3. B
4. A
5. B
6. A
7. D

PASSAGE #15—ANALYSIS

QUESTION 1

1. Which of the following is NOT mentioned as a Soviet attempt to impinge upon scientific freedom?

   (A) a strong emphasis on planned science
   (B) governmental interference with scientific research
   (C) charges respecting the relevance of scientific research performed in other countries
   (D) criticism of scientific inquiry relating to theories that conflicted with the Soviet regime's political ideology
   (E) dissemination of the notion of two types of science: socialist and naturalist

Question Type: Explicit Detail
Difficulty Level: Easier

(E) **is the best response.** The two types of science that the Soviet regime identified included socialist and capitalist (or bourgeois) science, not naturalist science; the term "naturalist" is not used anywhere in the passage.

Incorrect Responses

Each of the other responses is either mentioned explicitly or is described in either the fourth or fifth paragraph.

QUESTION 2

2. In stating that scientific knowledge had become closely linked with national security and could no longer be freely communicated, the author implies that

   (A) expensive research projects such as the particle accelerator and space programs apply technology that can also be applied toward projects relating to national security
   (B) governments have subordinated the ideal of scientific freedom to national security interests

      (C) **without free access to new scientific knowledge,
             scientists in different countries are less able to
             communicate with one another**

      (D) **governments should de-emphasize scientific projects
             related to military defense and emphasize instead
             research that can be shared freely within the
             international scientific community**

      (E) **government funding of scientific research undermines the
             ideal of scientific freedom to a greater extent than does
             private funding**

Question Type: Inference
Difficulty Level: Easier

(B) is the best response. Governments are placing a higher value on national security than on scientific freedom since scientific knowledge related to military defense is typically kept secret (presumably to prevent advantageous knowledge from leaking to enemy countries).

(E) is the second-best response. Response (E) is the second-best answer, since an argument can be made from the information in the second paragraph that government-funded research is more likely than privately-funded research to relate to matters affecting the national security (i.e., military defense). However, if this inference is to be based upon the excerpt mentioned in the question stem, the inference is far more speculative than is Statement (B).

Other Incorrect Responses

(A) is unsupported. No connection is implied between the particle-accelerator and space programs and national security.

(C) is not responsive to the question and is a bit nonsensical. Even if (C) were turned around to make some logical sense (e.g., "Without the ability to communicate with scientists from other countries, scientists do not have free access to new scientific knowledge"), the statement would still not respond to the question.

(D) is unsupported. The author neither states nor suggests which areas of scientific research should be emphasized.

QUESTION 3

    3. **The author quotes an article from *Literatunaya Gazeta* (line 53)
       most probably in order to:**

      (A) **illustrate the general sentiment among members of the
             international scientific community during the time period**

      (B) **underscore the Soviet emphasis on the notion of a
             national science**

      (C) **show the disparity of views within the Soviet intellectual
             community regarding the proper role of science**

(D) underscore the point that only those notions about
    science that conformed to the Marxist-Leninist ideal
    were sanctioned by the Soviet government
(E) support the author's assertion that the Marxist-Leninist
    impact on Soviet scientific freedom continued through
    the decade of the 1970s

Question Type: Purpose of Detail
Difficulty Level: Moderate

(B) is the best response. The fourth paragraph is concerned exclusively with pointing
out evidence of the Soviet emphasis on a national science; given the content of
the excerpt from *Literatunaya Gazeta*, it can be reasonably inferred that the author
is quoting this article as one such piece of evidence.

(D) is the second-best response. The quoted article does indeed reflect the Marxist-
Leninist ideal (at least as interpreted and promulgated by the government) and
may in fact have been published only because it was sanctioned (approved) by
the Soviet government. However, statement (D) is not likely to be the author's
purpose in quoting the article, since this conclusion would require speculation
and since the quoted excerpt makes no mention of government approval or
disapproval of certain scientific notions.

Other Incorrect Responses

(A) distorts the nature of the quoted article and runs contrary to the passage. The
article illustrates the official Soviet position and possibly the sentiment among
some members of the Soviet intellectual or scientific community. However, the
article does not necessarily reflect the views of scientists from other countries. In
fact, the reaction of Western scientists mentioned in the same paragraph suggests
that scientists from other countries disagreed with this view.

(C) is not likely to be the author's purpose in quoting the article since the author
argues in this paragraph that the notion of a national science pervaded the Soviet
consciousness, not that there was a great deal of disagreement and debate among
Soviet intellectuals.

(E) is not likely to be the author's purpose in quoting the article. Although the
assertion mentioned in Response (E) may in fact be true and is indeed supported
by the information in the passage, the author gives no indication as to when the
article was written or published; thus, the article itself lends no support to the
assertion mentioned in statement (E).

QUESTION 4

4. Which of the following statements is LEAST supported by the
   passage?

   (A) Intervention by the Soviet government in scientific research
       reached its zenith during the Stalinist era of the 1930s.

(B) Soviet attempts to suppress scientific freedom during the 1970s resembled those made by the Argentinean government.

(C) Like the Soviet regime, the Nazi regime promoted the notion of a national science and attempted to distinguish it from other science.

(D) Western scientists opposed the notion of planned science on the grounds that it restricts the scientist's freedom.

(E) The notion of "world science" runs contrary to the Nazi's *Deutsche Physik*.

Question Type: Explicit Detail
Difficulty Level: Challenging

(A) is the best response. Statement (A) provides the best response since it calls for an unwarranted inference that is unsupported by the passage. Although the author does refer in the fifth paragraph to the Stalinist purges of the 1930s, nowhere does the author state or suggest that the events of this particular time period marked the peak (zenith) of government interference with scientific research.

Incorrect Responses

(B) is strongly supported; lines 91–93 mention scientists losing their jobs and being arrested in Argentina, while lines 75–78 mention similar acts of suppression against Soviet refuseniks (scientists were fired and/or imprisoned).

(C) is less explicit in the passage than either (B) or (D); nevertheless, (C) is supported by the passage; while the Soviets distinguished socialist science from capitalistic science, the Nazis distinguished their *Deutsche Physik* from Jewish physics.

(D) is mentioned explicitly in lines 42–46.

(E) is less explicit in the passage than either Statement (B) or (D); nevertheless, Statement (E) is inferable from the fourth and sixth paragraphs considered together. According to passage (lines 87–89), a nationalistic science in Germany proclaimed the existence of a *Deutsche Physik* and distinguished it from other science. It can reasonably be inferred from this statement that *Deutsche Physik* would run contrary to the idea of a world science (the notion of "world science" was mentioned in the fourth paragraph in the context of Soviet attempts to dismiss or redefine the concept).

QUESTION 5

5. Which of the following best characterizes the "ambiguous position" (lines 37–38) in which Soviet scientists were placed during the decades that followed the Bolshevik Revolution?

(A) The Soviet government demanded that their research result in scientific progress, although funding was insufficient to accomplish this goal.

    (B) **They were exhorted to strive toward scientific advancements, while at the same time the freedoms necessary to make such advancements were restricted.**

    (C) **While required to direct their research entirely toward military defense, most advancements in this field were being made by non-Soviet scientists with whom the Soviet scientists were prohibited contact.**

    (D) **They were encouraged to collaborate with Soviet colleagues but were prohibited from any discourse with scientists from other countries.**

    (E) **The Soviet government failed to identify those areas of research that it deemed most worthwhile, but punished those scientists with whose work it was not satisfied.**

Question Type: Interpretation
Difficulty Level: Easier

(B) **is the best response.** According to the passage, the ambiguous position of Soviet scientists was that the Soviet government encouraged (exhorted) and generally supported scientific research, while at the same time it imposed significant restrictions upon its scientists (lines 38–41). Statement (B) restates this idea.

Incorrect Responses

(A) is unsupported. The author neither states nor suggests that the Soviets lacked sufficient funding; moreover, although statement (B), if true, would indicate an ambiguous position for scientists, it is not the nature of the ambiguity referred to in the passage.

(C) is wholly unsupported. The author neither states nor suggests either assertion made in statement (C).

(D) is supported (albeit, not explicitly) by the passage and, if true, would present an ambiguous position for Soviet scientists. However, as with (A), (C), and (E), the ambiguity referred to in (B) fails to reflect the nature of the ambiguity referred to in the passage.

(E) is unsupported. Although some Soviet scientists were indeed punished by the government, the author neither states nor implies that the government failed to identify those areas of research that it deemed most worthwhile. Moreover, although statement (E), if true, would indicate an ambiguous position for scientists, it is not the nature of the ambiguity referred to in the passage.

QUESTION 6

6. **Which of the following does the author identify as a fundamental cause of twentieth-century challenges to scientific freedom?**

    (A) **the increasing role that science has played in national life**

    (B) religious intolerance, particularly in the Soviet Union and
          in Nazi Germany

    (C) the Bolshevik Revolution of 1917 and the Marxism-
          Leninism political ideology

    (D) increasing disloyalty on the part of scientists to their
          governments

    (E) proliferation of nuclear weapons throughout the world

Question Type: Explicit Detail
Difficulty Level: Moderate

(A) is the best response. The passage states explicitly in the second paragraph that twentieth-century challenges to science's normative assumptions (i.e., scientific freedom) have grown "out of the increasing importance of science to social and national life."

(C) is the second-best response. The question asks for the fundamental cause of a general phenomenon, not of the specific challenges of the Soviet regime. Thus, (C) is too narrow.

Other Incorrect Responses

(B) is unsupported. The passage makes no mention of religious intolerance in the twentieth-century Soviet Union and alludes only briefly in the last paragraph to Jewish physics, which reference suggests more of a racial bias than a religious one on the part of the Nazis.

(D) is unsupported; nowhere in the passage does the author either state or suggest that disloyalty of scientists prompted restrictions upon their freedom.

(E) is far too narrow. Although nuclear weapons may have played a significant role in establishing a link between science and national security (and thus to restrictions on scientific freedom that are necessary to protect those security interests), the author makes no attempt to establish a specific cause-and-effect relationship between nuclear-weaponry development and challenges to scientific freedom; in fact, the passage makes no mention of nuclear weapons specifically.

QUESTION 7

    7. The author's primary purpose in the passage is to

        (A) examine the events leading up to the suppression of the
             Soviet refusenik movement of the 1970s

        (B) define and dispel the notion of a national science as
             promulgated by the post-revolution Soviet regime

        (C) describe specific attempts by the modern Soviet regime
             to suppress scientific freedom

        (D) examine the major twentieth-century challenges to the
             normative assumptions that science requires freedom
             and that it is inherently international

(E) point out the similarities and distinctions between
scientific freedom and scientific internationalism within
the context of the Soviet Union

Question Type: Primary Purpose
Difficulty Level: Moderate

(D) is the best response. The first paragraph identifies the two normative
assumptions, while the remainder of the passage discusses how those
assumptions have been challenged. Although the passage looks primarily at the
Soviet Union, the last paragraph briefly discusses other attempts at suppression
of scientific freedom in the twentieth century.

(C) is the second-best response. While the fourth and fifth paragraphs are indeed
concerned with describing Soviet attempts to suppress scientific freedom, (C) is
too narrow in that ignores the rest of the passage, omitting the broader historical
perspective.

Other Incorrect Responses

(A) is off focus and far too narrow; moreover, the author does not actually discuss
any specific events that might have caused the suppression of the refusenik
movement; rather, this historical phenomenon is mentioned simply as another
example of the Soviet regime's long-term pattern of suppression.

(B) is off focus and misses the author's attitude. Although the author does define the
concept of national science, no attempt is made to dispel or disprove the concept.

(E) is too narrow and is off focus. Although the author does make the point in the
first paragraph that scientific freedom and scientific internationalism are related,
no attempt is made to examine their differences; moreover, the author's broader
concern is quite different than to examine the relationship between these two
types of scientific freedoms.

SHORTER PASSAGES (for the GRE and GMAT)
BEGIN ON THIS PAGE

GMAT and short GRE passages are 200–300 words in length and are accompanied by 2–3 questions each. Try to LIMIT YOUR TIME TO 5 MINUTES for each of the following five question sets (#16 through #20).

NOTE TO LSAT AND MCAT STUDENTS:
Although sets 16–20 are shorter than the ones on your exam, go ahead and try them anyway—they're comparable in style and difficulty to the ones on your exam.

PASSAGE #16

Dorothea Lange was perhaps the most notable of the photographers commissioned during the 1930s by the Farm Security Administration (FSA), part of a U.S. government plan to revitalize the nation's economy and
(5) to communicate its human and social dimensions. The value of Lange's photographs as documents for social history is enhanced by her technical and artistic mastery of the medium. Her well-composed, sharp-focus images reveal a wealth of information about her subjects and
(10) show historical evidence that would scarcely be known but for her camera. Her finest images, while according with conditions of poverty that prompted political response, portray people who appear indomitable, un-vanquished by their reverses. "Migrant Mother," for
(15) example, portrays a sense of the innocent victim, of perseverance, of destitution as a temporary aberration calling for compassion, solutions, and politics to alter life for the better. The power of that photograph, which became the symbol of the photographic file of the FSA,
(20) endures today.

The documentary book was a natural genre for Lange and her husband Paul Taylor, whose narrative accom-panied Lange's FSA photographs. In *An American Exodus*, produced by Lange and Taylor, a sense of the
(25) despair of Lange's subjects is heightened by the cap-tioned quotations of the migrants, forming a powerful synthesis of image and voice. Taken from 1935 to 1940 during a period of almost constant travel and hardship, the *Exodus* pictures became the accepted vision of the
(30) migration of Dust Bowl farm workers into California.

1. According to the passage, the photograph entitled "Migrant Mother"

   (A) appeared in the documentary book *American Exodus*
   (B) was accompanied by a caption written by Lange's husband
   (C) was taken by Lange in 1935
   (D) is considered by the author to be one of Lange's best photographs
   (E) portrays the mother of a Dust Bowl farm worker

2. The passage provides information for responding to all of the following questions EXCEPT:

   (A) What was the FSA's purpose in compiling the photographic file to which Lange contributed?
   (B) How did the FSA react to the photographs taken by Lange under its commission?
   (C) In what areas of the United States did Lange take her *American Exodus* photographs?
   (D) Why did Lange agree to work under the commission of the FSA?
   (E) What qualities make Lange's photographs noteworthy?

3. Among the following characterizations, the passage is best viewed as

   (A) a survey of the great photographers of the Depression era
   (B) an examination of the photographic techniques of Dorothea Lange
   (C) an argument for the power of pictures to enact social change
   (D) a discussion of the goals and programs of the FSA's photographic department
   (E) an explanation of Lange's interest in docu-menting the plight of Depression victims

STOP.

PASSAGE #16—ANSWER KEY

1. D
2. D
3. C

PASSAGE #16—ANALYSIS

QUESTION 1

1. According to the passage, the photograph entitled "Migrant Mother"

    (A) appeared in the documentary book *American Exodus*
    (B) was accompanied by a caption written by Lange's husband
    (C) was taken by Lange in 1935
    (D) is considered by the author to be one of Lange's best photographs
    (E) portrays the mother of a Dust Bowl farm worker

Question Type: Explicit Detail
Difficulty Level: Moderate

(D) is the best response. The author cites "Migrant Mother" as an example of "[h]er finest images" (line 12)—i.e., as an example of her best photographs.

Incorrect Responses

(A) calls for speculation. The photograph might have appeared in Lange's book; however, the passage does not explicitly indicate so.

(B) calls for speculation. Lange's husband wrote narrative captions for the photographs appearing in *American Exodus*. However, there is no indication in the passage that "Migrant Mother" was accompanied by a caption or even that it appeared in the book.

(C) provides information not mentioned in the passage. Although it is reasonable to assume that the photograph was taken by Lange during the 1930s, the passage neither states nor implies what year the photo was taken.

(E) calls for speculation. According to the passage, the photographs appearing in *American Exodus* "became the accepted vision of the migration of Dust Bowl farm workers to California" (lines 31–33). However, the author does not indicate either that "Migrant Mother" appeared in the book or that the woman portrayed in the photograph was indeed the mother of a Dust Bowl farm worker.

QUESTION 2

2. The passage provides information for responding to all of the following questions EXCEPT:

  (A) What was the FSA's purpose in compiling the photographic file to which Lange contributed?

  (B) How did the FSA react to the photographs taken by Lange under its commission?

  (C) In what areas of the United States did Lange take her *American Exodus* photographs?

  (D) Why did Lange agree to work under the commission of the FSA?

  (E) What qualities make Lange's photographs noteworthy?

Question Type: Explicit Detail
Difficulty Level: Moderate

(D) is the best response. The passage provides absolutely no information about Lange's motives or reasons for accepting her FSA commission.

Incorrect Responses

(A) is answered implicitly in the first sentence of the passage: the FSA was part of a U.S. government plan to revitalize the economy and to communicate its human and social dimensions. Thus, the photographic file was compiled in furtherance of that purpose.

(B) is answered implicitly by the last sentence of the first paragraph. The FSA thought highly enough of one of Lange's photographs to use it as a symbol for its photographic file.

(C) is answered implicitly in the second paragraph. According to the passage, the Exodus pictures recorded the migration of Dust Bowl farm workers into California. Thus, some (and probably all or nearly all) of these photographs were taken in the "Dust Bowl" region of the U.S. and/or in California.

(E) is answered in the first paragraph, where the author mentions Lange's "well-composed, sharp-focus" images (line 9).

QUESTION 3

 3. Among the following characterizations, the passage is best viewed as

  (A) a survey of the great photographers of the Depression era

  (B) an examination of the photographic techniques of Dorothea Lange

  (C) an argument for the power of pictures to enact social change

  (D) a discussion of the goals and programs of the FSA's photographic department

  (E) an explanation of Lange's interest in documenting the plight of Depression victims

Question Type: Primary Purpose
Difficulty Level: Moderate

(C) is the best response. Admittedly, (C) is not an ideal characterization of the passage, which seems more concerned with Lange's work than with making a broader argument about the power of pictures. Nevertheless, the author does allude to Lange's ability to convey a need for social change through her photographs. Accordingly, the passage can be characterized as presenting one example (Lange) to support the broader point suggested by Response (C).

Incorrect Responses

(A) is far too broad. The only photographer discussed in the passage is Lange.

(B) is too narrow. Although the author mentions some of Lange's techniques (e.g., her "well-composed, sharp-focus images"), the author does not examine them in any detail.

(D) distorts the passage and is too broad. First, the passage does not indicate that a distinct photographic department within the FSA existed; in this sense, (C) distorts the information in the passage. Second, although the author alludes to the overall purpose of the FSA (in the first sentence), there is no further discussion of its goals or program, other than the discussion of Lange's involvement in compiling its photographic file; in this sense, (C) is far too broad.

(E) distorts the passage. There is no discussion in the passage of Lange's motive or reasons for photographing Depression victims other than that she was commissioned by the FSA to do so.

PASSAGE #17

The Pan-American land bridge, or isthmus, connecting North and South America was formed volcanically long after dinosaurs became extinct. The isthmus cleaved populations of marine organisms,
(5) creating sister species. These twin species, called "geminates," then evolved independently. Scientists observe, for example, that Pacific pistol shrimp no longer mate with those from the Atlantic Ocean. Yet the two oceans had already begun to form their
(10) distinctive personalities long before the isthmus was fully formed. As the seabed rose Pacific waters grew cooler, their upswelling currents carrying rich nutrients, while the Atlantic side grew shallower, warmer and nutrient poor. In fact, it was these new
(15) conditions, and not so much the fully-formed isthmus, that spawned changes in the shrimp population.

For terrestrial life the impact of the isthmus was more immediate. Animals traversed the newly formed bridge in both directions, although North American
(20) creatures proved better colonizers—more than half of South America's mammals trace direct lineage to this so-called Great American Biotic Exchange. Only three animals—the armadillo, opossum, and hedgehog— survive as transplants in the north today.

1. Which of the following statements finds the LEAST support in the passage?

(A) Population divergences resulting from the formation of the Pan-American isthmus were more a process than an event.
(B) The divergence in ocean temperature during the formation of the Pan-American isthmus resulted in a divergence in the ocean's nutrient value.
(C) Genetic differences among pistol shrimp have grown to the point that there are now at least two distinct species of these shrimp.
(D) The part of ocean which is now the Pacific grew deeper due to the geologic forces that created the Pan-American isthmus.
(E) Not until the Pan-American isthmus was fully formed did geminate marine organisms begin to develop in that area of the ocean.

2. The author mentions the mating habits of pistol shrimp in order to show that

(A) some species of marine organisms inhabiting the Pacific Ocean are now entirely distinct from those in the Atlantic Ocean
(B) twin species of marine organisms can each survive even though one species can no longer mate with the other
(C) since the formation of the Pan-American isthmus some marine geminates no longer mate with their sister species
(D) geminate species that do not mate with one another are considered separate species
(E) the evolutionary impact of the Pan-American isthmus was greater for marine organisms than for land animals

3. Which of the following statements is most readily inferable from the information in the passage?

(A) Species of marine organisms in the Atlantic Ocean number fewer today than before the formation of the Pan-American isthmus.
(B) The number of terrestrial animal species in South America today exceeds the number prior to the formation of the Pan-American isthmus.
(C) Of the indigenous South American species that migrated north across the Pan-American isthmus, more than three survive to this day.
(D) Since the formation of the Pan-American isthmus, fewer terrestrial animals have traveled north across the isthmus than south.
(E) As the Pan-American isthmus began to form, most pistol shrimp migrated west to what is now the Pacific Ocean.

STOP.

PASSAGE #17—ANSWER KEY

1. E
2. A
3. C

PASSAGE #17—ANALYSIS

QUESTION 1

1. **Which of the following statements finds the LEAST support in the passage?**

    (A) Population divergences resulting from the formation of the Pan-American isthmus were more a process than an event.
    (B) The divergence in ocean temperature during the formation of the Pan-American isthmus resulted in a divergence in the ocean's nutrient value.
    (C) Genetic differences among pistol shrimp have grown to the point that there are now at least two distinct species of these shrimp.
    (D) The part of ocean which is now the Pacific grew deeper due to the geologic forces that created the Pan-American isthmus.
    (E) Not until the Pan-American isthmus was fully formed did geminate marine organisms begin to develop in that area of the ocean.

Question Type: Inference
Difficulty Level: Moderate

(E) is the best response. It can reasonably be inferred that the "new conditions" which sparked the divergence in pistol shrimp are an aspect of the two oceans' "distinctive personalities," which the author states began to emerge "long before the isthmus was fully formed." Statement (E) contradicts the inference.

(D) is the second-best response. Although the passage states explicitly that the Atlantic area of the ocean grew shallower as the isthmus formed, it does not state that the Pacific area grew deeper. However, (D) is consistent with the common sense notion that deeper water is colder than shallower water. In any event, because (E) contradicts the passage information it is a better choice than (D).

Other Incorrect Responses

(A) is readily inferable. Based on the first sentence of the second paragraph, it is reasonably inferable that the impact of the isthmus on marine life was less immediate—in other words more gradual—than on terrestrial life. It is fair to characterize this more gradual impact as a process, while characterizing the Great American Biotic Exchange as an event.

(B) is reasonably inferable. The passage implicitly suggests that cooler water serves to increase nutrient value, while warmer water serves to decrease it.

(C) is reasonably inferable. The author cites pistol shrimp as an example of the development of geminates (twin species)—exactly what (C) describes.

QUESTION 2

2. The author mentions the mating habits of pistol shrimp in order to show that

(A) some species of marine organisms inhabiting the Pacific Ocean are now entirely distinct from those in the Atlantic Ocean
(B) twin species of marine organisms can each survive even though one species can no longer mate with the other
(C) since the formation of the Pan-American isthmus some marine geminates no longer mate with their sister species
(D) geminate species that do not mate with one another are considered separate species
(E) the evolutionary impact of the Pan-American isthmus was greater for marine organisms than for land animals

Question Type: Purpose of Detail
Difficulty Level: Moderate

(A) is the best response. The author discusses pistol shrimp as an example of twin species, or geminates. Thus, (A) expresses the author's immediate purpose in mentioning the mating habits of pistol shrimp.

Incorrect Responses

(B) distorts the author's purpose; whether a twin specie can survive without mating with another specie is irrelevant to the author's point that the formation of the isthmus resulted in the development of twin species.

(C) distorts the author's purpose, as expressed in answer choice (A). (C) also overstates the passage information by suggesting, at least implicitly, that *not until* the isthmus was formed have some marine geminates been unable to mate across species. This assertion is far too broad and is unsupported by the passage.

(D) distorts the author's purpose here. The author is not concerned with distinguishing geminates according to whether they can mate with their sister species. (D) is also factually unsupported by the passage, which makes no attempt to articulate when or whether "geminate" species are considered "separate" species.

(E) is irrelevant to the author's concern in the first paragraph, which does not deal with terrestrial animals at all—although the passage as a whole does lend support for statement (E).

QUESTION 3

3. Which of the following statements is most readily inferable from the information in the passage?

(A) Species of marine organisms in the Atlantic Ocean number fewer today than before the formation of the Pan-American isthmus.

(B) The number of terrestrial animal species in South America today exceeds the number prior to the formation of the Pan-American isthmus.

(C) Of the indigenous South American species that migrated north across the Pan-American isthmus, more than three survive to this day.

(D) Since the formation of the Pan-American isthmus, fewer terrestrial animals have traveled north across the isthmus than south.

(E) As the Pan-American isthmus began to form, most pistol shrimp migrated west to what is now the Pacific Ocean.

Question Type: Inference
Difficulty Level: Moderate

(C) **is the best response.** The second paragraph provides ample support for this inference. The author states that the terrestrial species migrating south were "better colonizers" than the ones migrating north, that *more than half* of those in the south today came from the north, and that *only three* animal species migrating north across the isthmus survive today. It is readily inferable, then, that more than three species that migrated south across the isthmus survive today.

Incorrect Responses

(A) is not as readily inferable as (C). Admittedly, the passage information that the shallower, warmer Atlantic is relatively nutrient poor lends support to statement (A); but nowhere in the passage does the author compare the total number of species in the two oceans.

(B) is unsupported by the passage, which suggests only that a great number of species (more than half) in South America today did not inhabit that continent prior to the Exchange. The author makes no attempt to compare the *total* number of species today with the number prior to the Exchange. (It is possible, for example, that some species have migrated entirely away from South America or have become extinct since the Exchange.)

(D) distorts the passage information, which indicates only that today there are more species that migrated south than there are that migrated north. Nowhere in the passage does the author compare the total number of animals (or species) that migrated each way during the exchange.

(E) confuses the passage information. It is the migration of terrestrial animals, not marine organisms, that the author discusses. Nowhere in the passage does the author suggest that shrimp migrated from one ocean area to another as the isthmus began formed.

PASSAGE #18

The eighteenth-century work *Encyclopédie* coincided with nascent industrialization, and what distinguished the work from its predecessors was its mix of the theoretical with the practical. While twenty pages
(5) were devoted to metaphysical speculation about the human soul, nearly as many were devoted to the machine manufacture of stockings, a principal industrial product of the day. In fact, 17 volumes of text were accompanied by 11 volumes of illustrations, at
(10) the insistence of chief editors Denis Diderot and Jean d'Alembert, known as the "Encyclopedists."

Prior to the mid-eighteenth century scholars had not dared to publicly assert the intellectual freedom to reason about the mundane tools of daily life with the
(15) same seriousness as the human soul. Understandably, in 1759 Pope Clement XIII listed *Encyclopédie* in the Church's Index of prohibited books, and the French government refused to license its printing. But due in part to the surreptitious assistance of one enlightened
(20) government official and in part to greedy booksellers, the work quickly became a best-seller throughout Europe.

Few people today share the Encyclopedists' ingenuous faith that human knowledge could be
(25) satisfactorily summarized in 28 volumes. But in a sense the work has triumphed. Recently when the Catholic Church wished to determine whether the Shroud of Turin was used for the burial of Jesus Christ, it did not rely on ancient authorities, as Pope Clement XIII
(30) would have done, but rather sent the Shroud to a laboratory—just what Diderot would have advised.

1. The author mentions the machine manufacture of stockings (line 7) most likely in order to

(A) show that for the Encyclopedists illustrations were just as important as text
(B) underscore the Encyclopedists' skepticism about prevailing metaphysical notions
(C) demonstrate the Encyclopedists' concern for the practical realm of human endeavor
(D) point out the Encyclopedists' great attention to detail
(E) explain why it was necessary to include eleven volumes of illustrations in the work

2. Based on the passage, which of the following best explains why the author characterizes the French government's suppression of *Encyclopédie* as "understandabl[e]" (line 15)?

(A) Pope Clement XIII had already called for the suppression of the work.
(B) The same government official who aided the Encyclopedists also refused to grant a license to print the work.
(C) The work's commercial success was the result of illegal printing.
(D) In challenging the general status quo, the work might incite readers to question political authority.
(E) The government had previously banned similar works.

3. Which of the following best expresses the main point of the passage's last paragraph?

(A) Although their efforts were admirable, the Encyclopedists were naively optimistic about the potential impact of their work.
(B) The ultimate success of *Encyclopédie* is born out by its detractors' later acceptance of the Encyclopedists' principles.
(C) Although obsolete today, *Encyclopédie* nevertheless continues to inspire not only scientists but also theologians.
(D) Were the Encyclopedists alive today, they would have followed the same course of action as the Catholic Church regarding the Shroud of Turin.
(E) History shows us that the Encyclopedists were overly ambitious in their attempt to systematize and record all human knowledge.

STOP.

PASSAGE #18—ANSWER KEY

1. C
2. D
3. B

PASSAGE #18—ANALYSIS

QUESTION 1

1. The author mentions the machine manufacture of stockings (line 7) most likely in order to

   (A) show that for the Encyclopedists illustrations were just as important as text
   (B) underscore the Encyclopedists' skepticism about prevailing metaphysical notions
   (C) demonstrate the Encyclopedists' concern for the practical realm of human endeavor
   (D) point out the Encyclopedists' great attention to detail
   (E) explain why it was necessary to include eleven volumes of illustrations in the work

Question Type: Purpose of Detail
Difficulty Level: Easier

(C) **is the best response.** The sentence to which question 1 refers parallels the preceding sentence, in which the author indicates the Encyclopedists' concern for both the theoretical and the practical. The author seems to be provide one example of each—the subject of the human soul is theoretical while the subject of stocking production is practical.

Incorrect Responses

(A) is true but does not respond to the question. While the statement is strongly supported by the passage, it does not express the author's purpose in mentioning the manufacture of stockings.

(B) is unsupported by the passage. The author neither states nor suggests that the Encyclopedists' were skeptical about prevailing metaphysical notions.

(D) is not well supported by the passage and does not respond to the question. Admittedly, it is reasonable to assume that Encyclopedists must necessarily pay great attention to detail. But nowhere does the author make this point or suggest that the article about the manufacture of stockings illustrates this point.

(E) confuses the author's purpose here. Admittedly, statement (E) finds support in the next sentence of the passage; one might reasonably conjecture that articles such as the one about stocking production were accompanied by illustrations. But the author's point in mentioning stocking production relates more clearly to the preceding sentence—about the editors' concern not just for the theoretical but also the practical.

QUESTION 2

2. **Based on the passage, which of the following best explains why the author characterizes the French government's suppression of _Encyclopedie_ as "understandabl[e]" (line 15)?**

    (A) Pope Clement XIII had already called for the suppression of the work.
    (B) The same government official who aided the Encyclopedists also refused to grant a license to print the work.
    (C) The work's commercial success was the result of illegal printing.
    (D) In challenging the general status quo, the work might incite readers to question political authority.
    (E) The government had previously banned similar works.

Question Type: Inference
Difficulty Level: Moderate

(D) is the best response. (D) is reasonably inferable from the passage information. Notice that in the preceding sentence the author uses the phrase "dare to assert the intellectual freedom...." This phrase suggests a challenge to political authority. Although the inference in statement (D) is not palpable, (D) is nevertheless a more reasonable explanation than any of the other four choices for the author's use of the word "understandably."

Incorrect Responses

(A) is unsupported by the passage, which neither states nor implies that it was due to the Pope's actions that the government suppressed of the work. (Although this was in fact the case historically, you're to respond based solely on the passage information.)

(B) is unsupported by the passage, which neither states nor implies that the official who refused to issue the printing license was the same official who then surreptitiously (secretly) somehow helped the Encyclopedists to disseminate the work.

(C) finds some support in the passage, but it does not respond to the question. Admittedly, it is reasonable to infer that the book was printed illegally (at least in France) and therefore that illegal printing contributed to the book's commercial success. But this fact is irrelevant to why the French government refused to issue a printing license in the first place—before the book was ever sold.

(E) is wholly unsupported by the passage, which mentions no government ban on any other work, similar or otherwise.

QUESTION 3

3. **Which of the following best expresses the main point of the passage's last paragraph?**

(A) Although their efforts were admirable, the Encyclopedists were naively optimistic about the potential impact of their work.

(B) The ultimate success of *Encyclopedie* is born out by its detractors' later acceptance of the Encyclopedists' principles.

(C) Although obsolete today, *Encyclopedie* nevertheless continues to inspire not only scientists but also theologians.

(D) Were the Encyclopedists alive today, they would have followed the same course of action as the Catholic Church regarding the Shroud of Turin.

(E) History shows us that the Encyclopedists were overly ambitious in their attempt to systematize and record all human knowledge.

Question Type: Main Idea
Difficulty Level: Moderate

(B) **is the best response.** The Catholic Church is the detractor (critic or opponent) to which statement (B) refers. The same Church that denounced *Encylopédie* later embraced the Encyclopedists' rigorous intellectual inquiry. This fact is the ultimate "triumph" to which the author refers in lines 25-26.

Incorrect Responses

(A) is too narrow in scope. Statement (A) expresses the author's point in the first sentence of the final paragraph, but does not embrace the larger point that the Encyclopedists eventually triumphed over their detractors.

(C) is unsupported by the passage. Admittedly, a large portion of the work is in all likelihood outdated today, and perhaps the work does continue to inspire scientists and theologians. Yet nowhere in the final paragraph—or anywhere else in the passage—does the author make either of these two points.

(D) distorts the author's purpose. Although statement (D) is reasonably inferable from the last sentence of the passage, again the author's larger point is that the Encyclopedists ultimately triumphed over their detractors [answer choice (B)].

(E) distorts the author's purpose. Although statement (E) is reasonably inferable from the first sentence of the passage, once again the author's larger point is that the Encyclopedists ultimately triumphed over their detractors [answer choice (B)].

PASSAGE #19

During the process of embryonic development, cells become progressively restricted in their developmental potential and finally acquire the biochemical and morphological specialization necessary for their
(5) respective functions in an adult. Since enzymatic and structural proteins are required for the appearance and maintenance of this specialization, the differentiated state results from the synthesis and activity of cell-specific proteins during development.

(10) Since all cells of an organism contain the same genotype as the fertilized egg, cellular differentiation is the result of variable gene activity rather than selective gene loss. Thus, cellular specialization and cell-specific protein synthesis result from the expression of
(15) appropriately selected groups of genes in each cell type. As development proceeds, the progressive differentiation of cells is correlated with changes in the population of protein species within the embryo, which reflect the accurate programming of the time and sequence of the
(20) biosynthesis of different proteins by the genome. In the absence of opportunities for genetic analysis, determining the mechanisms involved in the regulation of protein synthesis is key to understanding genome control during development.

(25) The majority of studies on gene activity in embryo-genesis have been done on the sea urchin system, where large numbers of embryos undergoing relatively synchronous development can be easily obtained. Also, sea urchins' permeability to radioactive isotopes and to
(30) inhibitors of RNA and protein synthesis provide a distinct advantage for study over amphibian material. Especially well documented are the maternal programming of early development and the genomic control of later differentiation in the urchin. Maternal
(35) products, stored in the egg cytoplasm from oogenesis, can support development from fertilization through the hatching blastula stage; however, development from the mesenchyme blastula stage is dependent upon gene products synthesized under the direction of the embryonic genome.

1. With which of the following statements would the author of the passage most likely disagree?

   (A) Morphological specialization requires the synthesis of cell-specific proteins.
   (B) Embryonic development involves differentiation in cell genotype.
   (C) The population of protein species with the embryo is dependent upon the timing of protein biosynthesis.
   (D) Enzymatic proteins are required for an organism's full development.
   (E) Selective gene loss is not a factor in cellular differentiation during embryonic development.

2. Which of the following statements about embryonic development in sea urchins is best supported by the passage?

   (A) Genomic control over early embryonic development is especially well documented.
   (B) Permeability to RNA inhibitors is comparable to that in amphibian embryos.
   (C) Development during the hatching blastula stage requires gene products synthesized under the direction of the embryonic genome.
   (D) Maternal products can support embryonic development following the mesenchyme blastula stage.
   (E) Genomic control of later cell differentiation has been studied extensively.

3. The last paragraph of the passage

   (A) compares two stages of biological development
   (B) describes a methodology for studying a biological phenomenon
   (C) illustrates a biological process by way of an example
   (D) defines and explains an important term mentioned earlier
   (E) provides an example which disproves a scientific theory

STOP.

PASSAGE #19—ANSWER KEY

1. B
2. E
3. C

PASSAGE #19—ANALYSIS

QUESTION 1

1. With which of the following statements would the author of the passage most likely disagree?

    (A) Morphological specialization requires the synthesis of cell-specific proteins.
    (B) Embryonic development involves differentiation in cell genotype.
    (C) The population of protein species with the embryo is dependent upon the timing of protein biosynthesis.
    (D) Enzymatic proteins are required for an organism's full development.
    (E) Selective gene loss is not a factor in cellular differentiation during embryonic development.

Question Type: Explicit Detail
Difficulty Level: Moderate

(B) **is the best response.** According to the passage, all cells of an organism contain the same genotype as the fertilized egg (lines 10–11). Thus, Response (B) contradicts the information in the passage.

Incorrect Responses

(A) restates the author's point in lines 5–9: "Since enzymatic and structural proteins are required for the appearance and maintenance of this specialization, the differentiated state results from the synthesis and activity of cell-specific proteins during development."

(C) accurately restates a point in the second paragraph. The author refers to "changes in the population of protein species within the embryo" (lines 17–18), then suggests that such changes "reflect the accurate programming of the time and sequence of the biosynthesis of different proteins by the genome"(lines 18–20).

(D) is inferable from the information in the first paragraph. According to the passage, biochemical and morphological specialization is necessary for cells' respective functions in an adult organism (lines 4–6). In turn, enzymatic and structural proteins are required for the appearance and maintenance of this specialization (lines 5–7).

(E) restates the author's point in the second paragraph that "cellular differentiation is the result of variable gene activity rather than selective gene loss" (lines 12–13).

QUESTION 2

2. Which of the following statements about embryonic development in sea urchins is best supported by the passage?

(A) Genomic control over early embryonic development is especially well documented.

(B) Permeability to RNA inhibitors is comparable to that in amphibian embryos.

(C) Development during the hatching blastula stage requires gene products synthesized under the direction of the embryonic genome.

(D) Maternal products can support embryonic development following the mesenchyme blastula stage.

(E) Genomic control of later cell differentiation has been studied extensively.

Question Type: Explicit Detail
Difficulty Level: Moderate

(E) is the best response. According to the passage, the maternal programming of early development and the genomic control of later differentiation are "especially well documented" (lines 32–34).

Incorrect Responses

(A) confuses the information in the passage. Genomic control of later differentiation, not early development, is especially well documented (see lines 33–34).

(B) runs contrary to the information in the passage. The permeability of sea urchin embryos to inhibitors of RNA "provide a distinct advantage for study over amphibian material" (lines 30–31). Thus, it is inferable that such permeability in sea urchins is greater than (not "comparable to") that in amphibians.

(C) confuses the information in the passage. Development "from the mesenchyme blastula stage" (not during the hatching blastula stage) requires gene products synthesized under the direction of the embryonic genome (lines 37–40).

(D) confuses the information in the passage. Maternal products, stored in the egg cytoplasm from oogenesis, can support development from fertilization through the hatching blastula stage (lines 34–37). The passage does not indicate that maternal products can also support such development following the mesenchyme blastula stage. Moreover, in the following sentence, the author suggests that development after the mesenchyme stage is controlled instead by other factors.

QUESTION 3

3. **The last paragraph of the passage**

   (A) compares two stages of biological development
   (B) describes a methodology for studying a biological phenomenon
   (C) illustrates a biological process by way of an example
   (D) defines and explains an important term mentioned earlier
   (E) provides an example which disproves a scientific theory

Question Type: Interpretation
Difficulty Level: Moderate

(C) is the best response. In the first two paragraphs, the author discusses the process of cell differentiation in embryonic development. While the author is particularly concerned with examining the mechanisms involved, no specific type of organism (animal) is discussed as an illustration until the final paragraph (which focuses on the sea urchin). Accordingly, Response (C) properly reflects the flow of the author's discussion.

(A) is the second-best response. In the final sentence of the passage, the author does compare different stages of embryonic development in terms of the controlling mechanisms at work during various stages. However, Response (A) distorts the author's point by suggesting that only two particular stages are compared.

Other Incorrect Responses

(B) is off focus. The only discussion of methodology is in the final sentence of the second paragraph, where the author indicates that while genetic analysis might be most instructive, absent the opportunity for such analysis it is most helpful to try to determine the mechanisms involved in the regulation of protein synthesis. However, in the third paragraph, the author does not go on to describe either methodology.

(D) distorts the information in the passage. There is no key term mentioned earlier in the passage that is defined and explained in the third paragraph.

(E) distorts the information in the passage. Although the function of the third paragraph is indeed to provide an example, the author is not concerned with disproving a theory but rather with illustrating a biological phenomenon more generally described earlier in the passage.

PASSAGE #20

The 35-millimeter format for movie production became a *de facto* standard around 1913, partially on the basis of a handshake agreement between George Eastman and Thomas Edison who wanted to standardize
(5) production and distribution for economies of scale. The mid-1920s through the mid-1930s, however, saw a resurgence of wide-film formats in Hollywood. During this time period, virtually all of the studios had their own formats, ranging in gauge from 55mm to 70mm.
(10) Research and development then slackened until the 1950s when wide-screen filmmaking came back in a big way in direct response to the erosion of box-office receipts because of the rising popularity of television. *This Is Cinerama* (1952) is generally considered to mark
(15) the beginning of the modern era of wide-screen film-making which saw another flurry of specialized formats, including CinemaScope, VistaVision, Todd-AO and Technirama. In 1956, Panavision developed Camera 65 for MGM Studios; it was first used during the filming of
(20) *Raintree Country*. Panavision soon contributed another key technical advance by developing spherical 65mm lenses which eliminated the "fat faces" syndrome that had plagued earlier CinemaScope films.

Some forty blockbuster or roadshow films, as they
(25) were called, were filmed in wide-screen formats during this period. But wide-screen formats floundered due to the deadly combination of expense, unwieldy cameras, and slow film stocks and lenses; the curtain finally came down with the release of *Ryan's Daughter* in 1970. And
(30) after the invention of a set of 35mm anamorphic lenses which could be used in conjunction with much more mobile cameras to squeeze a wide-screen image onto theatrical screens, film technology improved to the point where quality 70mm prints could be blown up from 35mm negatives.

1. It can be inferred from the information in the passage that wide-film formats were

   (A) in use before 1913
   (B) not used during the 1940s
   (C) more widely used during the 1920s than during the 1930s
   (D) not used after 1956
   (E) more widely used for some types of movies than for others

2. Based upon the information in the passage, which of the following was NOT a factor contributing to the increased use of wide-film formats for moviemaking?

   (A) spherical camera lenses
   (B) Panavision's Camera 65
   (C) television
   (D) anamorphic camera lenses
   (E) movie theater revenues

3. Which of the following statements is most strongly supported by the information in the passage?

   (A) If a movie does not suffer from the "fat faces" syndrome, then it was not produced in a wide-film format.
   (B) Hollywood's movie studios did not adhere to the standard established by Eastman and Edison.
   (C) The same factors that contributed to the resurgence of wide-film formats in the 1950s also led to the subsequent decline in their use.
   (D) The most significant developments in 35mm technology occurred after the release of *Raintree Country*.
   (E) Movie-theater revenues are not significantly affected by whether the movies shown are in wide-screen format.

4. Which of the following statements about the movie *Ryan's Daughter* is most readily inferable from the information in the passage?

   (A) It was the last of the blockbuster or roadshow films.
   (B) A wide-film format was used in its production.
   (C) Its release marked the end of the modern era of wide-screen filmmaking.
   (D) Since its release, movie theaters have generally not shown wide-screen films.
   (E) Anamorphic lenses were used in its production.

STOP.

PASSAGE #20—ANSWER KEY

1. A
2. D
3. B
4. C

PASSAGE #20—ANALYSIS

QUESTION 1

1. It can be inferred from the information in the passage that wide-film formats were

    (A) in use before 1913
    (B) not used during the 1940s
    (C) more widely used during the 1920s than during the 1930s
    (D) not used after 1956
    (E) more widely used for some types of movies than for others

Question Type: Inference
Difficulty Level: Moderate

(A) **is the best response.** The passage refers to the establishment of a *de facto* 35mm standard around 1913, followed by a "resurgence" of wide-film formats (in the mid-1920s to the mid-1930s). This resurgence suggests that wide-film formats were not new since they had been used before the 35mm standard was established—i.e., before 1913.

Incorrect Responses

(B) distorts the information in the passage. The passage does indicate that research and development slackened between the mid-1930s and the beginning of the modern era of wide-screen moviemaking (the early 1950s). However, the author neither states nor implies that wide-film formats fell into complete disuse during this interim period.

(C) distorts the information in the passage. The author makes no comparison between the 1920s and the 1930s in terms of the extent to which wide-film formats were used. The passage indicates only that "[t]he mid-1920s through the mid-1930s saw a resurgence"…"of wide-film formats in Hollywood."

(D) runs contrary to the information in the passage which indicates that the 1970 film *Ryan's Daughter* marked the end of the modern era of wide-film formats. If (D) were a viable response, then a much earlier film (released around 1956) would have marked the end of this era.

(E) alludes to information not discussed in the passage. Nowhere in the passage does the author either state or imply that wide-film formats were used more commonly for some types of movies than for others.

QUESTION 2

2. **Based upon the information in the passage, which of the following was NOT a factor contributing to the increased use of wide-film formats for moviemaking?**

   (A) spherical camera lenses
   (B) Panavision's Camera 65
   (C) television
   (D) anamorphic camera lenses
   (E) movie theater revenues

Question Type: Explicit Detail
Difficulty Level: Easier

(D) is the best response. According to the last sentence of the passage, anamorphic lenses, used with more mobile cameras, made it possible to create quality 70mm prints from 35mm negatives. In this respect, then, the invention of the anamorphic camera lens contributed to the demise (not the increased use) of wide-film moviemaking.

Incorrect Responses

(A) is discussed as a key technical advance in wide-film format technology. The spherical 65mm lens eliminated the "fat faces" syndrome (presumably, wide-film images were thereby made to appear more realistic). Accordingly, this new type of lens contributed to the increased use of the wide-film format.

(B) is referred to indirectly by the author as a key technical advance in wide-film format technology. In mentioning that "Panavision soon contributed another key technical advance" (lines 20–21), the author implies that Camera 65 was also a key technical advance.

(C) is mentioned in the first sentence of the second paragraph as one of two factors that prompted the resurgence in the 1950s of the wide-film format.

(E) is mentioned in the first sentence of the second paragraph as one of two factors that prompted the resurgence in the 1950s of the wide-film format.

QUESTION 3

3. **Which of the following statements is most strongly supported by the information in the passage?**

   (A) If a movie does not suffer from the "fat faces" syndrome, then it was not produced in a wide-film format.
   (B) Hollywood's movie studios did not adhere to the standard established by Eastman and Edison.
   (C) The same factors that contributed to the resurgence of wide-film formats in the 1950s also led to the subsequent decline in their use.

(D) The most significant developments in 35mm technology occurred
     after the release of *Raintree Country*.

(E) Movie-theater revenues are not significantly affected by whether the
     movies shown are in wide-screen format.

Question Type: Interpretation
Difficulty Level: Moderate

(B) **is the best response.** After stating that Eastman and Edison established a 35mm format as the
de facto standard for moviemaking, the author goes on to describe two subsequent eras of
resurgence in the use of wide-film formats. Accordingly, movie studios did not adhere to the
standard established by Eastman and Edison.

Incorrect Responses

(A) calls for an illogical inference that contradicts the information in the passage. The author states
that the invention of the spherical 65mm lens "eliminated the 'fat faces' syndrome that had
plagued earlier CinemaScope films" (lines 23–24). CinemaScope was one of the specialized
wide-film formats. Thus, if a particular movie does not suffer from the "fat faces" syndrome, it
could very well have been produced in wide-film format with a spherical 65mm lens.

(C) runs contrary to the information in the passage. According to the passage, it was the advent of
television and the resulting decline in box-office revenues that prompted the resurgence of
wide-film formats in the 1950s. The author identifies several factors as contributing to the
subsequent demise of wide-film formats: expenses, unwieldy cameras, slow film stocks and
lenses, the invention of the anamorphic lenses, and mobile cameras. However, the passage
does not mention the popularity of television or box-office receipts among those factors.

(D) distorts the information in the passage. The only post-*Raintree Country* technological
developments mentioned in the passage are the invention of anamorphic lenses and more
mobile cameras. While such developments were probably significant in the development of
35mm technology, to suggest that these innovations were the most significant developments in
35mm technology [as Response (D) suggests] exaggerates the author's point.

(E) runs contrary to the information in the passage. The information in the second paragraph
suggests that it was in response to eroding box-office revenues that the movie industry
stepped up its efforts to improve wide-screen technology. Moreover, based upon the author's
discussion of the modern era of wide-screen filmmaking, it seems that these attempts were
successful, at least until other problems (expense, unwieldy cameras, slow film stocks and
lenses) made continued use of wide-film format unfeasible.

QUESTION 4

4. **Which of the following statements about the movie *Ryan's Daughter* is most readily inferable from the information in the passage?**

   (A) It was the last of the blockbuster or roadshow films.
   (B) A wide-film format was used in its production.
   (C) Its release marked the end of the modern era of wide-screen filmmaking.
   (D) Since its release, movie theaters have generally not shown wide-screen films.
   (E) Anamorphic lenses were used in its production.

Question Type: Inference
Difficulty Level: Challenging

(C) **is the best response.** The author metaphorically states in the third paragraph that "the curtain finally came down with the release of *Ryan's Daughter* in 1970." Considered in the context of the preceding discussion about the floundering of wide-screen formats, it is clear that the author considers this movie to mark the end of the wide-screen era.

Incorrect Responses

(A) and (B) both call for the same unwarranted inference. It is unclear from the information in the passage whether *Ryan's Daughter* was one of those forty blockbuster films or, for that matter, whether it was even produced in a wide-film format. All the reader knows from the information in the paragraph is that the author considers this movie as marking the end of the modern era of wide-screen moviemaking.

(D) distorts the information in the passage. The author is suggesting that since 1970 wide-screen movies have not been produced. However, the author is not suggesting that theaters have discontinued showing wide-screen movies made prior to 1970.

(E) calls for two unwarranted inferences. First, it is unclear from the information in the passage whether *Ryan's Daughter* was produced in a wide-film format. Second, the author's discussion of anamorphic lenses is independent of the author's reference to *Ryan's Daughter*. Even if *Ryan's Daughter* was filmed in 35mm format, it is unwarranted to assume that anamorphic camera lenses were used in its production.